SHUTDOWN at
YOUNGSTOWN

SUNY Series in Urban Public Policy
Mark Schneider and Richard C. Rich, Editors

SHUTDOWN at YOUNGSTOWN

Public Policy for Mass Unemployment

Terry F. Buss

Center for Urban Studies
Youngstown State University

F. Stevens Redburn

Office of Policy Development
and Research
U.S. Department of
Housing and Urban Development

State University of New York Press   Albany

Published by
State University of New York Press, Albany

© 1983 State University of New York

Printed in the United States of America

For information, address State University of New York
Press, State University Plaza, Albany, N.Y., 12246

Library of Congress Cataloging in Publication Data

Buss, Terry F.
  Shutdown at Youngstown.

  (SUNY series on urban public policy)
  Bibliography: p.
  1. Plant shutdowns—Ohio—Youngstown—Case studies. 2. Iron and steel
workers—Ohio—Youngstown—Case studies. 3. Youngstown Sheet and Tube
Company.
I. Redburn, F. Stevens. II. Title. III. Series.
HD5708.55.U62Y683   338.6'042   82-5686
ISBN 0-87395-646-X   AACR2
ISBN 0-87395-647-8 (pbk.)

10   9   8   7   6   5   4

For our parents

Contents

Individuals Interviewed

Figures

Tables

Acknowledgments

The research reported here would not have been possible without the generous funding from the Ohio Department of Mental Health. We are particularly indebted to Dee Roth, Chief of Program Evaluation and Research, for her cooperation and her encouragement and support of this project.

A project of this scope and magnitude requires contributions from a great many researchers in order to bring it to fruition. Carla Wilson, project research manager, expertly coordinated the activities of researchers in the field and conducted much of our data analysis. Mindy Kimmelman, George Cheney, and Becky Grenga were responsible for completing many of our personal and case study interviews, as well as field editing and coding questionnaires. George Cheney also conducted several supplemental studies which provided information on the project.

The project received a great deal of technical support from various departments at Youngstown State University. The Reference Department of our library, most ably headed by Hildegard Schnuttgen and her staff, Louise Karns and Debbie Beronja, was extraordinarily helpful in locating and obtaining reference materials that were assimilated in this manuscript. Staff members of our Computer Center, particularly Fred Ulam, Tom Davidson, and Rich Rolland helped us to develop the complex computer programs and data files required in our data analyses, and were instrumental in assisting us in our data-processing activities. The Media Center technicians and artists, primarily Mary Ann Murray, Carl Leet, and Sue Greer, were responsible for producing most of the excellent figures in the manuscript. Judith Ferrett and Kathy Kiger, staff members at the Center for Urban Studies, expertly and efficiently typed and prepared the manuscript in its many drafts and revisions. We owe a great debt to Carla Wilson and Debbie Aberbach-Deutsch for their careful proofreading of our manuscript.

We benefitted a great deal from the comments and criticisms of nearly a hundred scholars, practitioners, and researchers who formally and informally examined our manuscript. Deserving of special mention are Hal Vreeland and Elliott Liebow, Center for Work and Mental Health, National Institute of Mental Health; George Cheney, Purdue University; Joseph Waldron, Youngstown State University; Marc Bendick, Urban Institute; and John Toogood, Clywd, North Wales. We, of course, bear sole responsibility for the contents of the manuscript.

1. Introduction

The Youngstown Sheet and Tube Company plant, east from Center Street Bridge, is a unit of the largest steel mills in the Youngstown area. In the blast and open-hearth furnaces, the rolling and strip mills, together with all the other divisions of a giant steel plant, are employed more than 7,500 men. Most of America's steel pipe and tubing comes from the new seamless-tube mill which simply plunges a hole through a solid cylinder of steel to furnish completed tubing far stronger than was possible under the old lap-and-butt welding process.

The Ohio Guide (1940)[1]

In September 1977, the directors of the Lykes Corporation, owners since 1969 of the Youngstown Sheet and Tube Company, announced the closing of its huge Campbell Works facilities and began laying off over 4,000 workers. Thus began a sequence of mill closings that permanently eliminated over 10,000 jobs in one metropolitan area in less than three years.

What follows is, first, an account of the initial shutdown's impact on the steelworkers, their families, and their community. Secondly, it is an exploration of public policies to deal with the immediate and longer-run human aspects of such closings.

* * * *

The closing at Youngstown Sheet and Tube can teach us much about our kind of society—about how fast the new becomes old, how fast useful know-how and technology becomes useless, how quickly apparent strength becomes weakness. The closing can also teach us about how people respond to adversity and, perhaps, about how to help them respond more successfully and creatively.

1

Youngstown—the Industrial City

Industrial America has grown, flourished, and begun to decline in hardly more than a century. Youngstown—the essential industrial city—was a village of fewer than 3,000 people on the eve of the Civil War. The first steel mill in the Mahoning Valley, the Union Iron & Steel Company, was not founded until 1892. In 1900, Youngstown was a city of 45,000. By 1940, its population had reached 167,000; in the meantime, steel-making had come to dominate every aspect of life.

The men and women who have worked in the 'Ruhr Valley of America' are either immigrants or the children of immigrants. In 1930, 54 percent of Youngstown's population was of foreign birth or extraction—Slovaks, Slovenians, Italians, Poles, and many others. Blacks from the South were recruited to work in the mills during labor shortages brought on by war or boom times. Today, they are approximately one-fourth of the city's population.

Youngstown grew quickly and with minimum attention to amenities not associated with steel.[2] Its reliance on steel has been both its strength and a source of vulnerability. During strikes, economic downturns, and especially during the Depression of the 1930s, the city's people suffered. Nevertheless, the productivity of the mills, the struggles of the union, and the prosperity generated by the success and growth of this industry and the nation's entire economy, gave thousands a living and, in time, made Youngstown's steelworkers one of the most productive, best-paid, and seemingly secure industrial labor forces in the world.

That apparent security is now gone. In historical terms, the city's era of stable prosperity was very short indeed. Youngstown, the prototypical American industrial city, has become the prototypical city in economic crisis.

Plant Closings—the National Problem

Every year in the United States, hundreds of manufacturing facilities are permanently abandoned. No one knows the exact number of such events or the numbers of workers affected.[3] However, a careful census of 410 major manufacturing corporations, accounting for about 40 percent of total U.S. manufacturing employment, identified over 1,000 plant closings during the 1970s.[4] Altogether, these shutdowns eliminated more than 280,000 jobs. Major physical contractions short of actual closings accounted for many more lost jobs.

Plant closing decisions are not made casually. Roger Schmenner (1980: 326) has determined that, in most cases, "by the company's accounting practices, the plant that is closed is one that has lost money. That it was even considered for closing is due to recognized poor performance over a number of years." The economics of the industry often accounts for this poor performance. However, these particular plants are more vulnerable to closing than others because of their greater costs of production, often attributable to obsolescent production technology. A financially troubled company may not close its oldest facilities first, since these may be more integral to the company's primary operations and represent larger unrecoverable capital investments. Rather, the first closed plants may be middle-aged or smaller facilities not closely tied in with other company operations. However, seriously troubled companies may eventually be forced to close larger, older plants that do not lend themselves to modernization; a prolonged period of decline in the company's or the industry's fortunes could, therefore, bring not only increasing numbers of plant closings but also closings that affect more workers and are larger in proportion to local labor forces.

Some (cf., Goodman, 1979) have argued that many closings result from corporate decisions to flee the unionized, highly taxed, and decaying Frostbelt cities for the warmer business climates of rural communities and Sunbelt cities. However, the best available statistical evidence suggests that interregional relocations are rather rare. Schmenner, for instance, finds that less than 15 percent of traceable plant relocations even cross state boundaries.

Barry Bluestone and Bennett Harrison (1980: iv–vii) claim that conglomerates account for a disproportionate number of closings, including many profitable, viable facilities. They believe that "managers of the giant corporations and conglomerates often create greater inefficiency through 'overmanaging' their subsidiaries, milking them of their profits, subjecting them to at best strenuous and sometimes impossible performance standards, interfering with local decisions about which the parent's managers are poorly informed and quickly closing subsidiaries down when other more profitable opportunities appear." Schmenner's manufacturing census confirms that in the last decade conglomerates closed plants more frequently than other companies, although their closings typically affected fewer workers per plant than those of other firms.

Plant closings have been somewhat more frequent, since 1970, in New England, the Pacific states, the Mid-Atlantic states, and the states of the East-North Central region around the Great Lakes. During this period, the latter two regions also experienced lower rates of new plant openings and very sluggish or negative job growth at established manufacturing facilities. Thus, the impacts of closings are concentrated regionally and often reinforced by the relative lack of new offsetting economic opportunities.

A more fine-grained picture of the pattern of closings would show a substantial clustering within regions as well. There is an easily observed tendency for industrial facilities to cluster geographically, and a corresponding tendency for communities to become overspecialized in a particular industry group or even a single industry. The consequence of this is that when a major U.S. industry declines, the impact is concentrated in a small, but heavily populated, area of the nation. Either a series of relatively small closings over a period of years or the sudden closing of a major facility can produce a state of localized economic crisis in which a community's supply of people able and willing to work exceeds, for a long period, the number of steady, secure, well-paid jobs available. The closing of hundreds of industrial facilities thus affects the future economic opportunities of thousands or millions of people and the future quality of life in communities all over the country.

The Decline of Industrial Cities

We are currently witnessing the decline of industrial America, the bankruptcy or deterioration of some once-mighty manufacturing enterprises, and with it all the sporadic but increasingly frequent closing of major industrial facilities.

The areas where these closings are concentrated are not as attractive as other communities to new investment, nor as supportive as they once were of technical innovation and entrepreneurship (Thompson, 1980; Kasarda, 1980). Even the largest, most economically diversified industrial metropolises of the East and Midwest, once thought to be immune from decline (Thompson, 1965), have lost population and employment. Prior to 1970, the few middle-sized metropolitan areas that lost population were found to be "overspecialized" or to otherwise possess some unusual vulnerability (Rust, 1975). Today, as many more major urban areas experience economic stagnation or decline, it is harder to argue either that growth is irreversible or that some unusual local weakness accounts for the loss of vitality.

Instead, the economic decline of older industrial centers appears to be mainly a function of changes originating outside these communities and beyond their short-run control. Plant closings reflect the decline of traditional industries and the nation's decline as a world competitor. The failure of new industries to arise in place of those lost results from changing production and transportation technology and other external factors that make these areas seem relatively unattractive to investors.

Other trends weaken the capacities of industrial cities to avoid or respond to economic crisis. A major change affecting many older cities is the trend toward ownership of a community's major industries by corporate conglomerates headquartered elsewhere. In Youngstown, the earliest attempts by outsiders to acquire Youngstown Sheet and Tube were resisted successfully by Ohio capitalists. However, in 1969, the Lykes Corporation takeover occurred; suddenly the massive steel mills were owned by a much smaller New Orleans–based shipping firm.[5] This was the climax of a series of political losses that changed Youngstown from a community based primarily on industries developed and controlled locally to one controlled by people not associated or identified with the community, and beyond its influence. These political losses foreshadowed, and perhaps guaranteed, the economic losses to follow.[6]

The current position of the older industrial areas is weak, both economically and politically; yet they must struggle to meet the needs of those losing their jobs and to maintain themselves as viable communities. Little is known, however, about how they are coping with the still recent reversal in their fortunes.

The Consequences of Major Plant Closings

Many communities and many working people have felt the concentrated force of changes in the nation's economic fortunes. When the national economy shudders, corporations go bankrupt, and jobs die. What then happens to those whose jobs suddenly disappear and to those with whom they live? When the basic industry of a community closes its gates, what happens to that community?

A few attempts have been made to calculate the adverse effects of plant closings on workers and their communities (cf., Bluestone and Harrison, 1980: Chapter 4). However, very few comprehensive community studies have been conducted in the wake of major closings and none that deal with the full scope of effects from the massive job losses recently experienced by many industrial cities. Although plant closings are generally believed to cause substantial harm to workers and communities, the research base for such beliefs is very thin.

When the existing literature on plant closings is reviewed from the viewpoint of the communities and people affected, two limitations are apparent. First, the literature overwhelmingly measures the problem in narrowly defined economic terms, to the neglect of noneconomic impacts and of public policies to address these directly.[7] Much of the discussion focuses on the reasons for interregional and urban-to-rural shifts in economic activity and population, on whether government contributes to these dynamics, and on how well government policies take them into account. Second, the literature contains little of practical value to local and state policy-makers struggling to organize an effective response amid cries of doom and intensive political competition. There is no published blueprint for local response to economic crisis. In contrast to research and writing about natural disasters, there is little practical emphasis in the literature on economic crisis: on how to organize and implement programs to soften the blow felt by terminated workers or how best to address the broadening circle of problems that may emerge in the wake of a major plant closing.

Thus, there are many unanswered questions about what happens to people and communities following a massive loss of jobs. How severe are the immediate emotional shocks to workers and their families? Is some form of trauma, breakdown, or violent reaction a common response? How do workers affected at different stages in their working lives, with different amounts of skill and education, and in different social situations differ in their responses? How many look for and find new work? Must they often accept, and are they willing to take, jobs that are less satisfactory in pay, status, location, or working conditions? And, very important from the standpoint of the community, what is the timing of various impacts and responses?

Other questions concern the broader circle of community impacts. How extensive is the "ripple effect" of job and income losses to others in the community? How many supplier or supporting firms also lay off workers? How many small businesses close? What is the impact of diminished cash flows on expansion and development decisions by other commercial interests? How do financial institutions respond to diminished economic prospects? What is the impact of property tax and other revenue losses on local jurisdictions, and how do they manage these while addressing the new needs created by an underemployed work force?

How do local human services agencies respond to an economic crisis? How appropriate and successful are their efforts to reach and help affected workers?

Finally, there is a set of unanswered questions about the longer-term effects of chronic underemployment, diminished economic expectations, and reduced government capacity brought on by one or a series of major plant closings or reductions in force. Since so many communities that once formed the heavy industrial backbone of the nation's economy now face longterm decline, we need to ask: How does economic distress alter the experienced quality of life in a community?

The Youngstown Study

Only when many of these questions can be answered with greater confidence will there be an adequate intellectual basis for devising effective social policies to meet the needs created by major plant closings. The present study explores the consequences of the Youngstown closing along the following dimensions: (1) the short-term emotional and financial stresses experienced by terminated workers and their families; (2) the ways workers in various circumstances responded to the experience of termination; (3) the "ripple" effect of massive job and income losses throughout the community's economy; and (4) indications of social stress and political response by the larger community in the two years following the Youngstown Sheet and Tube shutdown. See Appendix A for an overview of the study methodology.

Although primarily a case study, its conclusions concerning the impact of such events are set in a larger context of research on individual unemployment and community economic distress. A number of other studies have looked at the impact of economic change on various dimensions of personal, emotional, and material well-being. The combination of this evidence with more detailed information on the Youngstown closing yields some unexpected conclusions about the nature, severity, and timing of impacts.

Over a two-year period, beginning just after the first steelworker layoffs, the authors and their associates gathered many kinds of data. Multiple methods were used in order to construct a detailed, comprehensive picture of the psychological and social impacts of the closing. Particular efforts were made to go beyond previous studies in the range of indicators employed. The aim was to assess the whole community's reactions to the shutdown. But, the principal focus remained on the affected workers and their families:

Major sources of data included:

—Two interviews, one year apart, with a representative sample of more than 146 terminated steelworkers, their spouses, and their children.

—Comparable interviews with representative comparison groups of employed steelworkers and autoworkers in the Youngstown area.

—Telephone interviews with a representative sample of the Youngstown area adult population.

—Formal interviews with 30 key leaders of the Youngstown political and business community, as well as many informal conversations.

—A telephone survey of the adult population of Lowellville, Ohio, a small neighboring community that lost its steel mill, the only major industry, 10 years ago.

—Interviews with management terminated from Youngstown Sheet and Tube.

—Participant observation of efforts by the area's leadership to develop a comprehensive strategy for economic reconstruction and specific proposals to restore lost jobs.

—Design, leadership, and evaluation of a systematic research and planning process with more than 20 area human services administrators to develop a human services response to the crisis.

—A series of in-depth interviews with 15 local labor union leaders and 20 rank-and-file union members. These focused on the perceived role of the steelworkers union.

—Fifteen case studies of families directly affected by the crisis. Each was contacted several times over a two-year period.

—Telephone interviews with area workers focusing on geographic mobility and mobility plans.

—Collection of time-series indicators concerning 15 key dimensions of social life and economic conditions in the metropolitan area over multiyear periods, before and after the closing.

Social Policies for Communities in Economic Crisis

By intensively studying the short-term impacts of one major industrial plant closing and by reviewing the existing research that relates to such events, a partial knowledge base is established for considering public policies to ameliorate the short-run impacts of economic losses and also to improve the longer-term institutional capacity to maintain an acceptable economic standard and life quality in affected communities. The knowledge base is partial because no single community is representative of all communities and because, despite its varied components and detail, the present study cannot fully explore all of the questions raised above nor can it anticipate the full eventual impact of a weakened economy on the community's social life. Nevertheless, the authors have attempted to make full use of available insights in order to offer practical recommendations for human services and other social policies to meet the needs created by economic crisis.

Plan of the Book

The following chapter examines the context for the Youngstown closing, and how the nature of the industry, the behavior of the company's management and the union's leadership, and the weakness of government and public policy affected the community's capacity to respond to the crisis. Chapter 3 assesses the closing's impacts on workers and their families. Chapter 4 examines the broader circle of community impacts using a variety of data and approaches, including time-series analysis of several indicators of social and economic conditions.

In later chapters, the perspective shifts to that of policymakers and human services professionals concerned with developing social programs to meet the needs generated by major plant closings and similar events. Chapters 5 and 6 focus on the responses of workers and social agencies to the Youngstown closing. Chapter 5 examines three categories of worker response: reemployment, retraining, and relocation and how local agencies assisted in these efforts. Chapter 6 deals with other efforts by workers to cope with this personal crisis and, again, the efforts by local agencies to assist in the process of adjustment.

Chapters 7 and 8 use the evidence of impact and response presented in earlier chapters to draw conclusions about social policies appropriate to communities in economic crisis. Chapter 7 addresses employment, training, and mobility policy options. Chapter 8 examines the broader problem of developing a coordinated and effective local human services response. The final chapter looks at possible long-term effects of one or a series of economic losses on the quality of community life and local institutional capacity. The analysis ends with suggestions for social policies aimed at rebuilding such communities' economic and political vitality.

PART 1

BACKGROUND

2. Black Monday: The Closing of Youngstown Sheet and Tube

Without context, words and actions have no meaning at all.

Gregory Bateson
Mind and Nature

So fire runs in, runs out, runs somewhere
    else again,
And the bar of steel is a gun, a wheel, a
    nail, a shovel,
A rudder under the sea, a steering-gear in
    the sky;
And always dark in the heart and through it,
    smoke and the blood of man.
Pittsburgh, Youngstown, Gary—they make their
    steel with men.

Carl Sandburg
Smoke and Steel

On September 19, 1977, the Lykes Corporation announced it would close most of the Campbell Works of the Youngstown Sheet and Tube Company. Within weeks, some 4,100 workers permanently lost their jobs.

The impact of an event depends heavily on how those affected interpret its significance—an interpretation in turn dependent on other events, both past and present, and on the explanations offered by leaders and the media. The context of the Youngstown mill closing gave it its meaning, a meaning shared to some extent by all who were affected. This context included:

13

1. an industry in decline nationally and internationally;
2. a corporation whose control had passed from local people to outsiders who were viewed as, and proved to be, indifferent to the future of the community and its workers;
3. a union that had been rendered powerless; and
4. a community political leadership that had ignored the inevitable and was incapable of either resisting the closing or restoring lost jobs.

In short, the context of the crisis suggested that the closing was inevitable; and that it was the result of forces beyond the control of the community, its leaders, and, very definitely, the workers themselves.

On the other hand, there were elements of the crisis context that encouraged hope. The religious leadership of Mahoning Valley joined together to attempt the nearly impossible—to reopen the mill. Youngstown's only daily newspaper, *The Vindicator,* speculated about one proposal after another to restore or replace the lost jobs. The federal government expressed its concern and funded feasibility studies. For many, there seemed good reason to hope that jobs would be restored.

This added ambiguity to the context. One could await economic salvation, one could try to construct a personal solution, or both. The situation gave the individual worker some opportunity to fashion his own interpretation of what the future was likely to be and of his best course of action.

This chapter first examines the economics of the American steel industry. Second, it examines the behavior of the Lykes Corporation. The actions of its corporate executives largely determined the fate of 4,100 workers. Next, the chapter reviews the many failed schemes for reemploying the terminated workers. Finally, it describes the reactions of the steelworkers' union to the closing. This brief history of the crisis reveals the weakness of local unions and political leadership. Weakness is a central theme of the context in which workers attempted to understand and deal with the loss of their jobs.

Decline of the Domestic Steel Industry

According to its own statistics, the domestic steel industry is more efficient, productive, and profitable than almost any foreign competitor (e.g., American Iron and Steel Institute, 1980). This is a statistical irony that grows in proportion to the industry's decline.

According to this view, in 1978 and 1979, the United States produced lower-cost steel than any major foreign steel competitor, with the exception of Japan, which was only slightly more efficient (Marcus and Kirsis, 1979). By conventional measures, the United States steel industry has, over the last 10 years, operated at a higher rate of capacity, producing at a higher percentage of its total capability, than any other steel producer (Council on Wage and Price Stability, 1977). And, in absolute terms, the profitability of the industry greatly exceeds that of its foreign competitors, many of which operate at a loss prior to public subsidies.

In spite of the impressive comparisons above, the domestic steel industry is experiencing major problems which may ultimately reduce it to a fraction of its former size. From 1969 to 1978, employment in the American Steel industry declined 17 percent, a loss of approximately 95,000 jobs. Many steel-making facilities which were once the backbone of the steel industry have permanently closed; others will soon follow.

The American steel industry's domestic market and its share of the world market have declined dramatically. Following World War II, American steel accounted for approximately 50 percent of the world market (American Iron and Steel Institute, 1980: 9). In the five years

Table 2.1   Recent Steel Mill Closings and Layoffs in the United States, 1977-1980

Company	Location	Estimated Number Laid Off
U.S. Steel	Duluth (MN) Ellwood City (PA) Youngstown (OH) Torrance (CA) Waukegan (IL) Joliet (IL) and elsewhere	13,300
Bethlehem Steel	Johnstown (PA) Lackawanna (NY) and elsewhere	12,000
Youngstown Sheet & Tube	Youngstown (OH)	5,400
Alan Wood Steel	Conshohocken (PA)	3,000
Cyclops Corporation	Mansfield (OH) and Portsmouth (OH)	1,300
Phoenix Steel	Phoenixville (PA)	5,700

SOURCE: Individual steel companies.

ending with 1979, American steel's world market share was only 15 percent. A similar, although more erratic, trend has developed within the domestic steel market. Since 1975, foreign steel imports have accounted for as much as 18 percent of the domestic market (Council on Wage and Price Stability, 1977). The industry is in trouble.

Reasons for the Decline

There are many complex, interrelated reasons for the U.S. steel industry's decline (see Ignatius, 1979; Crandall, 1981; American Iron and Steel Institute, 1980; Hayes, 1979; "The Reindustrialization of America," 1980).

Sagging profitability. Decline can be measured in terms of return on capital. Profits in the American steel industry have been declining slowly over the last 30 years. From 1950 to 1978, profits as a percentage of net worth in the steel industry declined from 11.5 percent to 8.2 percent. This contrasts with the trend of all U.S manufacturing over the same period up from 13.8 percent to 14.6 percent. The result of this trend is that steel has become less and less attractive as an investment (Citibank, 1950–1978). This, in turn, reduces the industry's access to the capital needed to modernize and to maintain its international competitiveness.

Capital expenditures and recovery. Continuing reinvestment in facilities and equipment is necessary for any industry's growth. The American steel industry invests less in replacement capital than any major foreign steel producer. Over the last five years, the U.S. has reinvested about $19 per ton of raw steel production. Foreign competitors have invested substantially more: Japan, $26; West Germany, $24; United Kingdom, $35; and France, $28. After years of disinvestment, the U.S. steel industry is antiquated. In the Mahoning Valley, the newest blast furnace, an essential component in most steel-making activities, was constructed in 1921.

The costs of new facilities and equipment must be "recovered" over time. One reason for the low rate of capital expenditure in steel has been the long time period required for the recovery of new investment. The steel industry has one of the longest periods for capital recovery of any major industry—15 years. In contrast, the electronic, chemical, textile, and wood product industries require less than 10 years to recover capital investments. Moreover, in the last 10 years, inflation has doubled the costs of steel-making equipment. Consequently, the industry is unable to replace its existing capacity. The profit motive encourages management to allow existing mills to deteriorate and to invest profits from them in other industries.

Some observers (e.g., McConnell, 1963) also attribute the low rate of capital expenditure to factors related to management. Steel managers tend to be overly cautious in their approach to reinvestment. They have been unwilling to accept even moderate levels of risk in investing in their own industry. This may have led them to reduce capital investment.

Still another plausible explanation for the decline in reinvestment relates to the acquisition of previously independent steel companies by conglomerates and to the diversification of major steel producers into other industries (Bluestone and Harrison, 1980). Testimony taken in connection with the Lykes-LTV merger in 1978 indicates that following its purchase of Youngstown Sheet and Tube Company in 1969, Lykes used the bulk of its profits from the steel subsidiary to subsidize its other investments. Virtually none of the profits were used to modernize or maintain the Youngstown steel facilities (Greenman, 1979).

Finally, some observers see the steel industry's capital problems as part of a larger syndrome of costly federal government regulation and federal government–induced disincentives to investment.

Regardless of the cause, capital investment rates have declined, casting further doubt on the industry's future.

Labor productivity. Largely due to low reinvestment rates, the number of manhours required in the United States to produce a ton of steel has decreased only about 2.2 percent over the last decade (Marcus and Kirsis, 1979). Other countries—Japan in particular—have decreased required manhours required by almost twice the U.S. amount over this period.

Production costs and price increases. Steelworkers are among the highest-paid industrial workers. The average hourly wage for steelworkers in 1977 was approximately $13 per hour. Since 1950, steel industry wages have steadily risen above the average industrial wage. For example, on the average, steelworkers earn about 14 percent more than autoworkers (Ohio Legislature, 1980). The productivity lag has not prevented the industry and the union from reaching agreements that have substantially and steadily increased real wages over the past 30 years.

The steel industry also has experienced rising costs for raw materials and energy. Since 1950, the steel industry has reduced energy consumption by 28 percent; but the cost of energy to run the mills has increased six times (American Iron and Steel Institute, 1980: 61). Since 1972, the cost of raw materials has more than doubled. This has been the result of higher energy, mining, and transportation costs, passed on to the steel industry.

Steel prices have not kept pace with increased costs. Steel industry executives have argued that several political/economic events may be contributing factors (American Iron and Steel Institute, 1980; Ohio

Legislature, 1980). From 1960 to 1970, steel price increases were discouraged by political pressures, characterized as "jawboning" (e.g., McConnell, 1963). From 1971 to 1974, President Nixon instituted mandatory wage and price controls. And from 1974 to 1980 prices were held down, relative to the cost of living, by the Ford and Carter Administrations' voluntary wage and price guidelines (American Iron and Steel Institute, 1980: 79)

The domestic oligopoly in steel also may have contributed to the current profitability problems. Many have argued that the major steel producers have engaged in price-fixing, based on rates established by U.S. Steel, the nation's largest steel producer (Ignatius, 1979: 11). Such actions, in the absence of foreign competition, would enable most companies—even those which were less efficient—to remain in the black. However, it may also have discouraged reinvestment that would have headed off the current foreign steel inroads in the U.S. market.

Research and development. The American steel industry has also failed to invest in research and development which would make the industry more efficient and profitable (National Academy of Science, 1978). "The steel industry's total R & D spending as a percentage of sales is the lowest of all U.S. industries except for food and textiles." (A Comprehensive Program for the Steel Industry, 1977: 33) Moreover, much of existing industry research activity is: (1) not focused on basic processes but rather on operational problems that will only produce marginal increases in the efficiency of *existing* facilities and technology and (2) oriented to the competitive position and marketing requirements of individual companies. Inventions and information generated are not immediately shared by the remainder of the industry. Basic research spending by the steel industry actually declined from an annual average of $16,250,000 during 1968 to 1971 to an average of $9,250,000 from 1972 to 1975. Not only is 97 percent of this activity company-supported, but the overall level is low relative to other industrial categories.

Federal contributions to industry R & D are heavily imbalanced in favor of a few industries. Despite the fact that steel is an important basic industry, federal contributions to the industry's R & D was only $2 million as compared with $240 million for the chemical industry, $335 million for the automotive industry, and $2.5 billion for the electrical equipment industry.

Ironically, up until the late 1960s, the U.S. steel industry was a leader in technological breakthroughs in steel-making. But these break-throughs have not found application in the domestic production of steel. The Japanese employ several U.S.-developed processes which are highly efficient and cost-beneficial—continuous-slab casting to name but one example. The process accounts for 50 percent of their steel production, while only 16 percent of the production in the United States employs this method. Again, capital shortage and sagging profitability account for the lack of innovation in the domestic steel industry ("The Reindustrialization of America," 1980: 75).

Foreign steel dumping and the trigger price mechanism. Many major, foreign steel producers are heavily subsidized by their home governments. Some 69 percent of the French producers and 79 percent of British producers are government-owned and not necessarily profitable. Since American steel is not government-subsidized to any great extent, it cannot sell steel below production costs. Foreign competitors can afford, in the short run at least, to sell steel in foreign markets while taking a loss. Once they have expanded their shares of world production and sales, foreign producers can raise prices to recover losses incurred while undercutting competition. This practice is referred to by American steel producers as "dumping."

In an effort to inhibit dumping, the Carter Administration established the trigger price mechanism.[2] If the estimated costs of foreign production exceed the price being charged by the foreign producers, U.S. sales are restricted. There is debate about the trigger's effectiveness in preventing foreign inroads (Ohio Legislature, 1980; Comptroller General, 1980).

Slackening of demand. Aside from all of the above problems, the steel industry is experiencing slackening demand for many of its products, both domestically and internationally (Petzinger, 1978a). This is the case even though worldwide demand for steel is increasing. Industries such as automobiles, appliances manufacturing, and building construction, which once utilized enormous quantities of steel, have begun to find substitutes. These include plastic, glass, graphites, aluminum, and others. For an increasing number of uses, steel is too costly to transport, harder to shape, and now relatively more expensive in comparison with substitutes (cf., Arthur Andersen, 1980).

The steel industry in the United States has come to a turning point. If it continues along its present course, it will probably decline to such an extent that America will no longer be self-sufficient in meeting its steel needs. This also will mean that hundreds of thousands of jobs will be lost and many communities across the country will be disrupted.

Corporate Decisions and the Closing

Youngstown Sheet and Tube Company was established in 1900 by two Youngstown residents, George D. Wick and James A. Campbell (see Youngstown Sheet and Tube, 1975; Peskin, 1978g). Wick and Campbell originally had managed the Republic Iron and Steel Company (the forerunner of Republic Steel Corporation) for the "steel trust" of Andrew Carnegie of Carnegie Steel Company (the forerunner of U.S. Steel). They were dissatisfied with Carnegie for exploiting local interests to benefit absentee owners, and moved, therefore, to establish their own company.

In 1923, the company acquired the Brier Hill Steel Company, located in Youngstown, and the Sheet and Tube Company of Chicago. These acquisitions soon made the company the third largest steel producer in the United States.

The company continued to prosper through the 1950s. This was primarily a result of America's domestic growth, its dominance in the world steel market, and high steel demand during World War II.

Youngstown Sheet and Tube always prided itself on its local ownership. But in 1969 it merged with Lykes Corporation (Kelley, 1978), a conglomerate headquartered in New Orleans. Although Lykes had sought to maintain a low profile, it was a far-reaching consortium involved in shipbuilding, real estate, banking, and ranching.

George Schueller, U.S. Department of Justice attorney, studying the merger for the federal government, recommended that Attorney General John Mitchell find the merger in violation of the Clayton Antitrust Act. He stated that the merger would eventually destroy Sheet and Tube (Kelly, 1978). However, Schueller's recommendation was overruled, and the merger was permitted.

Officers of the Youngstown-based steel firm did not welcome the merger (Peskin, 1979: 50). Many top-level executives in Youngstown, including President Robert E. Williams, either left the corporation or chose to retire. As a result of the merger, the Youngstown area lost local control over its steel mills.

Almost from the beginning, the merger proved to be a mistake for both concerns. The decline in demand for steel after the Vietnam War made the steel industry a poor investment for Lykes Corporation. The corporation could more profitably invest its capital in its nonsteel-related subsidiaries. The shipbuilding industry also was retrenching. This reduced Lykes' own demand for steel from Sheet and Tube.

The declines in profitability were exaggerated by the inability of Youngstown Sheet and Tube to recapture its original share of the market for diversified steel products. The centers of these markets had shifted to the west and south, making shipment of products from Youngstown impractical. Other steelmakers laid claim to these markets.

Despite the fact that Lykes Corporation ranks number 144 in the *Fortune* 500 companies, the company appeared to be inept in managing Sheet and Tube. Eleanor Tracy (1978: 56) of *Fortune Magazine* provides the following glimpse of Lykes' Management:

The Lykeses must bear responsibility for a good deal of the failure at Youngstown Sheet and Tube. From the beginning, they viewed the steel company primarily as an investment; it was never thought of as an operation that young Lykes men might wish to manage. Notes one of them, "Steel just wasn't something we grew up with." Not only was there no tradition of interest in steel, there was no desire among Lykes men and women to leave Tampa and New Orleans for the bleakness of a northern steel town.

Toward Black Monday

Lykes Corporation decided to cut its losses at Youngstown Sheet and Tube by letting the steel-making operations flounder.[3] This was accomplished in several ways. First, capable managers were transferred into more profitable Lykes operations in nonsteel subsidiaries. Other talented personnel, seeing the writing on the wall, left the corporation. Second, Lykes began investing capital needed for renovating the steel mills into its nonsteel subsidiaries. This accelerated the decline of the already antiquated mills. Third, Lykes, in its absentee-ownership role, virtually abandoned contact with daily operations at Youngstown Sheet and Tube. Local managers were left without guidance or direction.

After seven years of neglect, Lykes Corporation began reporting quarterly losses amounting to hundreds of millions of dollars. Lykes had lost interest in steel-making. And Youngstown Sheet and Tube was now a major liability for the corporation, so Lykes began to search for a way to rid itself of the "problem."

Ironically, Lykes could not simply sell its steel mills even at heavy financial loss. There were no buyers outside the steel industry willing to expend over $600 million to purchase the antiquated facilities. Lykes also was forbidden under antitrust law to merge or sell its facilities to any other major steel-maker because of the advantage it might afford over competitors. At this time, Lykes was literally stuck with the mills.

On September 19, 1977, the only apparent solution to the problem was at hand. Lykes announced that it was permanently shutting down the Campbell Works portion of its Youngstown Sheet and Tube facilities.[4] Approximately 4,100 workers were told they would lose their jobs.

One Way to Shut Down a Plant: A Guide for Machiavellian Managers

The Lykes Corporation's handling of the closing of Youngstown Sheet and Tube provides a guide for managers who wish to pursue

Machiavellian[5] strategies in their dealings with laid-off workers and local communities. The components of the Lykes' guide are as follows.[6]

First, no advance warning of the shutdown was given to the workers and the community. Although it is difficult to pinpoint the motivations of the corporate executives, some felt that the sudden announcement was an effort to catch the community and workers off guard. Then, the closing could proceed with less resistance from workers or the community.[7]

Second, the company provided no programs for workers which would ease the burden of unemployment or help workers find other jobs. Workers simply had a job one day and no job the next. No transition period was provided. The corporation opted for a "clean" break.

Third, human and health service agencies which deal with unemployment problems were not permitted access, before or after the closing, to the mills or the company's records on workers. The company also refused to provide basic information to these agencies, such as names and addresses of the workers.

Fourth, the company virtually banned all communication by its employees with any organizations outside the corporation, especially the news media, Youngstown State University, and community organizations (e.g., Peskin, 1978a). The penalty for such communication, for white-collar as well as blue-collar workers, was "blacklisting," so that future job hunting, at least in the steel industry, would be impossible.

Fifth, key decision-makers who could speak for the company in terms of its plans, goals, and activities were not present in the community. Local managers merely served as messengers to absentee owners and out-of-state managers. These decision-makers, as noted above, were in the process of abandoning the company in Youngstown and were not responsive to communications from Youngstown's leadership.

Sixth, as will be discussed below, many community groups and worker committees attempted to contact the corporation to seek information, especially about the resale of the mills and workers' rights, problems, and expectations. These negotiations proved to be unproductive. Meetings were postponed or cancelled (e.g., Cook, 1979).

The effect of this policy by the Lykes Corporation is that a company, which had dominated the area economy for 77 years, closed its largest facilities in a matter of weeks. It left behind unemployed workers, empty buildings, and some rust-coated, antiquated, useless facilities.

Local Leadership and the Closing

The closing announcement in September 1977 caught the community entirely by surprise and totally unprepared. No human or health services were organized in advance to meet the needs of the affected workers. No economic recovery or revitalization plans had been developed, and the mechanisms for implementing them were not in place.

Within a few weeks of the closing, many community groups organized. Efforts were made to define the needs created by the closing and to examine alternative courses of action.

Figure 2.1   Chronology of the Youngstown Area Steel Mill Closings and Organizational Responses, 1977-1980

September 1977	Lykes announces closing of Campbell Works, idling 4,100 workers.
	Ecumenical Coalition formed.
October 1977	Mahoning Valley Economic Development Corporation (MVEDC) created.
February 1978	CASTLO created.
December 1978	Jones and Laughlin Steel takes over the shutdown Campbell Works and Brier Hill Works.
February 1979	Harvard Business School's study rejects worker-community ownership plan.
April 1979	Ecumenical Coalition's efforts officially terminated.
January 1980	U.S. Steel closes McDonald and Youngstown Works, idling 3,500 workers.
	Jones and Laughlin Steel closes Brier Hill Works, idling 1,400 workers.

The Ecumenical Coalition

In October 1977, religious leaders representing Catholic, Jewish, Protestant, and Orthodox faiths organized to meet the challenge of the steel mill closing. Bishop James Malone of the Catholic Diocese of Youngstown and Bishop John Burt of the Episcopal Diocese of Ohio provided the initial impetus for the organization. A "Steel Crisis Conference" in Youngstown was attended by religious leaders and representatives of a church-financed liberal-labor lobby and research organization, the Ohio Public Interest Campaign, and of two liberal "think tanks" based in Washington, D.C., the Institute for Policy Studies and the National

Center for Economic Alternatives. At the end of an intensive two-day session, the group reached consensus on its goals, which included (Collins, 1978):

—education of the community and the nation concerning the facts and events of the closing;
—exploration of the feasibility of a community/worker ownership takeover of the mills;
—advocacy of a national policy which would retain basic steel jobs in communities where steelworkers live;
—development of Youngstown as a model for the retention of jobs in severely distressed communities.

The Ecumenical Coalition, as the organization called itself, began its efforts by contracting with a Philadelphia engineering firm. It set out to determine the feasibility of acquiring and operating the closed portion of the Campbell Works (Beetle, 1977). This study was conducted jointly with the Western Reserve Economic Development Agency (WREDA). The study concluded that $120 million would be required merely to reopen the facility. Another $415 million would be necessary to modernize the plant to make it competitive and profitable.

In view of the large sums of money required for a community/worker takeover, the Coalition embarked on a fund-raising campaign to demonstrate the community's capacity and willingness to raise capital. The Coalition asked private citizens to establish "Save Our Valley" bank accounts. These accounts would remain under complete control of the depositor, but the aggregate amounts in participating banks would be reported to the Coalition. The Coalition hoped depositors would convert their accounts to stock in the new company when it materialized. By July 1978, almost 10 months after the closing, only $3.6 million had been raised. Most of this amount was contributed by large organizations.

The Coalition simultaneously began to seek federal grants and loan guarantees, as well as aid from the State of Ohio. The federal Economic Development Administration (EDA) initially pledged $100 million in federal loan guarantees in support of the community/worker ownership scheme. Later, Ohio Governor James Rhodes pledged $10 million in state assistance. But the amounts offered were far short of the necessary $500 to $600 million.

Political support for the Coalition in Ohio and in the local community was not spontaneous or unanimous. The Coalition sought to extract endorsement for their community/worker ownership plan by publicly demanding that state and local politicians rally around "the cause." Politicians, slow to respond to the challenge, were threatened with defeat in upcoming elections. Those who were against the Coalition were labeled as being against Youngstown. Using such methods, the Coalition was able to obtain begrudging, superficial support from virtually all elected leadership.

The Coalition also attemped to influence politicians on the national level, including President Jimmy Carter. Several mechanisms were employed. One strategy was to use the prestige and power of the national churches. Those churches holding substantial stock in Lykes-controlled corporations put pressure on executives, especially at stockholders' meetings.[8] The Coalition placed a $10,000, full-page ad in the *Washington Post*. The ad was signed by 2,000 Ohioans. It announced, "Mr. President, Youngstown's job crisis is a moral issue.... We need your help to keep self-help alive there and in the rest of Ohio." Another method employed by the Coalition was to demand meetings with major public officials in order to present their views. During the steel crisis, the Coalition met with every major official directly or remotely involved in the crisis.

The Coalition continued to bargain with the Lykes Corporation and federal government over reopening the mills. But during 1978 and early 1979 several reports were published which virtually destroyed the Coalition's efforts. In a study for the federal government, Professor Richard Rosenbloom of Harvard University's School of Business reported that the Coalition's community/worker ownership plan was not feasible ("Researcher's Report Hits Campbell Plant Reopening," 1978). Rosenbloom concluded that $525 million would not be sufficient capital to renovate the mills. An investment of more capital would not be prudent. In addition, it would be unwise to guarantee that the federal government would purchase its steel from the Campbell Works over the next 20 years. Rosenbloom questioned the conclusions of the National Center for Economic Alternatives feasibility study. This report eliminated any hope for securing federal loan guarantees or grants to reopen the mill.

During April 1979, the Coalition announced the end of its efforts at a community/worker takeover of the mills. A full post mortem of the failure of the Coalition must await more information on government and industry motives and internal decision-making. The following factors seem to have played a major role.

—Private-sector steel producers, notably in the Ohio and Pittsburgh region, resisted the Coalition's efforts by intensive lobbying in the U.S. Department of Commerce against the community/worker ownership plan. They rejected the idea of a federally subsidized mill in their market areas, especially when their own firms were in trouble (Peskin, 1979).

—The national leadership of the United Steel Workers (USW) did not fully support the Coalition's efforts (e.g., Howard, 1979) until March 1979. Perhaps this attitude reflected resistance to a plan that would place management responsibility in workers' hands, leaving the union in an ambiguous role. The best indication of the lack of union support was the fact that no public endorsements or funding by the USW were made for the Coalition during the crucial period of negotiations for government subsidies.

—The Coalition seems to have lacked enthusiastic grass roots support for its endeavors. Rallies and meetings held by the Coalition were poorly attended. Less than one hundred people attended a rally on September 19, 1978, to observe the first anniversary of the mill closing. The "Save Our Valley" program produced several large corporate and organizational contributions; but the several thousand contributions from the public were not impressive, given the apparent magnitude of the crisis and the extensive public relations campaign waged by the Coalition.

—The Coalition was not very realistic in its proposals or in its expectations of federal and state agencies. Loan guarantees of hundreds of millions of dollars were unprecedented at the time. The Carter Administration had designated only $500 million for loan guarantees to the entire steel industry.[9] Granting such a guarantee to the Coalition would have exhausted the reservoir of funds available for bailing out other companies experiencing similar difficulties.

—Another tangible factor was the perception by many that the Coalition was more interested in demonstrating an ideologically based program, independent of its efforts at saving the steel mills. Gar Alperovitz and Staughton Lynd, an activist attorney for the Coalition and United Steel Workers Local 1462, had jointly published a pamphlet advocating a "new American socialism." Since both were at the heart of the Coalition efforts, many potential allies equated community/worker ownership with an unacceptable radicalism. This unnecessary ideological baggage attracted national attention through numerous articles in liberal journals. On balance, this may have weakened the effort's chances of success.

Other Responses

The activities of the Ecumenical Coalition by no means represent the full range of community responses to the closing. In the first weeks after the closing announcement, new coalitions formed that were intended, first, to consolidate the Mahoning Valley's pursuit of federal and state funds and, later to administer a coordinated strategy for revitalization. The broadest of the coalitions, the Mahoning Valley Economic Development Corporation (MVEDC), was brought together by Congressman Charles J. Carney and chaired by the Mayor of Youngstown, J. Philip Richley (Garland, 1980). It included representatives of the two affected counties, Mahoning and Trumbull Counties, and their major cities, as well as of the business, labor, and other private leadership of the valley. MVEDC's formation was encouraged by the federal Economic Development Administration (EDA), which awarded it a $1 million grant to develop a new Comprehensive Economic Development Strategy (CEDS).

MVEDC thus supplanted an already-established two-county economic development organization, the Western Reserve Economic Development Agency (WREDA), as EDA's designated vehicle for development planning. WREDA, with funding from the steel industry and EDA, had conducted feasibility studies for restructuring the valley's fragmented, irrational, and antiquated steel production. WREDA had also nearly completed an area development plan required by EDA for designating the valley as a development district eligible for additional federal funds. This plan contained many elements of the later CEDS. Nevertheless, WREDA lacked support from key local leaders. While EDA shifted its attention to MVEDC, WREDA continued to work with the Ecumenical Coalition, the steel industry, and some elements of the valley's fragmented political leadership.

Meanwhile, the mayors of Struthers, Campbell, and Lowellville, three small communities in Mahoning County hard hit by the closing, became concerned that their interests were being subordinated by the Youngstown-dominated MVEDC.[10] While remaining part of the bigger umbrella group, they formed a new organization, CASTLO. Ohio Governor Rhodes and State Senator Harry Meshel provided strong political, as well as administrative, support to CASTLO, which then proceeded to develop its own plans and strategies.

Merely describing these three additional development coalitions oversimplifies the boiling pot of political rivalry, faction, and dealing that soon became apparent to federal agencies and hampered all efforts to plan and implement a long list of economic development initiatives after 1977 (see Appendix B). Major schemes included the community/worker ownership proposal backed by the Ecumenical Coalition; creation in the valley of a national center for steel technology development (pushed by MVEDC chairman, Mayor Richley); two proposals to rationalize the area's steel industry, one by building a huge joint blast furnace and the other to establish a modern coke plant in the closed Campbell Works (these backed by WREDA and a successor organization); creation of an industrial park on the mill site (by CASTLO); and a series of efforts to secure major new private industries for the valley, especially an aircraft manufacturer. Virtually all of these schemes relied on massive federal funding or loan guarantees. To date only the smaller CASTLO effort had been even partially realized. Ground had been broken for a new aircraft manufacturing plant, partly financed by a $3 million federal Urban

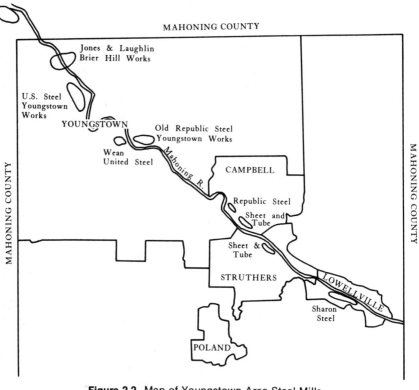

Figure 2.2 Map of Youngstown Area Steel Mills

Development Action Grant, that could employ workers by 1983. None of the planning and negotiation has as yet produced any significant number of new jobs for the area. The valley's inability to unite behind a single realistic approach to development has contributed to the long string of unrealized proposals, most of which would face long odds anyway.

The federal government's response to the closing helps to explain local actions during this period. The administration expressed a willingness to help. Vice President Mondale and Ambassador Robert Strauss visited the area and publicly pledged assistance. An interagency task force was established, chaired by Presidential Advisor Jack Watson, to oversee the federal government's response. Large grants and loan guarantees were promised once a feasible proposal could be found.

However, the federal administration wanted to deal with a united local leadership, to avoid offending either the steelworkers' union or the industry, and to insure that any massive government support would, in fact, be effectively used. Despite its desire to help and its interest in doing so, the government had great difficulty in finding a way to respond that would meet these criteria. Moreover, federal officials became increasingly appalled by the competition among local factions and proposals. The result was that funds were provided for planning and review of proposals but none for concrete job-creating actions.

Under pressure generated by their economic needs and the potential for massive federal support, the political leaders of the valley tried to coordinate their efforts. However, their individual interests and ambitions repeatedly drove them apart. Thus, mere necessity was insufficient to overcome an institutionalized fragmentation of government capacity.

The Unions

From 1936 to 1942, the CIO and U.S. steelworkers fought a series of bitter and often violent battles with the steel companies, culminating in creation of the United Steel Workers (USW) and its recognition as the workers' exclusive bargaining agent. Youngstown Sheet and Tube was one of the last to accept the union. It did so only under the combined pressures of federal government action and World War II (Galenson, 1956; Brody, 1960).

Forty years later, the USW faced a very different challenge from the companies. Its response, or lack of response, is another important element of the context in which workers reacted to the closing.

Once the steel mill closed, the USW leadership, headquartered only 60 miles away in Pittsburgh, all but abandoned local union leaders and workers. Apparently, the leadership determined that fighting to either avert the closing or reopen the mills was not in the best interests of the international union. The international reasoned that pressuring management to keep open unprofitable facilities would jeopardize high wages and benefits leveraged from the companies over the last decade. This position reduced the local elected leaders of the union to impotence in their dealings with the Lykes Corporation. Eventually, the international dismantled its regional offices in the area.

The corporation virtually refused any communication with local union leadership. Therefore, union leaders were continually caught by surprise when the company made decisions affecting workers and knew little more about the company's plans than the workers they represented.

Since the local unions could no longer mobilize their members and could not count on backing from the international, they were unable to effectively resist the closing. Workers, few of whom are very active in union affairs normally, distrusted leaders who appeared to be powerless in dealing with the closings and revitalization efforts. Some union leaders, expected by the workers to fight to the bitter end, probably misrepresented the nature of the closing and the possibility of revitalization to the workers and community in order to stay in power. Workers found themselves in an information-poor environment, being manipulated by their own leadership. Members of the two largest locals, sensing this situation, ousted their leadership in subsequent elections.

As a result of the general deterioration of local union organization, those in the community trying to help the workers could not assess their needs, could not contact them en masse, and found it still more difficult to mobilize or unite them in any way. Although victims of mass unemployment, the workers in this situation were surprisingly isolated and ill-served by their elected leadership.

Further Closings

The closing of the Campbell Works of Youngstown Sheet and Tube proved to be only the first chapter in a series of Youngstown area mill closings.

The Closing of Brier Hill

Even though Lykes Corporation had closed the Campbell Works, it was still not out of financial trouble. As a means towards a financial bailout, Lykes sought to merge with other corporate partners. The partner chosen was LTV Corporation, which owns the Jones & Laughlin Steel Corporation. LTV also was ailing financially, having reported at least $350 million in losses over the 1967 to 1977 period. By combining their individual debts into one large one and merging their steel subsidiaries into one larger company, Lykes and LTV hoped that they could make their steel facilities profitable, ostensibly by streamlining some operations, decreasing additional plant closings, and curtailing duplication of effort wherever possible.

On June 21, 1978, Attorney General Griffin Bell approved the Lykes-LTV union. As with the Lykes-Youngstown Sheet and Tube Company merger before, the Justice Department's antitrust division had counseled against approval. However, Bell invoked the "failing company" provision of the Celler-Kefauver Act, in rationalizing his action (see Kelley, 1978).

No sooner had the merger been approved than the new corporation announced that it was closing the Brier Hill Works, now a subsidiary of Jones & Laughlin Steel Corporation. In early 1980, the jobs of another 1,400 steelworkers were permanently lost.

The Closing of the McDonald and Ohio Works

U.S. Steel Corporation also operated two large steel-making facilities in the Mahoning Valley—the Ohio Works in Youngstown and the McDonald Works, a few miles to the north in the small city of McDonald. Together both works employed approximately 3,500 workers. With the closing of the Campbell Works and the impending closing of Brier Hill, as well as the rash of closings of other U.S. steel facilities, the USW demanded and received assurances from corporation Chairman David M. Roderick that both U.S. Steel works would not close. Roderick stipulated that the mills would remain open as long as they were profitable.

Keeping the facilities at both works operating profitably was an enormous task. They relied partly on equipment installed at the turn of the century. The workers made every effort—including foregoing pay raises—to keep the mills operational. Their efforts were successful until the last quarter of 1979, when the mills reported huge losses. One day before the closing of the Brier Hill Works, U.S. Steel announced that it was shutting down both facilities (see "U.S. Steel to Trim Fat," 1979).

The announcement of the U.S. Steel and Brier Hill closings reactivated the defunct Ecumenical Coalition, now the so-called Community Steel Corporation. In 1980, the group sued U.S. Steel for the right to purchase the shutdown facilities. A wave of feasibility studies, similar to those which accompanied the closing of the Campbell Works, was undertaken. However, there was little likelihood these mills would operate again.

Conclusion

To understand the Youngstown closing as the workers who were terminated experienced it, it needs to be looked at in the context of larger events and institutions. Here we have described four elements of that context which symbolized to workers both their own powerlessness to reverse or control the situation and the unwillingness or impotence of others, in or out of the community, to help them. These elements are:

—*the decline of the industry,* itself a symbol of the larger process of a national economic restructuring;

—*the indifference of the company,* a near-total refusal to acknowledge any responsibility for the personal and social consequences of its action

—*the incapacity of political institutions, at all levels,* symbolized by a ludicrous series of broken half-promises and failed proposals; and

—*the failure of the union,* including an absence of leadership from the international and a lack of vitality in the locals.

In this context, workers might be expected to pursue their interests individually rather than collectively. Although initially led to believe that the mills might reopen, they could be expected to realize quickly that there was little to be gained by waiting for external assistance. In this and less obvious ways, the context of the crisis influenced workers' interpretations of their situations and, in turn, their responses.

A review of the closing's context is thus helpful to those who would understand how it altered and will continue to change the community in which it occurred. The closing highlights a longer-term process in which the community lost control of its economic base, came to rely more heavily on decisions made elsewhere and on external financial assistance, and experienced a loss of vitality in major institutions, including local government and the unions. This loss of institutional capacity should be kept in mind while examining the reaction of the workers and the community to the closing.

PART 2

IMPACT OF THE CLOSING

The next two chapters examine the impacts of the Youngstown Sheet and Tube plant closing on workers, their families, and the larger community over a two-year period beginning with their closing announcement of October 1977. Most workers were terminated between November 1977 and March 1978, although some were retained for a longer period to aid in shutting down the plant and others were recalled for brief periods throughout 1978.

Chapter 3 focuses on the stresses experienced by workers and their families. Few households felt any financial hardship during the first year to 18 months, since a combination of regular unemployment benefits, supplemental benefits from a fund established through collective bargaining, and added and extended benefits provided under the Federal Trade Adjustment Act (TAA or TRA) kept most workers' incomes near the previous year's level. Workers who accepted TRA-approved retraining or who were called back to work for brief intervals were able to extend their benefit eligibility periods well beyond a year. Many terminated workers were able to find alternative work during this period; others accepted early retirement. However, some remained unemployed, either by choice or for lack of an alternative. Many of those who did find work reported that their new jobs were less satisfactory than their old positions in pay, in working conditions, or otherwise.

To say that most workers were insulated from immediate financial hardship is not to minimize the shock of the unexpected loss of seemingly secure employment. Many workers lost pension rights, status, and other advantages of accrued seniority. All workers, after a brief period, lost their group health insurance coverage. And most faced the uncertainty, anxiety, and stresses associated with the search for new work.

As time passes, the circle of impacts from a plant closing widens to touch the lives of many others in the community. Chapter 4 examines the

Youngstown closing's effects on the area's economy and social life over the following two years. This was a period in which the national and state economies were expanding; a fortunate coincidence that reduced the apparent "ripple effects" of the closing on area employment and business operations. However, in late 1979 and 1980, a major new wave of steel layoffs hit the Valley while the national economy turned downward. Thus, by the end of the period under study, there had been a massive permanent condition in the manufacturing base, and recession was exposing the underlying weakness of the area's economy.

3. Psychological Impact of the Shutdown

One of my best friends just had a heart attack which I know was brought about by this closing of the mill. He's 50, forced to retire, been to the South looking for work, sold his home, took to heavy drinking and then had a heart attack.

> Letter from former steel-
> worker to Steve Redburn
> (March 10, 1978)

The loss of a job is one of a class of stress-producing personal crises. These also include marriage, divorce, death of a close friend or relative, and similar events that suddenly change life's direction. The reaction to job loss may closely resemble reactions to other personal crises that involves some kind of loss; its importance depends, of course, on the meaning given to the job by the individual.

> ... The source of social legitimacy in capitalist society comes primarily from what a person does, and it is from this that inferences are drawn about who he essentially is. (Sennett and Cobb, 1972: 267-268)

While similar to other crises that involve a loss, termination of employment has distinctive aspects that may produce distinct effects. Job loss means, for many, the loss of a valued identity, as well as an immediate or prospective loss of income. Job loss is bound to heighten doubts about future security. It may alter relationships with family and friends. More obviously than similar crises of loss, it threatens one's self-esteem, sense of efficacy or usefulness, and sense of self or identity.

35

Job loss may also mean financial hardship. To some extent, this is mitigated where employment benefits are substantial and prolonged, where a spouse is still working, or where the general affluence of a community and of supportive relatives and friends provide substitute income or indirect assistance. The extent of financial hardship depends to a great degree on the duration of unemployment.

Economic Change and Behavioral Disorder

The extensive scholarship on economic change as a cause of psychological stress and behavioral disorder has been most thoroughly reviewed by David Dooley and Ralph Catalano (1980). Much of this work is highly sophisticated in its methodology, employing either cross-sectional or longitudinal research designs and either individual or aggregate levels of analysis. A variety of measures have been used for psychological "disorders;" time lags of typically one month to one year have been introduced in the longitudinal studies. The basic model that is suggested by most of this work is as follows: economic change (e.g., job loss) along with other environmental variables causes individuals to experience changes in their personal circumstances; depending on the extent of one's social support, social integration, and coping ability, the individual sooner or later may experience symptoms of stress; then, depending on the access to treatment, reactions of family and community, and other factors, the individual after some period of time may develop a behavioral disorder of severity sufficient to require professional treatment, which may or may not be received. In some studies, the onset of behavioral disorder is viewed as the uncovering of an existing disorder or intolerance of such personal life changes (Catalano and Dooley, 1977; Marshall and Funch, 1979). This model, as illustrated in Figure 3.1, is the same as that guiding the present study.

The Nature of Crisis

From an external viewpoint, job loss is a crisis in the sense that it represents a sharp discontinuity with previous experience. However, psychologists have defined crisis somewhat differently, by viewing the phenomenon as internal to the individual. From this perspective, crisis is a state of cognitive confusion wherein the individual literally does not know what to think of his problem, how to evaluate reality, and how to formulate and evaluate the outcome of the crisis and possibilities for problem-

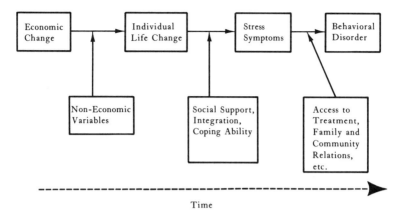

*Adapted from Dooley and Catalano (1980).

Figure 3.1 Major Causal Links between Economic Change and Behavioral Disorder

solving. Thus, it is recognized that the same experience can produce different degrees of individual "crisis" or, in fact, no crisis at all.

The psychological definition of crisis also implies a predictable pattern of responses by individuals to perceived crisis. Typically, the individual experiences a relatively severe, prolonged, and uncomfortable level of tension, perhaps accompanied by feelings of helplessness and ineffectiveness. The individual's usual problem-solving methods apparently offer no solution. Consequently, he or she will typically engage in innovative trial-and-error efforts to solve the problem. The individual may succeed and, in doing so, permanently add new coping capabilities to his personal repertoire.[1] The individual may fail due to lack of capability or bad fortune, and "a poor solution will inhibit future ability to cope with problems." (Halpern, 1973: 342) From this, it follows that a psychological crisis, induced by job loss or other external shock, may lead either to loss or gain in functional capacity, i.e., mental health.

The existing literature on crisis—which has a rather limited empirical base—also suggests that the success of crisis response is dependent both on one's personality and on current relationships (Cobb and Kasl, 1977). Thus, the crisis literature is consistent with the model of economic changes and behavioral disorder presented above.

Influences on Psychological Impact

The psychological meaning and impact of job loss can be altered by many variables.

To understand what termination may mean to the industrial worker, it is important to begin by examining the social and personal meaning of blue-collar work itself and of the social class position of such workers in U.S. society.[2] An essential dilemma experienced by these men (virtually all of the terminated steelworkers were men), especially those with families, is described by Sennett and Cobb as follows:

> A wage-worker is attempting to perform the most difficult of balance acts: on the one hand, he wishes to be with his wife and children, to play with and show concern for them; on the other hand, he knows that the only way he can provide decently for his wife and children, and give his life some meaning is by working longer hours, and thus spending much free time away from his family. [But] a working-class person has less chance than a middle-class person of sacrificing successfully; class definitions intrude to derail him from a sense that he has made an effective gift of his own struggle to someone else. (Sennett and Cobb, 1972: 125).

The relatively low status accorded blue-collar workers in this society, combined with the possibility that their children can move up in status, are said to produce complex, ambivalent feelings in these workers toward their work and toward their families. Frustration and anger are by-products of the inner tension produced by their position in the social structure.

This implies, also, that their reactions to loss of employment may be complex or ambivalent. If the above analysis of the worker's position is correct, the terminated man is suddenly released from the obligation that has produced both pride and frustration. Depending on family status, age, and other individual variations, this could be catastrophic or cathartic.

Another aspect of industrial employment often written about is the quality of the work experience itself (Terkel, 1974). The mass production worker is usually seen as engaged in dull, repetitive, sometimes dangerous, apparently meaningless labor that has few intrinsic rewards. In fact, there is great variety among steelworkers in the skill level and degree of responsibility associated with work. Moreover, the nature of steel-making produces considerable hour-to-hour and day-to-day variation in pace and the type of task performed. There is much idle time for some workers and therefore opportunity to socialize or rest. On the other hand, the noise, heat (or cold in winter), and supervision can be unpleasant or worse. Many employed steelwokers describe their reasons for working in materialistic terms. Perhaps this anecdote from an interview with a local representative to the United Steel Workers International union reflects the attitude of many steelworkers toward their jobs:

We had a meeting at the local union hall and I hoped we would have a good representation from the coke plant. Those fellows at the coke plant are making $20,000 to $25,000 a year working doubles. That place is unsafe to work in healthwise. This is a problem. They're worried about money instead of their health condition. If the company pays 60 cents an hour more, that means they'll die 20 years younger. That's what they're saying, give me the money, I'll die quicker.[3]

Studs Terkel's interview with a steelworker also gives some understanding of the worker's preoccupations:

When we were kids, we thought the steel mill was it. We'd see the men comin' out, all dirty, black. The only thing white was the goggles over their eyes. We thought they were it, strong men. We just couldn't wait to get in there. When we finally did get in, we were sorry. (Chuckles) It wasn't what it was cut out to be ...

Everyone looks forward to retirement, but there's a lot of 'em not makin' it. That's all they talk about is retirement. Where are you gonna go? What are you gonna do? And the poor soul never makes it. A lot of 'em, they're countin' the months instead of the years—and pass away. A lot of my friends are passed away already ...

If I retire right now, I would make $350 a month. There's a woman across the street got a half a dozen kids and no husband, and she's probably gettin' five hundred dollars a month from ADC. She gets more money than I would right now after workin' forty years. If I retire now, my insurance is dropped. I belong to this Blue Cross/Blue Shield insurance now. If I go on a pension, I would get dropped automatically. The day you retire, that's the day it's out.

I told my sons, "If you ever wind up in that steel mill like me, I'm gonna hit you right over the head. Don't be foolish. Go get yourself a schooling. Stay out of the steel mills or you'll wind up the same way I did." Forty years of hard work and what have I got to show for it? Nothing. I can't even speak proper. When you're a steelworker (laughs), you don't get to speak the same language that you would do if you meet people in a bank or a business office. (Terkel, 1974: 552-55)

Once again, it is unclear that job loss carries a wholly negative meaning for some industrial workers. For those who have invested fewer years and less of their personal identity in such work, the mill closing can be viewed as a challenging but potentially opportune event in their lives. The following anecdote suggests that a closing may be beneficial for some workers.

John Edwards had worked for Lykes for over 12 years as a crane operator. John was president of his local union and editor of the local union newspaper. John, as president and editor, established himself as a fair, although tough, union boss. He was respected by his fellow workers and company managers. John's union activities were conducted on his own time with only expenses compensated for by the union. He had to work full time in the mills. John felt that he could make a significant contribution to labor management relations in the mills, but at Lykes, he would rise no further than worker. John decided to get a college degree in his spare time of which he had very little. He estimated that a college degree would require six or seven years to complete while he worked full time and ran his union. Nevertheless, he persisted.

In February, 1980, John was told that his department in the mills was shutting down. This forced John to search for another job—something he had never done before. Instead of searching for a blue-collar job, John decided to apply for high-level labor-management positions in steel mills in the area. Much to his surprise, he landed a job as a labor relations representative in a large steel firm, making one and one-third his laborer's salary. The firm was impressed by John's handling of his union, as well as his efforts at obtaining a degree. The firm not only hired John, but also is paying the tuition for the remainder of his education.

John certainly was not an average worker with average skills and ability. He felt after a while that working in the mills thwarted his potential. John may have worked his way out of the mills had they not closed. Yet the closing gave John a reason to seek higher goals which he was able to realize. In his new job, he feels he is making a major contribution to labor-management relations in the steel industry.

Next, the psychological impact of job loss due to a plant closing may differ drastically from the impact of isolated job loss. For instance, in the midst of massive job losses, any shame or stigma is likely to be reduced because most people are not being fired due to any personal failing. Also, the group can be a source of mutual support and can give the experience a shared meaning. In particular, there is an opportunity for collective political response as well as individual response to the crisis.[4] Thus, massive job losses may be less likely than isolated firings to produce damaging psychological stress. On the other hand, massive job losses may reduce the capacity of community and family to offer social support at a time when it is most needed (Liem and Liem, 1979).

Finally, the psychological meaning of job loss depends on the particulars of individual personality, background, present social status, and resources. A fifty-year-old married worker with high-school-age children, limited education, no transferable job skills, and who is ineligible for a pension will not respond to job loss in the same fashion as a twenty-year-old apprentice electrician. Similarly, someone with a history of drug or alcohol abuse is more likely than others to react by increasing his/her use of these substances. Even these obvious examples are insufficient to capture the complexity of likely interactions with preexisting attributes of the individual and his situation.[5]

Mental Health and Mental Health Service Needs Defined

Before we can attempt to measure the impact of job loss on the mental health of those affected or assess the resulting needs for mental health services, it is necessary to define both "mental health" and "need" and to distinguish "mental health needs" from the need for mental health services.

"Mental health" may be defined either as proximity to a social average or norm, i.e., "normality," or as proximity to an ideal that is independent of a given societal context. Also, "mental health" may be defined either negatively, as in the "medical model," or positively, in terms of the possession of certain capacities or virtues. The "medical model" defines "mental health" as the absence of illness or disease defined "objectively, as a group of signs and/or symptoms, the existence of which is recognized by at least the mental health professional and, it is hoped, the patient...." (Cassimatis, 1979) In contrast, positive definitions offered by the various schools of psychoanalysis and existential psychology often equate mental health with individual autonomy or freedom. This includes the capacity for rational choice and implies active involvement with others, authenticity, empathy, independence of thought, and courage (Cassimatis, 1979).

Our theoretical and value preference is for a definition of "mental health" that is positive and independent of societal context. More pragmatically, we have had to translate an abstract definition into operational terms by which it can be reliably measured.

In addition, it is useful to stress those aspects of mental health that should come to the fore in a personal crisis calling for active response. In this sense, "an adequate conceptualization of good mental health refers to something more than passive adjustments, contentment, 'homeostatic balance', and freedom from inner tensions. Few persons would accept the healthy vegetable as a model. The more positive aspects of mental health, the active efforts of people to cope with their world, surely deserve attention." (Kornhauser, 1965 :38) Operationally, such an emphasis implies that terminated workers who are mentally healthy should:

1. acknowledge both the loss that has occurred and the likely benefits and costs to one's self, as well as to others, of alternative courses of action;

2. actively seek information, new skills, and resources in order to increase the likelihood of rational alternatives, including sources of income and, at least eventually, alternative employment; and

3. actively pursue the more likely of the rational alternatives.

In addition, an attempt has been made to measure emotional states and attitudes that are known to be associated with stress. It has not been assumed that in and of themselves these states indicate anything about a person's total state of mental well-being. The scales and other measures used to measure "mental health" of the affected workers, their families, and comparison groups of other workers are described in Appendix C.

To summarize, "mental health" has been defined and measured primarily in terms of the relative ability of individuals and groups to realistically assess their situation, cope with its actual or potentially harmful aspects, and exploit its opportunities.

The concept of "need" poses definitional problems of a different sort. Kimmel, writing on "needs assessment" methodology has concluded that ... need is an imprecise term. If the term is to be used for measurement and evaluation, it must contain precise standards which define the context for its application." (Kimmel, 1977; see also Varenais, 1977) Despite the pessimism of this statement, it leaves open the possibility that something can be said about the relative needs of various people or groups of people in a specified context. For instance, it may be possible to conclude that an economic crisis increases the *relative need* for particular subpopulations to exhibit certain kinds of coping capabilities or abilities to seek assistance in dealing with emotional stress.

We hypothesize that the needs of persons for increased coping or functioning capacity can be served—and perhaps served best—in ways that have nothing to do with mental health services or the services of any other formal institutional helping agency.

Most mental health needs assessments are conducted by mental health service agencies or their governing bureaucracies. These assessments involve (1) describing and understanding mental health needs in geographic areas and (2) evaluating information gathered in order to determine priorities for program planning and development (Hargreaves et. al. 1975). The link between assessing needs and planning services is made more directly in another widely circulated definition: "A needs assessment program is a research and planning activity designed to determine a community's mental health service needs and utilization patterns" (Warheit, Bell, and Schwab, 1974: 2), and usually emphasizes defining the problems exhibited and the resources hypothesized as needed to resolve these problems.

Given this emphasis on linking measurement of need to services planning, it is necessary to stress that mental health needs for the *community* (or population) and needs for mental health services for *individuals* are not equivalent. Logically and practically, it is possible to find mental health needs that do not require mental health services or the services produced by any institution. More positively, the most beneficial or cost-effective set of service responses to the mental health needs of a population may require a combination of mental health services, the services of other human services agencies, and the informal actions of other individuals or groups.

The implication of this distinction is that increased threats to the mental well-being of a community do not automatically dictate an increased need for the existing services of that community's mental health service providers. Although it is likely that mental health service agencies will be a useful resource for such communities, it is uncertain whether they should have the primary role in responding to an increase in mental health needs produced in economic crisis.

In order to arrive at such policy judgments, it is first necessary to examine evidence of change in mental health needs following massive job losses. Appendix C describes mental health measures used in personal interviews with the workers and their spouses as well as comparison groups of employed steel- and autoworkers. These measures are the primary basis for the discussion of the Youngstown workers' psychological responses to the closing, as presented below.

Evidence of Psychological Stress

Job loss, and the resulting unemployment, disruption of established social relationships, and financial strain, have been found in previous studies to produce significant psychological and physiological stress.

A study of industrial workers displaced by five plant shutdowns in 1959 and 1960 found "anger, resentment, bitterness, frustration, and bewilderment," but "surprisingly little radicalism or rejection of the social and economic system. Many accepted economic insecurity as part of the American way of life." (Wilcock and Franke, 1968: 92–93) When interviewed a year or less after the shutdown, many of those still unemployed had not given up hope of finding work; those over 40 were more often concerned that they would never again find decent jobs.

Intensive study of a small sample of suddenly terminated workers produced evidence of significant psychological and medical effects. Sidney Cobb and Stanislav Kasl (1977) followed 100 men who had lost their jobs due to plant closings plus 74 controls for up to a year, beginning with the closing announcement. The men were unemployed for an average of about 15 weeks during these two years. Most ended up in jobs similar in status and pay to those they lost.

> The men described their experience as somewhat disturbing, as requiring several months for return to normal, and as involving about as much life change as getting married. Those who had the most unemployment and the least social support viewed the experience as more stressful than others. (Cobb and Kasl, 1977: 174)

Cobb and Kasl's measures of psychological changes and health effects suggest the possibility that termination can lead to a number of short- and longer-term health effects, including ulcers. Health complaints were most prominent during the period of anticipation prior to job loss.

> ... Physiological changes suggesting an increased liklihood to coronary disease took place as did changes in blood sugar, pepsinogen, and uric acid, suggesting increased risk of diabetes, peptic ulcer, and gout. There was an increase in arthritis and hypertension and three men suffered attacks of patchy baldness. (Cobb and Kasl, 1977: vi)

Another small sample study, by James Manuso (1977), concluded that job abolishment induced depression in those predisposed to depression. A more intensive and detailed exploration of psychological responses to a plant closing concluded that "reactions... can be conceived of as large-scale separation, detachment process" that triggers denial in some workers, grief in others (Strange, 1978: 50–51). This study emphasized the inter-action of job loss with individual personality.

Indirect evidence for the effects of job loss is provided by Harvey Brenner's studies of the aggregate statistical relationship between unem-ployment rates and various indicators of personal well-being and stability (Brenner, 1977). He concludes that a "one percent rise in unemployment will increase stroke, heart, and kidney disease" and that "the 1.4 percent rise in unemployment during 1970 is directly responsible [nationally] for some 51,570 total deaths, including 1,740 additional homicides, 1,540 additional suicides, and for 5,520 additional state mental hospitalizations." The estimated cost to the society of lost income due to illness and mortality plus additional state prison and mental hospital outlays due to the 1970 unemployment rise is $7 billion.[6] These dramatic findings are a reminder that the personal impact of job loss on individuals constitutes in the aggregate a major national problem. When job losses are concentrated in a particular community, their similar effects are more concentrated.

Psychological Impact on Youngstown Steelworkers

Interviews with steelworkers and their spouses were conducted specifically to measure the psychological impact of the plant closing (see Appendix C for description of measurements used). Although the psychological measures used in interviews conducted with the Youngstown workers cannot match in depth or sophistication the small sample studies cited above, they do provide confirming evidence of short-term psychological stress among terminated workers who were unemployed when first interviewed.[7]

Few workers scored high on the mental health problem scales used;* yet those who were still *unemployed* showed significantly higher levels of aggressive feelings, anxiety, feelings of victimization, and alcohol abuse than other steelworkers, including those continuously employed, those who retired at the time of the closing, and those who were terminated but subsequently hired in other jobs. On all 12 scales, mean scores for the still-unemployed workers were above the mean for all steelworkers.

At the same time, it is surprising that terminated *reemployed* or *retired* workers showed no signs of elevated stress symptoms in the months following job loss. This suggests that the measured effects are related to continued unemployment and not to job loss per se. This is consistent with Cobb and Kasl's finding that terminated workers "with more unemployment did respond with strikingly, and very significantly, more anxiety and tension than those with less . . . ." (1977: 175)

When steelworkers, whatever their employment status, are compared with autoworkers, there are no consistent differences in average levels of stress symptoms. Even though a high proportion of the steelworkers sample had experienced job loss and unemployment, their average incidence of emotional problems was not noticeably higher (see Table 3.2).

---

*For the analysis that follows, we have elected to report the results of our findings in their most parsimonious form. We did, however, in the course of our investigation, perform a variety of higher-level statistical analyses to insure that no important statistically significant findings were being overlooked.

Table 3.1 Mean Scores and Mean Deviations of Steelworkers on Mental Health Scales According to Employment Status, First Wave, 1978

Mental Health Scale[a]	Steelworkers[b]				Steel worker Total[e]	Significance
	Unemployed	Retired	Rehired[c]	Employed[d]		
Alcohol Abuse	.38	-.13	-.10	-.10	.33	.013
Drug Abuse	.03	-.11	-.08	-.02	.95	.426
Victimization	.57	-.43	-.49	.02	1.11	.001
Apprehensive Avoidance	.36	.04	-.19	-.10	1.60	.335
Depression Immobility	.23	-.42	-.11	.02	.95	.218
Aggression/ Irritability	.66	-.58	-.10	-.14	1.96	.090
Acute Dependency	.32	-.09	-.42	.03	2.28	.273
Helplessness/ Depression	.38	-.55	-.01	-.05	.98	.144
Poor Family Relations	.22	-.35	.05	-.04	2.06	.017
High Anxiety	.62	-.59	-.03	-.12	1.67	.012
Trust/Suspicion	.46	-.38	-.04	-.10	1.67	.102
Hypochondriasis	.24	-.12	-.09	-.05	.60	.310
(N)	(58)	(36)	(50)	(112)	(256)	

a See Table A.1 for a list of items used in scale construction; b Figures are mean deviations; c Rehired other than at Youngstown Sheet and Tube; d Figures are mean deviations; e Figures are sample mean scores.

Percy Smith
Employed by Youngstown Sheet and Tube Company, 1973–1979
Age: 33
Spouse: Rachel, married 1972
Children: three daughters

Percy recalls when his father was laid off by a steel mill closing 18 years ago. His father, while unemployed, argued often with his wife, seemed to drink a lot more than usual, and could barely provide for his family. Percy lost his steel job in August 1978, was recalled twice briefly, and then permanently released. Rachel, his wife, considered this a crisis point in their marriage. During the brief recalls, Percy got into arguments at work and sometimes returned home late at night in a drunken rage, waking the children. He threatened to take his gun to work. In subsequent weeks, he drank heavily and the couple fought regularly and violently. Overspending and declining income created financial problems. After his third layoff notice, at Thanksgiving 1978, Rachel left with the three daughters, while Percy raged through the empty house screaming, crying, breaking windows and furniture. He was hired in June 1979 by Republic Steel and laid off in January 1980. The couple are now together but their financial situation is "uncomfortable" and their relationship still "shaky."

This information combined with the evidence of elevated stress sysmptoms among *unemployed* steelworkers may mean that employed autoworkers experience stress levels similar to those affecting the sampled steelworkers. More to the point is that relatively few in either group exhibit high stress symptom scale scores.

Timing of psychological impact

One reason why evidence of psychological stress may be weak is that measures are taken only at two points in time. For instance, workers may be under greatest stress soon after the mill closing is announced or between the time they receive their individual notice of termination and the actual date of layoff. Alternatively, some workers may be under greatest stress much later, as their unemployment benefits become exhausted and the prospect of comparable alternative employment fades away. It is quite plausible that the period of greatest stress will vary from worker to worker, depending both on personality and on individual circumstances.

Table 3.2 Mean Scores of Steelworkers, Spouses, and Autoworkers on Mental Health Scales, First and Second Waves, 1978 and 1979

Mental Health Scale:*	First Wave (1978)			Second Wave (1979)	
	Steelworkers	Spouses	Autoworkers	Steelworkers	Spouses
Alcohol Abuse	.33	.13	.36	1.44	1.24
Drug Abuse	.95	.99	.45	.67	.76
Victimization	1.11	.92	.99	1.13	.67
Apprehensive Avoidance	1.60	1.52	1.42	1.62	1.37
Depression Immobility	.95	.78	.75	1.42	.95
Aggression/ Irritability	1.96	1.65	1.76	1.49	1.30
Acute Dependency	2.28	2.02	2.50	1.76	1.14
Helplessness/ Depression	.98	.96	1.07	1.11	.89
Poor Family Relations	2.06	2.06	2.00	.81	.89
High Anxiety	1.67	1.54	1.88	2.53	2.29
Trust/Suspicion	1.67	1.32	1.51	2.67	2.23
Hypochondriasis	.60	.78	.60	.45	.30
(N)	(256)	(179)	(73)	(155)	(114)

* See Table A.1 for a list of items used in scale construction.

Cobb and Kasl devote great attention, in their longitudinal study, to this question of timing. Their data show that, averaged for all workers, concern over financial and job security are greatest at the time of termination, are also elevated during the "anticipation" period prior to layoff, have dropped off substantially six months after termination, and have declined still further one year, and then even more two years, after termination. Although their data and analysis are very detailed, it appears that psychological symptoms scale scores similar to those used in the Youngstown surveys do not vary as dramatically over time. Also, in their study, differences between those with higher and lower rates of unemployment had disappeared two years after termination.

The second wave of Youngstown interviews, conducted from 15 to 18 months following termination, offer some rather weak statistical evidence of continuing differences between those unemployed at that time and other steelworkers.[8] For instance, the unemployed report significantly more symptoms of acute dependency and victimization ($p < .10$); although not quite significant, there appear to be differences as well in levels of aggression and alcohol abuse. Moreover, the average difference of means, across all 12 stress symptom scales, between unemployed steelworkers and all steelworkers, was virtually the same on the second wave as on the first wave. This suggests circumstantially that differences are not part of a stage-by-stage reaction to initial job loss but rather a relatively stable pattern accounted for by difference in current employment status. In less complicated language, it appears likely that current stress has more to do with current status than with past events.

The interview evidence cannot be used to determine whether workers suffered greater stress in the anticipation period before termination or perhaps right around the date of termination than subsequently. However, there is anecdotal and case study evidence that this was the case for some workers.

Changes in Mental Health

Aggregate mean mental health scores for first and second wave interviews with steelworkers and their spouses were analyzed in order to determine how individual mental health scale scores had changed over the period of the study. Table 3.4 shows moderate correlations between first and second wave scores for both steelworkers and their spouses. Correlations appear to be strong overall for spouses, however.

This result suggests that many respondents were remarkably consistent in their psychological status from the first to the second wave of mental health

Table 3.3 Mean Scores and Mean Deviations of Steelworkers on Mental Health Scales According to Employment Status, Second Wave, 1979

Mental Health Scale:	Steelworkers[a]				Steel worker Total[d]	Significance
	Unemployed	Retired	Rehired[b]	Employed[c]		
Alcohol Abuse	.33	.17	-.27	.00	1.44	.119
Drug Abuse	.11	.25	-.15	-.01	.67	.171
Victimization	.70	-.29	-.34	.01	1.13	.095
Apprehensive Avoidance	-.01	.15	-.31	.08	1.62	.598
Depression Immobility	.58	.05	-.49	.03	1.42	.211
Aggression/ Irritability	.68	-.34	-.49	.07	1.49	.105
Acute Dependency	.46	-.60	-.55	.17	1.76	.055
Helplessness/ Depression	.22	-.42	-.25	.10	1.11	.382
Poor Family Relations	.42	-.19	-.36	.06	.81	.262
High Anxiety	.08	-.45	-.50	.21	2.53	.168
Trust/Suspicion	.22	-.36	-.22	.08	2.67	.398
Hypochondriasis	.07	.13	-.35	.08	.45	.336
(N)	(48)	(19)	(30)	(58)	(155)	

a See Table A.1 for a list of items used in scale construction; b Figures are mean deviations; c Rehired other than at Youngstown Sheet and Tube; d Figures are mean deviations; e Figures are sample mean scores.

Table 3.4 Pearson's r Correlations between Steelworker and Spouse Mental Health Scores and between Their First and Second Wave Scores

Mental Health Scale:	Steelworker Wave I-II r (significance)	Spouse Wave I-II r (significance)	Steelworker/Spouse Wave I r (significance)	Steelworker/Spouse Wave II r (significance)
Alcohol Abuse	.21 (.004)	.60 (.000)	.03 (.342)	.11 (.089)
Drug Abuse	.13 (.054)	.62 (.000)	-.03 (.352)	.03 (.338)
Victimization	.29 (.001)	.55 (.000)	.08 (.147)	.19 (.008)
Apprehensive Avoidance	.25 (.001)	.53 (.000)	.06 (.242)	-.04 (.301)
Depression Immobility	.30 (.000)	.55 (.000)	-.05 (.252)	.23 (.002)
Aggression/ Irritability	.32 (.000)	-.09 (.123)	.11 (.092)	-.08 (.174)
Acute Dependency	.31 (.000)	.50 (.000)	.12 (.065)	.20 (.006)
Helplessness/ Depression	.29 (.000)	.53 (.000)	.03 (.353)	.12 (.064)
Poor Family Relations	.08 (.169)	.52 (.000)	.25 (.001)	.30 (.000)
High Anxiety	.30 (.000)	.55 (.000)	.09 (.133)	.00 (.476)
Hypochondriasis	.11 (.094)	.57 (.000)	.07 (207)	.08 (.159)
Trust/Suspicion	.20 (.005)	.56 (.000)	.16 (.020)	.06 (.221)

* See Table A.1 for a list of items used in scale construction.

testing. For this group, the effects of the closing, either positive or negative, were either minimal or persisted during the period between the two interviews.[9]

In addition to determining the degree of change in scores it is also important to determine changes in direction (i.e., higher or lower mental health scores). Scores on the first and second waves were matched for each respondent. The number of increases or decreases in scoring were then summed. It happens that workers are just as likely to have scored lower. This result suggests that aggregating the scores for each sub-sample obscures important individual psychological changes, whether related to the plant closings or not.

Personal Characteristics and Psychological Stress

Earlier studies have suggested that older, less-educated, and minority workers are likely to be more severely affected by job loss than others. A plausible contradictory hypothesis is that less-educated and minority workers will be less severely affected because their job statuses tend to be lower and less secure to begin with, so that sudden termination is less of a loss and less of a shock than it would be for others.

Analysis of variance shows that among all affected workers all three background variables mentioned—education, age, and race—influenced

---

Jonathan Sherrill
Employed by Youngstown Sheet and Tube Company, 1950–1978; retired March 1978
Age: 59
Spouse: Marianne, married 1955
Children: two daughters

Jon is a black man who came from North Carolina during the Korean War to work in the mills. When working, Jon had little time or energy for hobbies or outside activities. Now he has large blocks of time which are difficult for him to fill. He tends a large backyard garden in summer and watches a lot of television. He has also looked for work, without success. To cut back on their expenses after his forced early retirement, he and his wife have canned and frozen vegetables. For the past thirty years, he has looked forward to returning to North Carolina and building a retirement home. Now, with a reduced pension, this is unlikely.

the response to loss to employment.[10] When first interviewed, older workers who had been laid off—whether unemployed, retired, or rehired—were more likely than younger workers to be in a condition of "stunned immobility." However, it was more rather than less educated workers who experienced the strongest stress reactions on the three indices of alcohol abuse, victimization, and aggression. Blacks were more likely than whites to express feelings of victimization. The sizes of these differences, although significant, do not suggest that such reactions were overwhelming for most workers, even among these subgroups of those affected.

The role of social support in determining response to job loss has been examined in earlier studies. To maximize the homogeneity of their samples, Cobb and Kasl studied only married workers. However, they found that social support—including spouse support—was an independent influence on the amount of stress experienced after job loss; they found that those with highest unemployment and least social support experienced greatest stress.

The Youngstown surveys indicate that social support should not be equated with marital status.[11] Single workers ($N = 40$) were not significantly different than married workers ($N = 242$) in the extent of psychological stress experienced. This is further supported by the rather surprising finding that current employment status of their husbands seems to have little or no relation to the amount of psychological stress reported by steelworkers' wives.

Gil Reeves
Employed by Youngstown Sheet and Tube Company, 1963–1977
Age: 58
Spouse: Myra, married 1962
Children: two daughters and one son

Myra said that since Gil's layoff more than a year earlier, he had become gradually more depressed and moody. Even though he was always looking for work, each job rejection became more difficult for him to accept. Myra believes her husband's joblessness and reduced income added to existing problems within the family. At about this time, they separated and she took the children to West Virginia, where her parents live.

Tom Cinelli
Employed by Youngstown Sheet and Tube Company, 1971–1977
Age: 26
Spouse: Betty, married 1977
Children: one son

Tom's unemployment benefits stopped in April 1979, after he completed a publicly funded drafting design course. By mid-1979, Tom and Betty were close to bankruptcy. Two-thirds of Tom's $500 monthly income was spent on rent and utilities. They were ineligible for food stamps because their income was considered too high. They could not afford medication for Betty's and her son's chronic sinus conditions. A year later, Tom was still without work, and the couple had divorced. Betty feels the layoff hurt their marriage but does not blame the divorce on that alone. She now has a part-time job in a local grocery store.

A more detailed examination of the role of the family would probably reveal wide variations in the level and success of supportive efforts. Walter Strange's case studies of terminated workers, as well as the much earlier work of Bakke (1944), indicate that "the wife's perception is [a] critical input in her husband's definition of their situation." (Strange, 1978: 55) However, there is also evidence in these studies that unemployment can either strengthen or weaken the marriage, depending on its preexisting basis and stability.

The question of social support is broader, of course, than the role of the traditional husband/wife relationship. Many more workers today than in prior years are likely to be single or to be members of less traditionally structured households. Moreover, the sources and forms of social support can show even more variation than reflected in household classifications. Consequently, more careful analysis of the interactions between social support and employment status is needed as a basis for mental health and social policy development (e.g., Figueira-McDonough, 1978).

Job Safety as an Indicator of Mental Health

Another way to measure psychological reaction to a plant closing is through changes in workers' on-the-job behavior. This reaction may begin as soon as a closing is announced. For some workers, the stress may surface as injuries on the job. Workers may become preoccupied with personal

George Kendik
Employed by Youngstown Sheet and Tube Company, 1946–1977
Age: 52
Spouse: Carolyn, married 1963
Children: one daughter, one son

George spent 31 years at Youngstown Sheet and Tube as a production foreman. It was the center of his social life. Although hard hit financially by the loss of his job, he and his wife, Carolyn, were not deeply in debt and had money saved. However, emotionally George was devastated. He could not leave the house for weeks and was unable to discuss the situation with friends. Not until several months later did he feel ready to look for work. He then found work in a state liquor store at considerably reduced income and benefits. He still feels cheated and deceived; he blames the company for doing nothing to aid him after the layoff. Now when he meets his old friends, he finds it hard to communicate. He says that the glue which held them together for so many years has become weak and unbinding.

matters, may abandon usual precautions, or may simply give up caring about their safety. For many in hazardous jobs, this lack of attentiveness could lead to serious injury or, in some cases, death. Also, actions taken to shut down the plant may create new hazards.

Ed Mann, President of the local union representing workers at the Brier Hill Mill, expressed his concern for what he perceived as a serious problem there when the LTV Corporation indicated in 1978 that it would close the facility in about one year (Peskin, 1978). Mann reported that injuries in the works were twice as high in the ten months after the announcement of the closing of Brier Hill as before. This union leader stated that two workers had been killed and 127 injured in plant accidents after the closing announcement. Safety records were acquired from both the Campbell and Brier Hill Works to test this claim concerning the stress-producing consequences of a plant shutdown. Jones & Laughlin Steel Corporation examined its safety records from the Lykes-owned Sheet and Tube Company for 1976, 1977, 1978, and 1979, and provided these statistics. Confirming data from the Ohio Division of Occupational Safety and Health Administration were also obtained. Table 3.5 shows the trend in plant safety for the last four years.

Mann's estimate was correct. In those facilities that remained open for some period after the closing plans were announced, lost work cases, lost

Table 3.5   Accidents at Youngstown Sheet and Tube Campbell and
Brier Hill Works, 1976–1979

	Manhours Worked	Lost Work Cases	Lost Work Days	Fatalities	Severity[a]	Frequency[b]
1976	16,361,995	339	6,113	0	75	4.14
1977	15,343,914	401	10,491	2	137	5.23
1978	9,670,509	311	8,705	2	180	6.43
1979	8,870,264	170	4,029	0	91	3.83

[a] Severity is an Occupational Safety and Health Administration (OSHA) overall rating.
[b] Frequency is based on the number of lost work hours per 100,000 manhours worked.
SOURCE: Jones & Laughlin Steel Company

work days, fatalities, accident severity, and frequency all increased dramatically from 1976 to 1978. In 1979, some time after the crisis, the rates declined sharply. If stress increases the likelihood of injury in this setting as it so often does in others, then these statistics may indicate that workers facing layoffs were under considerable pressure.

Why Psychological Effects Appear Relatively Mild

Several factors may have ameliorated short-run psychological distress due to the 1977–78 Youngstown job losses. *First,* the economy nationally and in Ohio was expanding; while unemployment fell less rapidly in Youngstown during this period than in other parts of Ohio, jobs were available in the community for unemployed workers. Twenty months later, approximately 95 percent of the laid-off workers had either found new jobs or had chosen early retirement (Bagshaw and Schnorbus, 1980). Although the new jobs were not always desirable or secure, the prospect of long-term unemployment which might necessitate moving, selling a home, modifying a lifestyle, and so on, was not an important consideration for most workers. The short-run capacity of the local labor market to absorb workers from shut-down plants may be a major factor in determining potential psychological impact.

Second, on the whole, workers probably had substantial financial resources upon which to draw. Steelworkers are among the highest paid industrial workers. In addition, unemployment compensation, supplemental union benefits (SUB pay) and trade readjustment allowance (TRA) provided workers with almost as much income as their prior wages. This compensation was provided for at least six and as much as 18 months. As a result of these two factors, workers could take their time in finding new employment. They could also pursue retraining in order to secure different jobs in the local market.[12] The options and resources available to the steelworkers were not available to most laid-off assembly-line workers studied in the 1950s and 60s. Consequently, the type of industry which is affected and availability of savings and insurance payments may be important factors in determining psychological impact.

Third, the Youngstown Sheet and Tube Company was for years a dominating part of the community. When it permanently closed, many— but not all—workers felt that it somehow would reopen. Indeed, it appeared that various legal battles, schemes for reopening the mills, corporate mergers, and renovation plans would somehow lead to a reopening. Steelworkers were accustomed to frequent layoffs, and had become accustomed also to "doom and gloom" stories of potential closings. The fact that so many workers were at first laid off following the closing announcement, yet subsequently called back for one or more short periods, may have supported these beliefs. In the past, somehow the mills always remained open; in this case, the closing was permanent. Nevertheless, for many months, a diminishing number of former workers maintained an unjustified optimism.

Fourth, relative to other U.S. metropolitan areas of similar size, the Youngstown community has been socially stable and relatively integrated. Intergenerational family ties, ethnic group identifications, the Catholic Church, and traditional machine-style political organization are relatively strong in this area and provide major social and spiritual support in times of personal crisis. This web of personal relationships not only offers emotional comfort but also constitutes an informal system of economic exchange and employment. Thus, it fulfills many functions similar to those also intended by the formal systems of financial assistance and human services.

For some or all of these reasons, the level and duration of psychological stress due to job losses may have been reduced.

Does Distress Constitute a Mental Health Problem?

It has been noted that, averaged for groups of workers, the measured effects tend to be relatively small, although statistically significant. Given the relative bluntness of the questionnaire as an instrument for recording psychological distress, it is difficult to determine: (1) whether the recorded intensity of distress is an accurate reflection of the intensity of what is felt by the workers and (2) whether what is measured constitutes evidence of mental health problems among at least some fraction of the workers. The latter question is complicated by differing definitions of mental health and mental health needs, as indicated earlier in the chapter.

For example, an arbitrary criterion can be applied to the scale scores to isolate individuals who gave "disintegrative" or "dysfunctional" responses which fall beyond two standard deviations from the mean scale scores. There are 12 steelworkers (about four percent of the sample) who meet this criterion. Subsequent detailed examination of their survey responses by a clinical psychologist confirmed that these constituted, at least, a population at "high risk" of mental illness.

Similar proportions of the spouse and autoworker samples were found to be at this level of risk. Thus, it may well be that the steel crisis had little effect on the proportion of workers under severe stress or "at risk" of needing professional treatment for mental health problems. At the least it suggests that, for most unemployed workers, the measured increases in stress probably do not constitute psychopathology of a severity that would customarily lead to a diagnosis of need for mental health services.

Two possibilities remain. One is that the measurement methods employed, although derived from traditionally used diagnostic tests, may not adequately capture the mental and emotional stress resulting from job loss or unemployment. This would be true, for instance, if the timing of the interviews did not correspond, for many workers, to the period(s) of greatest stress—which is probable. Second, it is possible to view the mental health of workers as having to do not simply with anger, anxiety, alcohol abuse, and other negative symptoms of stress but also with their abilities to cope creatively with the changes that have occurred. If the definition of mental health is broadened to include these positive attributes, then we may find considerable variation *within* the terminated and unemployed groups in individual coping abilities. This would lead to rather different conclusions about both the need for and the role of mental health services and other human services in relation to plant closings. Therefore, a closer look is needed at the various strategies—both individual and collective— used by workers to cope with the loss of a job and with the closing of the mill.

Conclusion

Evidence concerning the significant personal stresses produced by job loss and continuing unemployment is gradually accumulating. The Youngstown data suggest that the experienced stresses were relatively mild. However, a number of other studies indicate that economic change produces greater incidence of behavioral disorder and health problems among those affected.

Given the variety of environmental conditions under which job losses can occur and given the wide variations in personal circumstances and coping abilities, more research is needed to specify causal "pathways" between job loss and psychological impact (Dooley and Catalano, 1980). This research will be especially important to policy-makers trying to identify points of maximum leverage at which to intervene.

The evidence of short-term psychological effects on Youngstown steelworkers indicates that most short-term emotional stresses were manageable without professional intervention. Few workers experienced severe trauma or breakdowns. If, however, the concept of mental health is defined to include positive capacities to cope more effectively or creatively with personal crisis, then more information is needed on how workers managed this situation. Such evidence is examined in Chapters 5 and 6.

Before turning to an examination of more active responses to the crisis, however, it is necessary to complete the portrait of short-run impacts by looking at the closing's impact on the wider community. A variety of information is brought to bear on this question in Chapter 4.

4. The Community Impact of the Shutdown

Coauthored with Anthony Stocks

It seems like Youngstown will be that ghost town we all heard rumor of.... Will the last one leaving Youngstown, please turn out the lights?

former steelworker, Letter to the Editor,
Youngstown Vindicator, 1979

The unemployed worker who seeks new work immediately competes with, and perhaps displaces, someone with less experience and skill. The wife of a laid-off worker who finds a new part-time job is no longer able to spend her days as a hospital volunteer. The bar where workers gathered near the plant entrance, at first, gains patronage but some months later is forced to close. Workers on a railroad that carried steel between parts of the mill lose their jobs as well; two years after the shutdown, a residence hotel where these railroad men once stayed overnight between shifts, also closes down. Local governments that relied on property taxes paid by the steel company are forced to reduce services and lay off employees. Day after day, the media carry stories of both gloom and hope related to the local economy. Thus, effects of the closing move outward, from those directly affected, to touch significantly the lives of virtually all in the community.

The expectation that the Youngstown Sheet and Tube closing would drastically alter the community's future was expressed in letters such as the following:

The loss to the valley is impossible to define, for this decision will affect almost every aspect of life. Besides the 5,000 families whose livelihood is cut off, railroaders, truckers, and others who

60

serve the Campbell plant will be affected. Youngstown, Campbell, and Struthers, along with their schools, the county, the library, and other institutions will lose millions of dollars in tax income; even the "bedroom" townships will be affected. (Letter to the Editor *Youngstown Vindicator,* September 20, 1977)

I don't know if the people of Mahoning Valley realize that the closing of the Youngstown Sheet and Tube Campbell Works not only affects the steel workers and their families, but the community as a whole. Right now, not everyone is feeling the economical and emotional pinch of the mill closing but it is evident it is a matter of time if we don't do something now.

The unemployed steel workers won't be in the buying market as before, causing small independent businesses to close. Sunday church collections won't be as high, causing higher tuition fees for private schools and church bills.

The unemployed won't see their family doctors as they should for fear of high medical bills or for lack of hospitalization, thus reflecting on lower hospital census and calling for layoffs of hospital workers.

Those able to work will have a higher tax burden to compensate for those not working. Towns built around the steel industry, like Struthers, Lowellville, and Campbell, may be future "ghost towns." (Letter to the Editor *Youngstown Vindicator* October 8, 1978)

This chapter attempts to assess the nature and extent of the closing's impact on the community, using three types of information. The first is an analysis of employment rates. These are compared with rates which might have occurred had the Campbell Works not shut down.

The second type of information used are selected social indicators: number of divorces, real estate transfers, bankruptcy petitions, crime rates, mortality rates, number of new car sales, court cases, marriage license applications, United Way contributions, and liquor sales for Mahoning County, including Youngstown. Where available, social indicator data from Trumbull County, Mahoning County's sister county to the north, are included for purposes of comparison. Social indicator data were gathered where possible on a monthly basis from January 1975, more than two years before the crisis, up to and including May 1980.[1]

The third data source is a telephone survey with 302 adults, a representative sample of Youngstown area residents, conducted during the summer of 1978. The object was to ascertain the impact of the crisis on attitudes and perceptions of the general public, including people who may or may not have experienced the direct and indirect effects of mass unemployment.

Two analytical strategies were undertaken in order to assess the impact of the steel mill closings on the community. One strategy involved a comparison of actual events before and after the closing with an interpolation of what would have happened had the closing not occurred. The other was an examination of differences in events during equivalent time periods before and after the crisis (e.g., December 1976 with December 1977).

Employment in the Youngstown Area

Following the September 1977 closing announcement, various informal studies by local and state government agencies forecast additional, i.e., secondary, job losses ranging from 4,000 to 14,000.[2] These projections tended to overshoot the mark. They assumed status quo conditions in other local employment sectors, independent of or only partially dependent upon local steel for markets. They did not consider the impact of unemployment insurance, trade adjustment assistance, and other transfer payments in sustaining income and employment in the short run.

The actual employment changes which occurred in manufacturing and nonmanufacturing sectors in the Youngstown-Warren Standard Metropolitan Statistical Area (SMSA) in the year following the plant closure were less than expected. However, to assess the effect of the closing on employment, it is necessary to project, in the light of other changes in the local economy, what employment would have been had the mills remained open.

Employment Change in Manufacturing

Employment in manufacturing remained relatively stable despite the closing. However, this occurred during a period of surging economic activity nationally. Other methods of analysis indicate there were 3,000 to 4,200 fewer manufacturing jobs in the metropolitan area a year after the closing than would have been there if the mills had remained open.

Of particular note is the strength of transportation equipment employment in the months when jobs in primary metals and its basic steel component were declining. Between August 1977 and January 1978, the gain of 4,700 transportation equipment jobs more than offset the loss of 3,900 jobs in steel. This meant an absolute increase in area manufacturing employment over comparable months of the previous year. Undoubtedly, the shift from production of the ill-fated Vega automobile to a more successful selling mix of compact cars at the Lordstown Complex of

General Motors Corporation accounts for much of this gain in transportation equipment jobs.

Except for the strong performance of fabricated metal, most of the sectors in Table 4.1 reveal little change in employment. Moreover, as summarized by Figure 4.1, in all months after January 1978, except August, the loss of jobs in primary metals more than offset gains in transportation equipment. This left manufacturing equipment employment below the preceding year for the months of March through July. Yet there is no doubt that the expansion of jobs at the General Motors Lordstown plant did much to cushion the blow to the Youngstown-Warren economy and sustain its economic base. In fact, the mean values for manufacturing equipment employment for the 12 months preceding and following the closure are identical.[3]

While the historical record is important, it is equally interesting to inquire what manufacturing employment within the Youngstown-Warren Metropolitan Area might have been if there had been no partial shutdown of the Campbell Works. Two simple methods were employed to estimate this. First, trend analysis were conducted on monthly employment data[4] for the SMSA in the year prior to the partial closing of the Campbell Works. The best-fit trend for each sector was then used to project monthly employment for the succeeding year. Thus, it was possible to compare projected employment with actual employment to estimate the strength of each sector of manufacturing employment.[5]

A second method was used to determine the ratios of local employment to that of the entire State of Ohio, by sector, in each month for the year prior to the Campbell Works shutdown. The ratios for each sector were then multiplied by state employment, by sector, for each of the months in the following year. This produced an estimate of local projected employment. Such a "share-of-state" technique assumes that the Youngstown-Warren area's share-of-state employment by sector would remain constant over the two-year span, in the absence of any major events affecting the local economy.

Figure 4.2 illustrates both the trend projection and share-of-state estimates of manufacturing employment for the local economy in the year following the closing announcement. The share-of-state method produces consistently higher estimates of manufacturing jobs than the trend projection. By the end of the first year following the Campbell Works shutdown, actual manufacturing employment was 3,000 lower than the trend projection and 4,200 less than the share-of-state estimate. For primary metals employment, both the trend projection and share-of-state methods yield 4,700 more local jobs than those actually in existence by August 1978.[6]

Table 4.1 Paired Monthly Manufacturing Employment for the Youngstown-Warren SMSA; September 1976 – August 1978 (In Thousands)

Manufacturing Sectors	September 1976	September 1977	October 1976	October 1977	November 1976	November 1977	December 1976	December 1977	January 1977	January 1978	February 1977	February 1978
Durable Goods:												
Stone, Clay & Glass	2.5	2.7	2.4	2.7	2.3	2.7	2.2	2.5	2.1	2.6	1.9	2.6
Primary Metals	42.4	41.6	41.4	40.4	40.8	39.4	40.7	38.6	41.1	38.6	40.9	36.8
Blast Furnace & Basic Steel	27.0	26.3	26.2	25.2	25.6	24.0	25.3	22.9	25.8	23.0	25.6	22.3
Fabricated Metal Products	8.8	8.6	8.7	8.7	8.7	8.9	8.5	8.8	8.3	8.9	7.5	9.0
Fabricated Structural Metal Products	2.8	2.8	2.7	2.9	2.7	3.0	2.7	3.0	2.6	3.0	2.5	3.0
Nonelectrical Machinery	7.3	6.7	7.0	6.2	6.7	6.4	7.0	6.2	7.0	6.1	6.7	5.9
Metalworking Machinery	3.6	3.0	3.3	2.9	3.1	2.8	3.3	2.6	3.3	2.5	3.1	2.3
Electrical Equip. & Supp.	3.4	3.1	3.3	3.1	3.3	3.2	3.4	3.2	3.4	3.2	3.4	3.2
Transportation Equipment	9.6	11.3	9.5	12.9	7.5	12.3	9.9	13.1	7.3	12.7	9.5	12.7
Other Durable Goods	1.3	3.0	2.8	3.0	2.7	2.8	2.7	2.8	2.7	2.7	2.6	2.4
Total Durable Goods	75.3	77.0	75.1	77.0	72.0	76.2	74.4	75.2	71.9	74.8	72.5	72.6
Nondurable Goods	6.2	6.2	6.1	6.2	6.1	6.2	6.1	6.0	5.9	5.9	6.1	5.9
Total Manufacturing	81.6	83.2	81.1	83.2	78.1	82.4	80.5	81.2	77.8	80.8	78.6	78.6

	March 1977	March 1978	April 1977	April 1978	May 1977	May 1978	June 1977	June 1978	July 1977	July 1978	August 1977	August 1978
Durable Goods:												
Stone, Clay & Glass	2.4	2.6	2.5	2.6	2.6	2.6	2.6	2.7	2.6	2.5	2.7	2.7
Primary Metals	40.9	36.3	41.3	36.7	42.1	36.9	42.0	36.5	41.1	36.8	41.2	36.6
Blast Furnace & Basic Steel	25.7	22.2	26.0	22.0	26.7	22.2	26.8	22.3	26.7	22.7	26.9	22.6
Fabricated Metal Products	8.5	9.0	8.4	8.9	8.8	9.2	8.8	9.2	8.6	9.2	8.2	9.1
Fabricated Structural Metal Producs	2.7	3.0	2.7	3.1	2.7	3.1	2.7	3.2	2.8	3.2	2.8	3.2
Nonelectrical Machinery	6.7	5.8	6.8	5.8	6.7	5.8	6.7	5.7	6.7	5.8	6.7	5.8
Metalworking Machinery	3.1	2.2	3.0	2.2	3.0	2.2	3.0	2.2	3.0	2.3	3.0	2.3
Electrical Equip & Supp.	3.4	3.2	3.4	3.2	3.4	3.2	3.4	3.2	3.1	3.2	3.1	3.2
Transportation Equipment	9.6	12.8	9.7	12.9	9.8	13.0	10.2	12.9	10.2	12.6	8.0	12.7
Other Durable Goods	2.7	2.5	2.8	2.4	2.8	2.6	3.0	2.6	2.9	2.5	3.0	2.7
Total Durable Goods	74.2	72.2	74.9	72.5	76.2	73.3	76.7	72.8	75.2	72.6	72.9	72.8
Nondurable Goods	6.1	5.9	6.1	6.0	6.0	6.0	6.1	5.9	6.0	6.2	6.1	6.2
Total Manufacturing	80.3	78.0	81.0	78.5	82.2	79.2	82.7	78.7	81.2	78.8	79.1	78.9

SOURCE: Ohio Bureau of Employment Services, *Ohio Labor Market Information,* monthly issues.

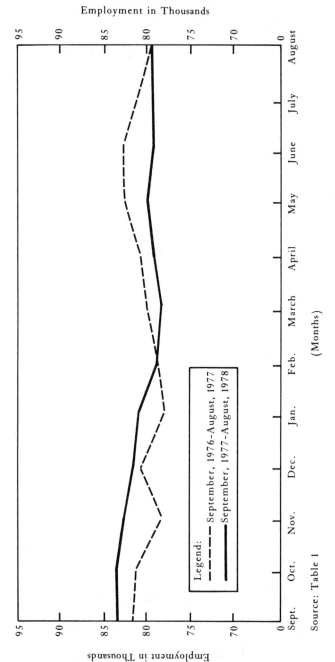

Source: Table 1

Figure 4.1 Manufacturing Employment in the Youngstown-Warren Area, September 1976—August 1978

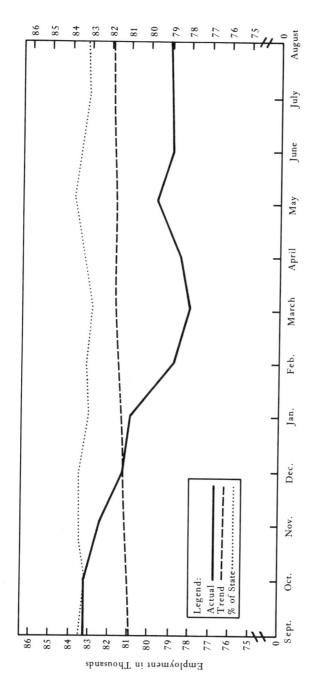

Figure 4.2 Manufacturing Employment for the Youngstown-Warren Area, Actual, Trend Projected, and Percentage of State Estimated, September 1977–August 1978

Nonagricultural Employment Change

Similar procedures were used to explore changes in nonagricultural employment in the Youngstown-Warren SMSA. Table 4.2 reveals that both retail trade, services and miscellaneous industry sectors consistently produced more jobs in the year following the Campbell Works shutdown than in the preceding 12 months. Such performance was aided by two things. Laid-off steel workers were provided liberal transfer payments. And the metropolitan area grew in importance as a retailing center for neighboring counties in Ohio and northwestern Pennsylvania. Construction showed similar strength.

It is gratifying to see that all nonagricultural employment in the local economy was higher in each of the 12 months following the shutdown at the Campbell Works than in the previous year. In contrast to manufacturing employment, the mean value for nonagricultural employment was significantly higher in the 12 months following the closure than in the 12 months prior.[7]

These numbers belie the fears that the Campbell Works shutdown could cripple the local economy. But once again they must be considered in relation to state and national trends. Between September 1977 and August 1978, nonagricultural employment increased by 4.1 percent nationally and by 2.1 percent in Ohio.[8] Over the same period, nonagricultural jobs fell off 1.3 percent in the Youngstown-Warren SMSA.[9] It is clear the local economy did not share in the employment growth of the nation, or in the more modest expansion within Ohio.

Trend projections and share-of-state estimates were developed to assess how nonagricultural employment might have changed if the Campbell Works had not closed. Figure 4.3 shows actual, trend projected, and share-of-state estimated nonagricultural employment in the 12 months following the shutdown. Unlike manufacturing, the share-of-state estimates only yield higher employment than the trend projections for September through December and the month of June. As of August 1978, trend projected nonagricultural employment was 8,400 larger and share-of-state 5,300 greater than actual employment.[10]

Subsequent Status of Employment

In June 1980, the unemployment rate for Mahoning County as 13.7 percent—at a time when the U.S. rate was 7.0 percent and the Ohio rate was 8.7 percent. This high unemployment rate reflects the loss of almost 10,000 basic steel jobs. Additional job losses were due to the 1980 recession and the multiplier effect for jobs related to or dependent upon the steel industry.

Employment in Thousands

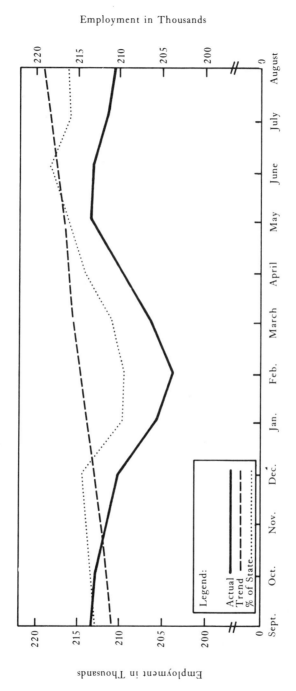

Figure 4.3 Nonagricultural Employment for the Youngstown-Warren Area, Actual, Trend Projected, and Percentage of State Estimated, September 1977–August 1978

Table 4.2 Paired Monthly Nonagricultural Employment for the Youngstown-Warren SMSA, September 1976 – August 1978 (In Thousands)

Employment Sectors	September		October		November		December		January		February	
	1976	1977	1976	1977	1976	1977	1976	1977	1977	1978	1977	1978
Mining	0.3	0.3	0.3	0.3	0.3	0.3	0.3	0.3	0.3	0.3	0.3	0.3
Construction	7.5	8.5	7.2	8.2	7.0	7.9	6.4	7.2	5.6	6.2	5.3	6.0
Manufacturing	81.6	83.2	81.1	83.2	78.1	82.4	80.5	81.2	77.8	80.8	78.6	78.6
Transportation and Public Utilities	9.9	9.9	9.8	9.9	9.7	10.1	9.8	10.1	9.6	9.8	9.7	9.8
Wholesale Trade	7.5	7.7	7.5	7.7	7.5	7.7	7.5	7.7	7.4	7.6	7.3	7.6
Retail Trade	36.4	37.1	36.3	37.2	36.6	37.5	37.4	38.4	35.5	36.5	34.7	35.8
Finance, Insurance & Real Estate	6.5	6.9	6.5	6.9	6.5	6.9	6.6	6.9	6.5	6.8	6.5	6.8
Services & Misc. Industry	33.8	35.3	32.6	34.2	32.5	34.0	32.5	32.6	32.2	32.3	32.2	33.0
Government	23.0	24.3	24.5	25.2	25.0	25.7	25.3	25.8	24.5	25.2	25.0	25.9
TOTAL	206.4	213.3	205.7	212.9	203.2	212.4	206.2	210.1	199.2	205.4	199.5	203.7

	March 1977	March 1978	April 1977	April 1978	May 1977	May 1978	June 1977	June 1978	July 1977	July 1978	August 1977	August 1978
Mining	0.3	0.3	0.3	0.3	0.3	0.3	0.3	0.3	0.3	0.3	0.3	0.3
Construction	6.2	6.8	7.1	7.8	7.4	8.1	7.7	8.6	8.5	9.1	8.7	9.2
Manufacturing	80.3	78.0	81.0	78.5	82.2	79.2	82.7	78.7	81.2	78.8	79.1	78.9
Transportation and Public Utilities	9.7	9.9	9.9	10.1	10.1	10.3	10.2	10.6	9.8	10.5	9.7	10.0
Wholesale Trade	7.4	7.7	7.6	7.8	7.6	7.9	7.7	7.8	7.8	8.0	7.8	8.0
Retail Trade	35.3	36.4	36.3	37.5	36.7	38.1	37.1	38.5	37.1	38.4	37.0	38.3
Finance, Insurance & Real Estate	6.5	6.8	6.7	7.0	6.8	7.0	6.9	7.1	6.9	7.0	6.9	7.0
Services & Misc. Industry	32.6	34.1	33.9	35.3	34.4	35.7	34.8	36.2	34.9	36.1	34.8	35.9
Government	25.2	26.1	24.8	25.6	25.3	26.1	25.0	25.3	23.2	23.5	23.1	22.9
TOTAL	203.5	206.1	207.6	210.0	210.8	212.7	212.4	213.0	209.7	211.8	207.4	210.6

SOURCE: Ohio Bureau of Employment Services, *Ohio Labor Market Information*, monthly issues.

In 1973, there were 211,000 jobs held in Mahoning County. Some 93,000 jobs were in the manufacturing sector. As of May 1980, Mahoning County had 207,600 jobs, or a loss since 1973 of 3,400 permanent jobs. The important manufacturing sector was reduced to only 68,800 jobs, a loss of 24,200 jobs, or 26 percent of the 1973 total.

Growth in other sectors prevents the unemployment rate from being still higher. The loss in manufacturing jobs was partly offset during the 1973–1980 period by increases in government jobs, from 22,500 to 27,500; in retail sales from 29,100 to 47,500; and in services from 20,700 to 39,300.

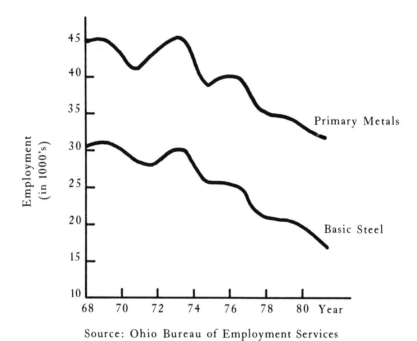

Source: Ohio Bureau of Employment Services

Figure 4.4 Steel-Related Jobs in the Mahoning Valley, 1968-1980

Jobs are important to psychological well-being. But the community and the workers may not return to normal even when the unemployed have found jobs. In the case of Youngstown, the average manufacturing jobs paid $10 per hour or about $20,000 per year. By contrast, retail jobs pay only $4.73 per hour and service jobs about $7.00. The loss of 24,200 manufacturing jobs compared to 1973, means that the local economy will lose $500 million per year in wages. Consequently, it appears that the overall standard of living in the community will decline, as workers are compelled to work for less.

Other Socio-Economic Consequences of Plant Shutdown

To assess the shutdown's impact on Youngstown's social fabric, time series data were collected for several key social indicators. These were: number of new car sales, real estate transfers, bankruptcies filed, court cases, divorce petitions granted, marriage license applications, mortality rates, crime, United Way contributions, and liquor sales. The analysis looked for trends over a time period spanning the shutdown.[11]

Each time series began, depending on data availability, sometime before the closing of the steel mills and continued to a time at least one year later. Where possible, we compared equivalent data for Trumbull County, bordering Mahoning County on the north so that some inferences could be made relative to a baseline. Where the data were rich enough, we performed a variety of trend analyses and attempted to project the indicators into the mid-1980s to see what might have happened had the Campbell Works not shut down.

Crime

Incidence of criminal activity has been directly related in numerous studies to economic depression (Hemley and McPheters, 1974). Two different types of data were gathered in order to test this hypothesis. One data source was the Youngstown Police Department's information on the number of traffic accidents, traffic arrests, and traffic tickets gathered monthly for the period 1976–1978. The other data were from the FBI Uniform Crime Reports for the City of Youngstown, gathered yearly for the period 1975 through 1979.

Youngstown traffic data. Of the three traffic indicators, only the number of accidents increased from 1977 to 1978. This increase was slight (5%). The Youngstown Police Department's Traffic Division data are difficult to interpret. Traffic enforcement programs varied during the years examined. In 1976, a comprehensive enforcement program known as the Fatal Accident Reduction Enforcement (FARE) program was initiated. It was suspended in 1977. In 1978, however, a new enforcement procedure called Selective Enforcement Program (SEP) was instituted. The effects of these programs are visible in Figure 4.5. The number of traffic tickets issued declined significantly in 1977 after the FARE program was suspended.

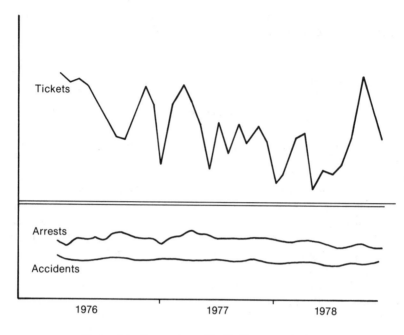

Figure 4.5   Youngstown Traffic Reports, 1976-1978

These varying enforcement techniques and the absence of any significant surge in the statistics following the closing are evidence that any impact resulting from the closings was either too small to measure or offset by other influences.

FBI uniform reports. Statistics excerpted from the Uniform Crime Reports compare the percentage change in the total crime index for the City of Youngstown with changes for the United States, North Central States (including Ohio), and all cities of 100,000 to 250,000 (Youngstown has a population of approximately 140,000). Data for 1976 and 1977 indicate that the volume of crimes committed in Youngstown increased by 6 percent and 8 percent, respectively. For these years, the crime index declined or remained the same for the U.S., the North Central States, and cities of 100,000 to 250,000 population. Figures for 1978 show only slight changes for any of the four categories: U.S. (-1%), North Central States (- 1%), cities of 100,000-250,000 population (+2%), and Youngstown (- 0.5%).

In 1979, the trend established in 1976 and 1977 was dramatically reversed. Youngstown showed a significant decrease in the crime index of

The Community Impact **75**

10 percent. The crime indices for the U.S., the North Central States, and cities of 100,000–250,000 population increased by 11 percent, 6 percent, and 12 percent, respectively. These comparisons suggest that Youngstown's crime rates were not responsive to the same influences as other areas during these years.

Table 4.3   FBI Crime Data for Youngstown City 1975–1979

Years:	Crime Index*	Murder	Rape	Robbery	Assault	Larceny	Vehicle Theft
	N	N	N	N	N	N	N
1975	8,001	38	48	518	318	3,527	859
1976	8,486	40	52	485	399	4,013	656
1977	9,162	28	54	449	442	4,795	684
1978	9,124	18	63	375	488	4,912	611
1979	8,574	29	54	362	564	4,360	673

* Refers to total number of serious crimes included in the uniform crime reporting system.

SOURCE: FBI, *Crime in the U.S.,* yearly issues.

The FBI annual crime index figures can be broken down also by type of crime, as shown in Table 4.3. Analysis of individual crimes produced a mixed pattern. The incidence of various crimes fluctuated across the years examined, rather than uniformly increasing or decreasing. Rape, assaults, and larceny all increased in the year following the closing. Assaults have shown a uniform increase since 1975. Rape, robbery, and larceny, however, showed some decline in 1979. As with traffic statistics, special programs instituted by the police department may account for part of the statistical fluctuation. Data are also subject to variations in reporting practices. Trend analysis of crime reports thus provides no support for a finding that the 1977–78 closing influenced rates of criminal activity in the community.

Mortality Rates

The numbers of death certificates filed in Mahoning and Trumbull Counties for the years 1976 through 1979 were divided by current population estimates for each year. This measure was then used to obtain a "mortality" rate per 1,000 persons for each county. National mortality rates were also included for comparison. Table 4.4 shows the results of this analysis.

Table 4.4   Mortality Rates for Mahoning and Trumbull Counties
1976–1979

Years	Number of Death Certificates Issued		Mortality Rate[a] (per 1,000)		
	Mahoning N	Trumbull[b] N	Mahoning	Trumbull	National[c]
1976	3,183	1,642	10.4	7.1	8.9
1977	3,251	1,649	10.6	7.1	8.8
1978	3,233	1,620	10.6	7.0	8.8
1979	3,227	1,590	10.5	6.9	8.7

[a] Computed by dividing Ohio Department of Health population estimates by 1,000, then dividing into number of death certificates.
[b] Girard, Ohio, keeps its own records and is not included in this computation.
[c] National Center for Health Statistics, *Monthly Vital Statistics Report,* yearly reports.

SOURCE: Ohio Department of Health.

Mahoning County has a death rate much higher than either the national average or Trumbull County. However, trends in the data for all three areas are similar: the death rate after 1977 shows a slight decrease.

Death rates for Mahoning County after its plant closing does not necessarily contradict the findings of Brenner (1977; see also Chapter 3). The fact that the unemployed steelworkers were soon reemployed may be one important factor. Another may be that two years after a closing is not sufficient time to observe its effects on death rates.

Liquor Sales

Liquor sales may constitute a good measure of stress for a community. If liquor sales increase after a closing, then perhaps more people are turning to alcohol as a way to cope with personal problems. Annual liquor sales from 1976 through 1979 in dollars per capita were charted for Mahoning and Trumbull counties.

Table 4.5 shows that sales per capita increased for both counties. The two counties experienced the same rate of change over the four year period. When dollar figures were converted to 1967 levels to offset inflation, the sales appeared to be more constant over the period. Thus, evidence does not support a finding of increased alcohol consumption in the community following the plant closing.

Table 4.5   Liquor Sales for Mahoning and Trumbull Counties, 1976–1979

Years:	Sales in Dollars		Rate (dollars per capita*)	
	Mahoning	**Trumbull**	**Mahoning**	**Trumbull**
1976	$11,590.790	$7,666,651	$37.80	$32.00
1977	11,668,846	7,729,969	38.10	32.30
1978	12,054,404	7,968,189	39.40	33.20
1979	12,530,458	8,347,729	41.00	34.70

* Computed by dividing Ohio Department of Health population estimates into yearly sales.

SOURCE: Ohio State Office of Liquor Stores.

United Way Contributions

The extent to which individuals see fit to help others by contributing to charitable or community activities may be a surrogate measure for the extent to which the community's morale is affected positively or negatively by an economic crisis. It also reflects the community's capacity to help its members. Presumably, when times are bad, individuals will tend to retain potential contributions either as savings or expenditures on personal needs. The crisis reduces directly the contributions by those companies which base their contributions on payrolls and have cut back their work forces. Contributions to the Mahoning and Trumbull County United Way Campaigns from 1975 to 1980 were charted. Mahoning County contributions dropped in 1978, the year of the closing, but rebounded in 1979. Trumbull County contributions, by contrast, show a steady and more rapid rate of increase. Thus it appears likely that the closing caused a temporary drop in the financial resources available to private human service agencies.

Other Socio-economic Indicators

Other socio-economic indicator data were gathered, including monthly frequencies of domestic relations court cases, divorces/dissolutions granted, new court complaints filed, marriage license applications, bankruptcies filed, real estate transfers, and new car sales in Mahoning and Trumbull Counties for the period 1975 to 1980. Next, the months preceding the closing of the Campbell Works—January 1976 to September 1977—were matched with corresponding months following the closing—January 1978 to September 1979. The periods were compared to determine

Table 4.6   United Way Contributions for Mahoning and Trumbull
Counties

| | County | | | |
| Year: | Mahoning | | Trumbull | |
	Total	% Change	Total	% Change
1975	$1,936,900	+1.6	$1,156,082	+2.6
1976	1,967,025	+2.9	1,186,719	+7.9
1977	2,025,410	-0.4	1,288,483	+9.6
1978	1,947,504	+7.5	1,424,702	+9.0
1979	2,106,122	+2.5	1,565,287	
1980	2,160,406		*	

*Not yet available.

SOURCE: Mahoning and Trumbull County United Way

whether any statistically significant changes occurred for any of the
indicators.[12]

Results of this analysis show that in only one case, new car sales, was
the period before the closing significantly different from the period after
the closing for Mahoning County. In that case, Mahoning County car sales
declined at the same time Trumbull County sales were rising. Further, the
data for Trumbull County for this period also yielded two significant
differences–increases in new court complaints and marriage applications.

A pairwise matching of periods before and after a crisis is only one
technique available for determining the impact of events on a community.
Another technique involves examining the trends in the data for the
preclosing period and comparing them with what would have happened
had the closing not occurred and with what actually happened after the
closing. In order to accomplish this, the monthly social indicator data were
deseasonalized, that is, the recurrent effects of seasonal changes in the data,
which occur on a regular basis regardless of other potential impacts, were
removed. Next, the deseasonalized trends were plotted (Figures 4.6–12).
On the same charts, two straight lines were plotted showing results of
regression analyses. The first regression analysis showed the approximate
straight-line trend for the 33 months preceding the closing. The regression
line drawn for this period was extended to May 1980 as shown in the
dashed line in the graph. This line indicates what might have happened had
the closing not occurred. The second regression analysis established the
straight-line trend for the entire period from 1975 to 1980.

As Figure 4.6 shows, in Mahoning County the number of complaints
filed in court began to decrease after the closing, whereas it had been
increasing in the preclosing period. In the case of divorces/dissolutions

Table 4.7   Pairwise *t*-Tests for Selected Social Indicators, January
1976–September 1977, January 1978–September 1979

Social Indicator:	21 mos. Before Closing		21 Mos. After Closing			
	Mean	g	Mean	g	t	p
Domestic Relations						
Mahoning	81.7	23.4	93.8	23.0	-1.61	.124
Trumbull	31.4	7.7	32.2	8.2	-0.29	.772
Divorces/Dissolutions						
Mahoning	155.0	33.4	150.4	30.7	0.42	.677
Trumbull	113.8	15.3	111.6	12.4	0.48	.633
New Court Complaints						
Mahoning	179.6	16.5	180.9	16.0	-0.22	.826
Trumbull	111.2	12.1	100.5	14.3	-2.32	.031*
Marriage Licenses						
Mahoning	203.3	13.8	200.7	16.2	0.52	.611
Trumbull	167.2	14.8	180.0	15.4	-2.49	.022*
Bankruptcies						
Mahoning	26.3	6.9	25.5	8.9	0.35	.732
Trumbull	25.0	5.3	20.6	6.6	1.89	.073
Real Estate Transfers						
Mahoning	879.0	67.2	882.8	59.3	-0.23	.823
Trumbull	717.1	162.9	779.6	169.5	-1.17	.258
New Car Sales						
Mahoning	1.258.6	78.1	1,178.6	71.7	3.01	007*
Trumbull	1,726.0	183.3	1,872.9	242.2	-1.91	.071

g = standard deviation
t = student's *t* distribution statistic
p = indicates statistical significance
* = indicates statistically significant at p > .05.

granted, Figure 4.7 shows that the decreasing trend in the preclosing period continued on well into the postclosing period.

Two indicators appear to turn in a negative direction after 1977. Domestic relations court cases (Figure 4.6) had been on a decline in the preclosing period. Although the regression line in the graph shows that this trend has abated somewhat, it appears from visual inspection that the trend in domestic relations court cases would best be described as nonlinear. If this were done, domestic relations cases would be shown to be increasing at an alarming rate.

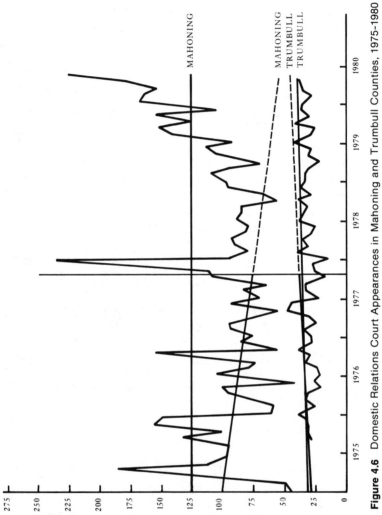

Figure 4.6   Domestic Relations Court Appearances in Mahoning and Trumbull Counties, 1975-1980

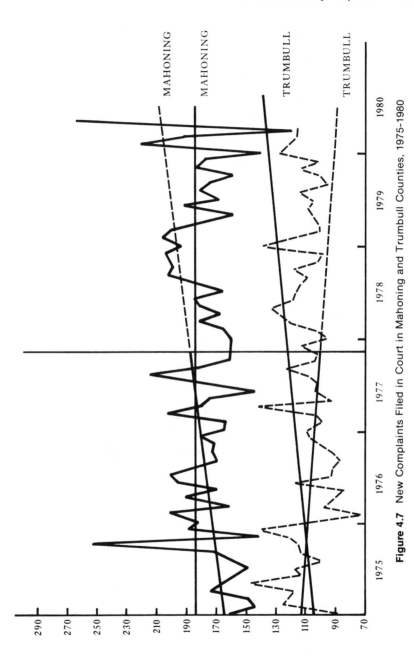

Figure 4.7 New Complaints Filed in Court in Mahoning and Trumbull Counties, 1975-1980

A related indicator of domestic relations is provided by data on child abuse and neglect. Requests to the Mahoning County Children Services Board (CSB) for services increased 14.5 percent from 1975 to 1976 and 3.2 percent from 1976 to 1977. In the next two years 1978 and 1979, requests for services increased 61.9 percent and 29.8 percent, respectively. Trumbull County's CSB, on the other hand, showed annual increases in services demand of 28.1 percent and 7.1 percent in the two years prior to the closing and decreases in demand of 2.1 percent from 1977 to 1978 and 2.8 percent from 1978 to 1979. Although the Mahoning County trend cannot be attributed to the steel mill closing based on this evidence alone, the pattern does suggest that family relations in the community were becoming more strained in the two years following the closing (see also Aronson and McKersie, 1980: 86-87). Another negative trend that may be a possible result of the crisis is the recent decline in marriage license applications filed. Residents appeared to be more likely to get married before the closing than they were after the closing (Figure 4.8).

The remaining three indicators—bankruptcies, real estate transfers, and new car sales—all reveal negative trends. However, inferences that they were affected by the closing are highly problematic. Bankruptcies, for example, were declining before the closing, but have recently begun to increase (Figure 4.10). This almost certainly is in part a function of a new, more liberal bankruptcy filing statute (Cocheo, 1980). Similarly, real estate (Figure 4.11) and new car sales (Figure 4.12) were increasing prior to the closing, but are now declining. However, these declines may be a function of high interest rates, reduced consumer buying power precipitated by the 1980 recession, or consumer uncertainty about the future.

On balance, therefore, the social indicators data suggest that the closing did not have the severe social impacts many people anticipated. In other words, the two-year period following the closing was very much like that preceding it. Looking over the whole pattern of community change before and after 1978, and taking into account all known alternative explanations for observed trends, the short-run impact of the massive layoffs appears slight. This is, in part, a function of the size of the community. It is, we believe, also in large part a function of the coincidence that this closing occurred when the state and national economies were rising.

However, the lack of immediate, dramatic impact is also consistent with other evidence pointing up the distinctive nature of economic crises. Many people misunderstand this. So frequent were the predictions of economic collapse and social disaster in early 1978 that Youngstown's mayor felt it necessary to hand out buttons bearing the message, "Youngstown is Alive and Well." It is certainly alive.

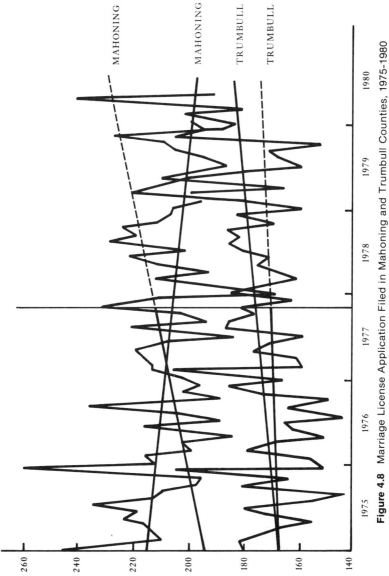

Figure 4.8 Marriage License Application Filed in Mahoning and Trumbull Counties, 1975–1980

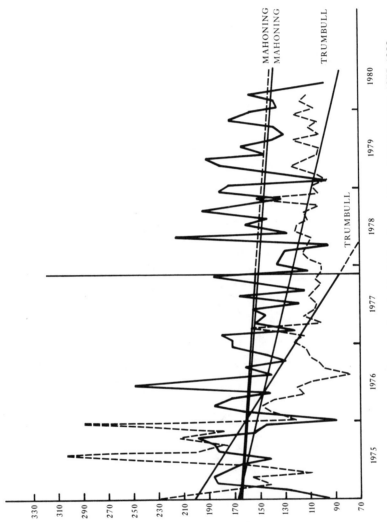

Figure 4.9 Divorce Decrees Granted in Mahoning and Trumball Counties, 1975–1980

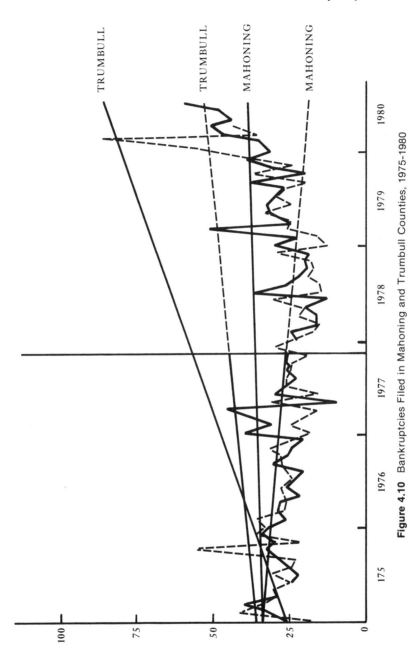

Figure 4.10 Bankruptcies Filed in Mahoning and Trumbull Counties, 1975-1980

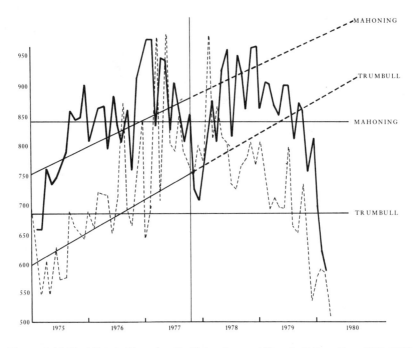

Figure 4.11 Real Estate Transfers in Mahoning and Trumball Counties, 1975-1980

Economic crisis differ from natural disasters in the timing of their impacts. In the latter case, the social stresses and economic costs are compressed into a small slice of time, after which they diminish sharply. By contrast, massive layoffs plant social and economic time bombs throughout the community, which may detonate long afterward. The effects of economic crisis thus have no obvious peak but persist far longer in the form of heightened personal and structural vulnerabilities. The latter includes a weakened economic capacity to resist and rebound from recession and a weakened political capacity to organize and implement programs of reconstruction.

General Public Reaction

A survey of a random sample of Youngstown area adults conducted in the summer of 1978 provides the final set of evidence used to assess the impact of the closing on the community.[13] The survey focused on political responses to the crisis. About 42 percent of Youngstown area residents

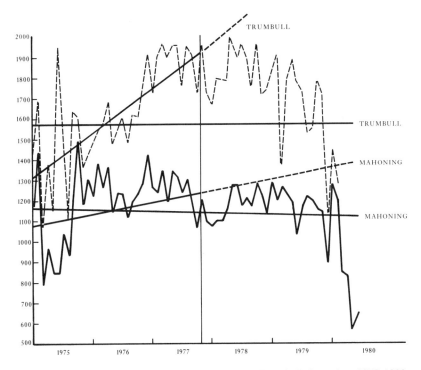

Figure 4.12 New Car Sales in Mahoning and Trumbull Counties, 1975-1980

claimed to be "very interested" in following events related to the steel crisis; 11 percent were "not at all interested." The community's average level of interest, while lower than that of the steel workers (70% "very interested") suggests the possibility of widespread, active involvement in efforts to meet the crisis. A majority of area residents also was able to accurately state the number of jobs lost, the corporate owner of the closed mill, and the Ecumenical Coalition's basic purpose.

In contrast to these percentages, one-fourth or less in the sample engaged in discussions about the closing. Only seven percent attended any rally or meeting, a fact confirmed by observed low attendance at various crisis-related political events open to the public. Fewer than five percent communicated with public officials about the closing orally or in writing.

The relative lack of mass community political involvement is additional evidence that continuity rather than change marked the period following the closing.

Conclusion

The statistical trends and averages reported in this chapter may be misread as evidence that most Youngstown area residents were not touched by the closing. The numbers do not capture the mix of fear, despair, and anger—powerful emotions—that swept over the area in late 1977. These could be heard in conversations at bars or on the street. A steady stream of letters to the editor also provided a gauge of such feeling. One letterwriter reported: "I am amazed at the venom I...hear spewed at the past and present steelworkers."[14] Such strong emotions led a few to talk or write in doomsday terms: "Perhaps in a few hundred years, people will remember the death of a steel mill and the death of a large part of a community."[15]

Despite the damage done so far—and still to be done—by the massive loss of steel jobs in the Mahoning Valley, the rhetoric of death is not appropriate. An economic crisis drains vitality from a community slowly in a thousand small ways. It alters the underlying economic structure of the community by removing its most obsolete elements. It does not produce a sudden, sharp break with the past. Therefore, its effects must be measured over a period of years.

Having said this, it is still surprising to note how few indicators show significant social impacts over the two-year period after the closing. This can be better understood once the responses of individuals and helping agencies have been examined.

PART 3

Responding to the Crisis

Part 2 treated consequences of the Youngstown Sheet and Tube closing as though individuals and the community were passive receptors of its effects. Obviously, however, people and organizations actively responded to the crisis. The next two chapters once again examine the short-run consequences of the closing, but this time from a perspective that reveals the dynamics of individual and collective response.

Responses to the closing are evaluated using the standard of positive mental health as defined in Chapter 3. This concept has very broad utility, capable of application not only to the coping efforts of individuals but also to the ameliorative or damage-prevention strategies pursued by agencies and institutions. For example, by comparing the community human services system's response to an optimal performance standard (as developed, in this case, through extended discussions by the system's leadership), it is possible to judge: (1) whether the system is functioning in a "healthy" manner; and (2) to what extent its actions support or increase individuals' capacities to cope successfully with job loss and unemployment.

Both chapters in Part 3 look first at individual responses and then at the responses of community agencies whose missions are to help individuals with service needs related to job loss. Chapter 5 focuses on individual and agency responses related to reemployment, retraining and relocation. Chapter 6 deals with personal efforts through other means to cope with the stresses and costs of job loss and with the roles of a broader range of local human services agencies seeking to help the workers.

5. Reemployment, Retraining, and Relocation

Preceding chapters revealed that workers and their spouses on the whole did not experience severe emotional problems as a result of termination. Similarly, the community showed little evidence of social upheaval as a result of ripple effects which might have been expected following mass layoffs.

What can account for the apparent absence of severe impact? One partial explanation is that many terminated workers coped with their situations in ways that ameliorated the potential negative impacts, especially by restoring some degree of financial stability (Sobel and Folk, 1967). Some workers effortlessly found jobs to replace those lost. Others participated in retraining activities which upgraded or changed existing skills so that jobs could be obtained. Still others decided to relocate in other communities where job opportunities were better. Some chose to retire under early retirement options of varying generosity. And some were able to insulate themselves by relying on an extensive social support network.

Public and private helping agencies in the community attempted to enhance workers' skills in gaining reemployment by offering a wide range of assistance programs.[1]

In light of worker coping behavior and agency assistance, this chapter will attempt to answer the following questions. *First,* do workers delay job hunting until unemployment benefits are terminated or do they seek work immediately? *Second,* what kinds of jobs do workers take to replace jobs lost? *Third,* how do workers search for jobs and how successful are their efforts? *Fourth,* to what extent do workers participate in retraining programs in order to enhance their qualifications for jobs, and how useful are these programs for obtaining jobs? *Fifth,* do workers consider migration from a depressed community a viable option for reemployment?

After considering strategies which workers pursue to gain reemployment, the chapter will focus on the responses by employment service agencies and programs—The Ohio Bureau of Employment Services (OBES), The Trade Adjustment Assistance (TAA) program, and services under the Comprehensive Employment and Training Act (CETA). More specifically, we will answer the questions: Are the efforts of OBES (including TAA) and CETA consistent with the evidence of worker needs and desires? Are there inadequacies in the system which militate against effective, efficient delivery of services to workers? Subsequent chapters will draw out the public policy implications of answers to these questions.

Finding a Job

The low incidence of severe mental or emotional problems among the terminated workers may be a result of their success in quickly finding good new jobs. To test this proposition, at least indirectly, we examined the employment status of the laid-off workers one and two years following the closing. The end of the first year marked the time at which unemployment benefits were expiring, so that workers were expected to have obtained jobs where possible to avoid cutting into savings or other resources. The end of the second year marked the time during which workers who had not yet found jobs would be experiencing severe financial difficulties because savings and resources might be near exhaustion, thereby necessitating either taking a job or going on welfare. Comparison of workers' strategies at the two points in time also permits examination of the pattern of employment status changes from the first to the second year.

More than two years after the closing, a 32-year-old former pipe-shop laborer and lifelong resident of the area was asked to describe the whereabouts and employment of laid-off workers known to him. He was able to locate 57 of his former coworkers and friends. Most were working in the area at other heavy industrial facilities. By and large, they have found jobs that are in one way or another—lower pay, poorer working conditions, long commuting distances—less satisfactory than their previous work. The exceptions are people with transferable skills, many of whom found high-paying work at the GM assembly plant 30 miles to the west. The ability of one worker to locate so many of his acquaintances two years later illustrates the stability and integration of the blue-collar community in the Mahoning Valley—an important factor in mitigating impacts of the closing.

One Year After the Closing

Based on the initial wave of interviews with 146 terminated workers, one third ($N = 50$) were reemployed one year after the steel mill closings. One-fourth ($N = 36$) of the workers were eligible for and opted to retire. Thus, about three out of every five workers had regained some financial security by this time. But approximately two-fifths ($N = 60$) were still unemployed. This latter group was either inclined or compelled to forego obtaining another job, even when unemployment benefits were expiring.

We attempted to account for the success or failure in finding another job in a variety of ways, as summarized below.

Analysis revealed that, on average, the unemployed were more educated than the reemployed or retired workers.[2] They were on average much younger than the reemployed workers and, of course, earned less than any other group. Age appears to be important in explaining unemployment. On closer inspection, two distinct age groups were identified: very young workers (early twenties) and middle-aged workers (forty or older). Although most of the younger unemployed had completed high school, many had not yet developed either saleable skills or an extensive job record. Hence, they had more difficulty finding a job. Older unemployed workers had less formal education, more job experience, but were likewise not highly skilled (see especially Sheppard, Ferman, and Faber, 1959).

Some 138 employed workers—those who still worked for Youngstown Sheet and Tube Company and constituted a "control group" for purposes of this comparison—were demographically the opposite of the unemployed workers. They were less educated and older, and had the highest current income of any group. Those workers who were rehired at places other than Youngstown Sheet and Tube were younger than the other groups. They now earned less income than the employed, but more than the retired. These workers were relatively highly skilled, and jobs to suit their skills were available at the time they were laid off; but since they were beginning a new career, they were forced to accept lower wages. In some cases, they were underpaid given their experience and skills. Retired workers were much older and less educated. Retired workers began working before higher levels of educational achievement were common in the labor force. They earned less from their pensions than any of the employed or rehired groups but more than the unemployed.

Two Years After the Closing

The second wave of interviews, a year later, enabled us to discover how a worker's employment status had changed over the past year. A comparison of employment status in the two years is presented in Table A.3 in the Methodological Appendix.

There was considerable and varied change in employment status from the first wave to the second. Of the 155 workers interviewed in the second wave, about nine percent were then unemployed (N = 14). This figure is confirmed by Ohio Bureau of Employment Services (OBES) statistics which then estimated that between 10 percent and 15 percent of the laid-off workers remained unemployed (see Bagshaw and Schnorbus, 1980). In our sample, only three percent of the workers were unemployed at both times when interviews were conducted. Two years following the closing, relatively few workers remained unemployed. The local labor market had been remarkably elastic or absorbent.

Even though many workers were laid off during the closing, many were called back at least once by Youngstown Sheet and Tube Company. Some were called back to assist others in closing down the works. Most were rehired in company departments which were kept open. Results showed that about 60 percent (N = 93) of the workers in the sample were recalled in this way.[3] Perhaps significantly, 13 percent gave up newly acquired jobs in order to be rehired temporarily at Youngstown Sheet and Tube. This pattern of reemployment is perhaps unique in plant shutdown studies. Others (e.g., Adams and Aronson, 1957) found that many workers quit their jobs before final notices were given to them. In this case, the high-paying jobs in the steel industry, even if only temporary, were a sufficient lure to workers to remain on the job or to consider returning.

Only about 19 percent (N = 30) were reemployed between the two interviews other than at Youngstown Sheet and Tube. This group was primarily made up of those who had been unemployed in the first year (N = 12) and those who, at the first interview, initially were not yet laid off by Youngstown Sheet and Tube (N = 11). A group of workers chose to retire (12%, N = 18) between year one and two. However, others left retirement to take new work (see also Hayes, 1979).

Results of this study defy simple explanations that suggest that "eager beavers" get jobs and "gold bricks" are wasting taxpayers' money by receiving unemployment benefits. Finding a new job is not necessarily an ideal or permanent solution (see Wilcock and Franke, 1968: 124). First, workers vary in their potential for finding jobs based on their age, race, sex, and skill. Some workers, then, may be systematically, although perhaps temporarily, excluded from the labor force unless and until other workers have been reemployed. Second, even finding a job immediately after a closing may not be a long-term solution to employment problems. Evidence suggests that there may be a high probability of losing a job after being reemployed. This job instability, especially among workers who have enjoyed job security, high wages, and excellent benefits, may take its toll on workers years later. Third, the significant number of workers for whom benefits had expired suggests that if workers do use unemployment compensation as a kind of paid, extended vacation, they do so in a personally costly fashion (see also Schlozman and Verba, 1979: 94-95).

Types of Jobs Obtained

A closer look at the types of jobs found by workers and the period during which they found them is revealing. Some 50 workers in the first wave sample sought new jobs immediately after old jobs were terminated. In this "rehired" group, only three were *not* hired into a manufacturing industry. The remaining 47 were primarily rehired in the metal-fabricating and basic steel industries in both skilled and unskilled positions. These industries thus appeared to skim off the more experienced workers to fill their current manpower needs, perhaps indirectly displacing less skilled or less experienced workers. Once the relatively few steel-related job opportunities were exhausted, other laid-off workers were reemployed in the automotive, transportation, and construction industries (see Chapter 4). Other workers were not so fortunate, however. These workers were forced to take low-paying or less prestigious jobs. An undetermined number either quit or lost one or more such jobs during the study period, only to accept similar ones once again.

By January 1981, the basic steel and metal-fabricating industries were again contracting. Even worse, the automobile and construction industries had experienced long-term layoffs and permanent job terminations; and other jobs related directly or indirectly to these industries had begun to lay off workers or to shut down altogether. This recession-related trend was reflected by unemployment rates of 16 percent in Mahoning County and 15 percent in Trumbull County (February 1981). The labor market had shrunk substantially.

Job Search by Workers

Workers have the option of either searching for jobs using services provided by the local Ohio Bureau of Employment Services (OBES) or using their own initiative for a personal search. Some workers, of course, will use both options.

Workers utilizing OBES were afforded direct access to job placement counselors who established a satellite office in the union halls which workers were assumed to frequent. These counselors were given no client responsibilities other than those concerning displaced steelworkers.

Ken Siegel
Employed by Youngstown Sheet and Tube Company: 1973–1978
Age: 27
Spouse: Susan, married 1977
Children: none
Education: high school diploma

Ken visited many places in search of work and talked with countless people who he felt might be able to help him find work. He has looked for the kind of job which could become a lifetime career.

During the summer of 1978, Ken had several work offers, but he did not find the kind of employment he wanted. In May 1978, Ken attended a six-week truck-driving development school funded by his Trade Readjustment Allowances. He said that the course, although helpful, did not adequately train drivers for the demands and pressures of hauling freight for long distances. By June, Ken had trained three weeks with a large local trucking firm. He was not paid during this period. He quit before taking his final road test or completing sufficient hours for certification. In August, Ken found work with another small steel-hauling company. Again, he quit soon afterwards.

Ken said he had two primary difficulties with these jobs. He felt that pressure on the job to deliver cargo in a minimum amount of time encouraged truckers to exceed safe speed limits, drive long hours without proper rest, and resort to using amphetamines to keep up the pace. In addition, Ken was reluctant to leave his wife alone for long periods because of her illness. He disliked these working conditions. He found them "not worth the money or the time." Ken does enjoy driving a truck, but would prefer to haul freight for a small local express company. In this way, he could work regular eight- to ten-hour daylight shifts.

Workers in our study were asked to rate the help they received from OBES in finding a job. Ironically, among those who found jobs during the first full year following the closing ($N = 50$), *not one worker reported having used OBES in finding a job.* Among those who were unemployed ($N = 49$) 22 percent rated OBES as "very helpful" in finding a job even though they had not found one. Some 59 percent found it not at all helpful. And 18 percent elected simply not to use the service.

Terry Turner
Employed by Youngstown Sheet and Tube Company: 1951–1977
Age: 51
Spouse: Nancy, married 1958
Children: three sons, 17, 14, 12
Education: high school diploma

Terry explains that he has now "put aside" much of the bitterness about losing his job. In December 1979, he and a friend were able to purchase a local service station. Terry says that his partner provided most of the money for the venture. Terry agreed to assume the bulk of the management responsibilities.

"For now," Terry says, "we are surviving with the station." He hopes their franchise can become more profitable in the future, if gasoline consumption by the public begins to increase again.

At the present time, Terry "is not quite sure" how his family and his friends are going to cope with future problems. Nancy, with cautious optimism, says, "We'll have to do the best we can." Terry looks back on the past and says, "all of this was unnecessary. We were sold down the river." When asked if he meant the Mahoning River, Terry laughs and says, "Yeah."

Apparently, the public employment service played a very minor role in helping secure jobs for the unemployed (see Thompson, 1965: 214; Wilcock and Franke, 1968: 117). And, when it did play a role, it was not very effective in helping workers (see also Blau, 1964).

If workers did not use OBES, then how did they find jobs? With few exceptions, workers employed a so-called "plant gate" strategy (see Foltman, 1968; Wilcock and Franke, 1963: 125–128) in applying for jobs. This strategy was one in which workers went directly to plants they believed might be hiring, and filed applications. With an average of 10 applications filed per worker for jobs, workers must have canvassed possible employers in the area very thoroughly. Interviews revealed that this strategy was buttressed through the use of an informal social network or "grapevine" through which workers passed valid (and invalid) information about possible jobs to one another. Clearly, the utility of individual initiative and the informal network vis-a-vis the public employment service should not be overlooked.

The preceding analysis shows that even after two years, many workers had not achieved job stability. But having even a temporary job, or a series of jobs, or receiving various forms of financial compensation in lieu of work may have lessened the incidence of emotional problems, not to mention financial problems. It remains to be seen whether or not the predominant pattern of job instability continues and, therefore, takes its toll on workers over a longer time period. The possibility of longer-term effects is discussed in Chapter 9.

Jobs Through Retraining

Education and retraining are means some workers can use to cope with job loss, perhaps turning it into an opportunity for long-run self-improvement. Upgrading existing skills can allow them to qualify for higher-level jobs, modify skills somewhat to qualify for a wider range of comparable jobs, or convert to an entirely different set of skills necessary for a new type of occupation. The community's education and training programs provided workers a long menu of options: adult education programs in vocational schools; adult basic education, high school completion, and preparation for the General Equivalency Development (GED) examination in the public school system; one- and two-year technical training programs in community and technical colleges; business courses in business schools; occupational training through proprietary schools; skills training in programs provided by Comprehensive Employment Training Act (CETA) funding;[4] bachelors and graduate degrees available in public and private institutions of higher education; and skills-training programs established under the TAA program. Workers in both waves of the study were asked if they had enrolled in any education or retraining programs following the closing. They were also asked if they planned to enroll in any education or retraining programs in the future.

Seeking Additional Education and Retraining

In a regional economy where worker skills related to steel-making are no longer in demand, our expectation was that laid-off steelworkers would be likely to seek educational programs or courses providing nonsteel-related skills in order to make themselves more employable. Seeking additional education would be more likely among the unemployed and rehired workers than it would among retired workers or workers still employed at Youngstown Sheet and Tube. Further, the longer a worker remained unemployed, the more likely the worker would be to seek out and enroll in additional education and retraining programs.

Table 5.1   Mean Scores for Steelworker Educational Enrollment by
Employment Status, First and Second Waves,[a] 1978 and 1979

First Interview (year one)			Second Interview (year two)		
Employment	Enrolled Mean Score	N	Employment	Enrolled Mean Score	N
Unemployed	1.81	37	Unemployed	1.89	18
Retired	1.90	21	Retired	1.92	13
Rehired	1.94	31	Rehired	1.76	29
Employed	1.88	59	Employed	1.91	89
TOTAL	1.88	148	TOTAL	1.88	148
$F(3,144) = .88, p = .45$[b]			$F(3,144) = 1.69, p = .17$		

[a] First and second wave data are composed of workers who responded on
both waves. The question posed was: "Have you enrolled in any educational
courses or programs since the shutdown of Youngstown Sheet and Tube
Company?" (coded: 1=yes, 2=no).
[b] "F" refers to F-test, "p" refers to statistical significance.

These hypotheses were tested by examining responses to the first- and
second-year interviews. From Table 5.1, it can be seen that additional
education and retraining was not often sought by any group in either the
first or second years (see also Aronson and McKersie, 1980; Ferman, 1980;
Foltman, 1968). In addition, the four groups in the analysis did not differ
significantly from one another in their behavior, suggesting that differences
in employment status during this period did not influence decisions to seek
retraining. Change in employment status between the first and the second
years also was unrelated to the likelihood of enrollment. This finding is
consistent with other research on plant shutdowns (e.g., Foltman, 1968:
116; Wilcock and Franke, 1963).

Lack of interest in additional education and retraining may be
explained in various ways (see also Foltman, 1968: 116-117). First, laid-off
workers who were able to find jobs elsewhere, especially in manufacturing
industries (Bagshaw and Schnorbus, 1980), may have felt no need to
upgrade their skills. Second, the continuous efforts by various groups
inside and outside the community to either keep the mills from closing or to
reopen them under a worker or community ownership plan (see Chapter 2)
may have caused some workers to postpone seeking further education.
Third, many workers feel that steel making is not only a job, but a way of
life. Some of these simply do not want to learn skills not involved in steel-
making. Fourth, some workers must have believed that retraining would
not help them in finding a job.

Retraining Opportunities Sought

Few workers who are unemployed are expected to expend scarce personal resources to educate or retrain themselves for future employment (Wilcock and Franke, 1963: 192). The U.S. Department of Labor through its TAA program attempted to overcome this problem by subsidizing workers who wanted retraining.

The TAA program was a major source of support for workers in seeking education and retraining (see Employment and Training Administration, 1979). Workers received a weekly stipend from the Labor Department for up to 52 weeks which when added to unemployment compensation will yield 70 percent of the worker's original take-home pay. An additional 26 weeks of payments could have been awarded to complete training once begun. Workers could have participated in a variety of programs, including vocational and higher education. TAA benefits were awarded only to workers in industries which have closed as a result of foreign competition.

OBES administered the retraining program at the local level. Retraining programs and classes were "purchased" by OBES from local training providers based on worker demand and perceived need for skills in the labor market by OBES administrators. In some cases, workers participated in retraining programs not "purchased" by OBES. Some, but not all, were made eligible for reimbursement by TAA.

Administrators at OBES at our request examined the files of individual unemployed workers from Youngstown Sheet and Tube in order to provide data on retraining. Results of this examination showed that 757 workers received funding for education and retraining in 1978 and 1979. Of this number, 128 workers (17%) were funded so that they could complete training in apprenticeship programs related to the basic steel industry. By participating, these workers automatically received TAA benefits.

In addition to apprenticeship programs, some 311 workers (41%) participated in retraining programs contracted for by OBES. A breakdown of these programs is presented in Table 5.2 By participating, these workers were automatically eligible for benefits. Also contained in Table 5.2 is a list of programs in which workers enrolled on their own initiative (i.e., "self-enrolled"), and then were paid for retraining rather than for looking for a job. Of the 412 enrollees (54%), 94 (12%) were denied benefits because retraining was determined to be inconsistent with TAA restrictions.

It is important to notice that apprenticeship and self-enrolled or purchased programs concentrated on vocational retraining at an "entry level" for those occupations. For example, programs in electronics do not

Table 5.2   Numbers and Percentages of Ex-Steelworkers in Types of Retraining Self-Enrollment and Purchased Contracts,* 1978–1979

Courses:	Self-enrolled N	%	Purchased Contract N	%
Single college courses	12	3	0	0
Air conditioning & refrigeration	34	8	49	16
Welding	45	11	60	19
Accounting	33	8	13	4
Secretarial	12	3	12	4
Janitorial	11	3	4	1
Electronics	42	10	28	9
Business management	48	12	3	1
Police	8	2	2	1
Nursing	13	3	1	0
Electrical appliance/ machine repair	16	4	26	8
Business machines	10	2	0	0
Small gas engine	13	3	21	7
Automotive maintenance	16	4	11	4
Advertising/marketing	13	3	5	2
Technicians	17	4	1	0
Real estate	8	2	0	0
Teaching	5	1	0	0
Trade (e.g., beautician, drafting, upholstering)	25	6	44	14
Truckdriving	6	1	27	9
Machine operation	4	1	0	0
Computer-related	17	4	4	1
Adult Basic Education (ABE)	1	0	0	0
Other	3	1	0	0
Total	412	100%	311	100%

*Data available from OBES do not show how many workers dropped out of retraining programs.

SOURCE: Ohio Bureau of Employment Services.

concern such engineering or highly technical skills as might be required for jobs in the computing industry, but instead are oriented toward elementary skills required for initial employment in electronics manufacturing firms. Most other studies of retraining after mass unemployment have also found heavy concentration on these kinds of skills (e.g., Wilcock and Franke,

1963; Schultz and Weber, 1966; Foltman, 1968; Ferman, 1980).

CETA and Retraining: Retraining programs funded under the Comprehensive Employment and Training Act (CETA) (see Hallman, 1980) are designed to provide skills or opportunities for the "hard-to-employ" in order to stimulate their entry into the labor force (see also Council for Economic Development, 1978). The hard-to-employ are primarily people who have been denied work experience, received inadequate education, or developed ineffective personal qualities, all of which may have excluded them from the work force.

CETA programs' eligibility restrictions make most laid-off steelworkers ineligible for participation because they are not disadvantaged as defined above. Steelworkers, having held high-paying manufacturing jobs in either skilled or unskilled occupations, do not appear to require this kind of employment assistance, in any case.

Even though some steelworkers were made eligible for the CETA program in Youngstown, it is questionable whether this was in their best interest or that of the CETA program. Having had a high-paying job, even as an unskilled laborer, only to be relegated to entry-level status of hard-to-employ workers, may have been difficult for some workers to accept. But more important, placing experienced workers in the CETA program may have pushed aside the truly hard to employ. The intent of the program, then, may have been defeated.

It appears that policies which intend to place experienced workers in direct competition with inexperienced workers for the same jobs must be carefully examined.

Contribution of Retraining to Finding a Job

OBES kept no records concerning how many workers actually found jobs in fields related to the retraining they received. This was the case, in part, because workers were not required to report this information to OBES and because OBES administrators elected not to request it from workers.

Based on our own data, among those finding jobs (N = 50) up to one year after the closing, only three reported having participated in retraining to secure a job. By the second year, some seven out of 29, or 32 percent had taken retraining and found a job. Research on plant closings in other communities supports the conclusion that retraining is of dubious value in securing jobs (see Schultz and Weber, 1966; Samuelson, 1981; Ferman, 1980; Hansen, et al., 1980).

Retraining may be beneficial to some workers even though it may not lead to specific job opportunities. Workers might, for example, utilize retraining to extend unemployment benefits. For some, more time might be required to secure a desired job so that retraining promotes some financial security. Other workers might view retraining as the best means of profitably and constructively occupying enforced leisure time.

Although we did not establish in our analysis that retraining programs might lead to undesirable reemployment, other researchers have. Stern (1973), for example, found that workers who received retraining tended to accept lower skill and hence, lower-paying jobs than others (see also Hansen, et al., 1980; McCarthy, 1975; Pursell, et al., 1975). This resulted because retraining programs did not train the workers for high-skill jobs. Therefore, the retrained found themselves at the entry level for their new occupations. This is especially true for vocational retraining programs, as shown in Table 5.2.

If retraining has the effect of stimulating workers to accept lower-paying jobs, then retraining, if it is useful at all, may be most beneficial to already low-paid, unskilled apprentice workers who upon completion of their training will at least have a skill. The completion of apprenticeships by less-experienced workers was a major benefit of the Youngstown retraining programs (see also Schultz and Weber, 1966).

Retraining may have negative impacts on workers if jobs are not obtained (Schultz and Weber, 1966). Workers may believe that retraining would not be offered unless it leads to a job. Those who build up rising expectations about job possibilities may experience subsequent difficulties when hopes are dashed in the labor market.

Jobs Through Relocation

A third option besides reemployment and retraining for coping with job loss is to migrate to another community in search of employment. Initially, workers were asked whether or not they intended to move and then an effort was made to determine if workers had moved. These results were also compared to results from a similar study (N = 302) of Youngstown area residents generally.[5]

Intentions of Migrating

Steelworkers interviewed in the first and second years after the closing, and a sample of Youngstown area residents, were asked if they planned to move. Steelworkers in the first year were only slightly more likely (20%) than the general public (15%) to report they planned to move

Averill Thomas
Employed by Youngstown Sheet and Tube Company: 1965–1978
Age: 42
Spouse: Joyce, married 1965
Children: two sons, 8 and 9
Education: two years' high school

With trade readjustment allowances (TRA), an unemployed worker is eligible for an extension of benefits in order to obtain additional or new types of training. Averill enrolled in a program which would last no longer than six months. He knew that when his benefits expired, with no chance of extension, he would have to pay for the balance of his schooling on his own. At that time, he says, his primary concern would be to find work, not to continue going to school. So for now, his chief aim is to learn a high-paying skill as long as the money holds out.

Averill said he would have preferred to go to semi-truckdriving school, but TRA benefits were no longer being provided for this, since the course's tuition was raised. The only other occupation Averill was interested in was welding. This course did not really appeal to Averill but he would be certified at the end of six months and a certificate would mean greater employability for him. He stated that, given the range of vocational choices available today, he would have preferred a more mentally stimulating field instead of hard physical labor. He said he might even have opted for an associate degree in some technical area offered by Youngstown State University. Though he quit high school early, Averill had obtained his graduate equivalency diploma certificate while in the Navy.

Shortly before he was due to begin his TRA-funded welding course, Averill was notified by his employment services counselor that his maximum 26-week training extension had been rescinded. He was provided with no rationale for the decision. He was merely informed one week prior to the start of classes there was suddenly and inexplicably no money available for him. Needless to say, Averill was disappointed and very angry with the news. He was told that even if his benefits were shortly restored, he would be unable to attend a training session until 1979.

(see Wilcock and Franke, 1963: 168–70). By Summer 1979, the proportion of terminated workers reporting an intention to move had dropped to 15 percent. Although the intention to move is not necessarily followed by migration from an area, this rather large pool of potential migrants in the steelworker and general public samples is consistent with census information indicating substantial out-migration of population from the City of Youngstown between 1970 and 1980.[6]

Reports of an intention to move were examined for employed and unemployed groups in the steelworker and general public samples. Some fairly complex patterns were observed. Unemployed steelworkers were more likely (32%) to plan to move than their employed counterparts (17%) on the first wave. By contrast, employed workers in the general public were more likely (22%) to desire to leave than the unemployed (9%). During the second wave interviews, the unemployed steelworkers were much less likely (11%) to plan to leave than they themselves had been on the first wave (32%) and less likely even than the employed in the second (14%) and first (17%) waves to desire to leave.

One possible explanation for these results would be that the initial loss of a job for steelworkers produced a desire to escape. After an adjustment period, perhaps as evidenced in second-year responses, this desire for escape was reduced. Some employed steelworkers in both waves may have been apprehensive about losing their jobs with the inevitable decline of the steel industry. These workers, then, planned to leave. The general public responses may not be related to the loss of jobs in the steel industry, but instead may constitute the perception by the employed that there are greener pastures elsewhere.

Relocation Program

Under one section of the Trade Adjustment Assistance Act, workers may be given financing to relocate following a plant closing. Workers may receive funding either to move their households from an impacted community or to visit other communities to apply for jobs. These programs are administered in Youngstown by OBES.

OBES records indicated that only 231 workers, about six percent of the laid-off work force, applied for assistance to relocate. Only slightly more, 283 workers, about seven percent, applied for travel assistance to look for other jobs before moving. Records were not kept to indicate how many workers applied for funding for both purposes.

These figures give credence to the hypothesis that many who expressed an intention to move were unlikely to follow through. It seems likely that potential migrants would seek subsidies when moving rather than assuming the financial burden themselves. Other evidence also suggests that public programs which attempt to send people to jobs find little acceptance among workers (Samuelson, 1980).

Other studies have shown that workers might accept interplant transfers where relocation would be necessary (e.g., Schultz and Weber, 1966). In the Youngstown case, Youngstown Sheet and Tube had virtually no openings for workers in its Indiana Harbor Works near Chicago. As a result, only a handful of workers were permitted and indeed chose to relocate by means of interplant transfers. Similarly, when Jones & Laughlin Steel Corporation acquired the Brier Hill Works of Youngstown Sheet and Tube and then shut them down, the corporations steel mills in the Pittsburgh area were unable to absorb any but a handful of displaced workers, most of whom were temporarily rehired. Consequently, although the unions had interplant transfer agreements with management, these made little difference in a declining industry.

Where the Unemployed Planned to Move

OBES did not record whether workers had moved and where they might have moved. To get some idea of the places to which workers might migrate, we asked workers who expressed an intention to move where they planned to move. Of the 27 laid-off workers who mentioned a specific place on the first wave of interviews, nine intended to migrate to Trumbull County, immediately to the north of Youngstown. Some 14 workers mentioned a Sunbelt state. The remaining four mentioned locations in the Northeastern United States. By the second wave, only four were still considering a move to Trumbull County and only one to a Sunbelt state.

These results suggest that some workers will move short distances to obtain jobs. The chances of workers finding jobs in Trumbull County after the first steel mill closing were good. Other workers, however, appeared to be doubtful about job prospects in the region. These workers were considering the Sunbelt as a new location. Their intentions may have been buttressed by rumors that the Lykes Corporation might be hiring workers in the Houston area.

Social Support Networks

As observed in Chapter 1, the Youngstown area was originally populated by immigrants who were drawn primarily from Europe to work in the steel mills. The community has evolved so that persons of various ethnic backgrounds have clustered in particular neighborhoods, often in extended families. It has not been uncommon to find three generations of a family all working in the same steel mill.

Neighborhoods in Youngstown composed of these groups are special places. Families and relatives appear to watch out for one another. A worker with skills in plumbing will offer his services at cost to his family and neighbors. A laid-off worker, having trouble finding a job, may move in with a relative. Several workers may get together at local neighborhood bars to discuss their problems. Local business men may offer credit to long-time customers who are down on their luck. The elaborate social support network in these neighborhoods may account for worker reluctance to leave the area (see LaRocco, et al., 1980 and Gore, 1978, for a literature review on this subject). Why trade the certainties and security of the known for the vagaries of the unknown (see Smith and Fowler, 1964)?

A separate survey of 76 unemployed steelworkers from Youngstown Sheet and Tube was conducted in August 1979 to determine if the above impression could be substantiated.[7] The survey measured the relationship of perceived "quality of life" and "sense of belongingness" to respondents' intention to migrate. Results of the study confirmed our expectation (see also Foltman, 1968: 97–105). Some 82 percent of these unemployed workers had a deep "sense of belongingness" on the measures used, while

---

Ken Siegel
Employed by Youngstown Sheet and Tube Company: 1973–1978
Age: 27
Spouse: Susan, married 1977
Children: none

When Ken was first laid off, the Siegels lightly considered the prospect of relocating in search of work. They really didn't give this much serious thought, as Ken was hopeful he would find a local job soon. However, when he saw no solid offer in sight at a wage and the hours he would accept, out-of-state "help wanted" ads became more enticing. He was impressed by the relocation benefits offered to prospective skilled workers. He felt that such a move might be in his interest. "At least warmer places don't have to deal with seasonal employment periods. The cost of living in the South is generally a little cheaper than Youngstown," said Ken. Ken was open to such a change and appeared enthusiastic about finding work where competition for steel-related jobs is not as fierce.

only eight percent appeared to be isolated. About ten percent gave ambiguous responses.

Because of the apparent integration of workers in the social support network and community, mental and emotional problems may have been minimized. Even more important, financial problems which might plague isolated unemployed workers might have been delayed or ameliorated because of the resources upon which many workers could draw.

Those who were less deeply embedded in the support network, and those who were willing to abandon it, tended to be those with easily marketable skills and/or high levels of education, or young single workers without family ties. These groups may well have insulated themselves from negative impacts because, as a group, they might be more individually resourceful or at least less encumbered than those who depended on extensive social support.

Ironically, the informal network might be on the decline as an indirect result of the steel mill closings and the economic depression of the area. A March 1981 study of 700 graduating seniors from Youngstown area high schools revealed that some 60 percent were considering moving from the community.[8] Some 80 percent of this group reported that lack of job opportunities was the major reason for their decision. The prevalence of such views holds bleak long-term implications for the community. If fewer graduates remain in the community to replace older workers leaving the labor market, the community will have difficulty in supplying the manpower needs for new or existing industry. These possible long-term effects are discussed further in Chapter 9.

Local Employment Services

Employment Services Responses

Employment services agencies, like the Ohio Bureau of Employment Services (OBES), have been called the cornerstone of community response to plant closings (Thompson, 1965). On the one hand, OBES must provide compensation to the mass unemployed in order to ameliorate the impact of job loss. On the other, OBES must assist workers in finding or qualifying for jobs. Indeed, its programs to reemploy, retrain, or relocate workers encompass many of the services needed by the mass unemployed. Administrators and staff implemented these programs with enthusiasm and in accord with guidelines governing their operations. Unfortunately, as will be shown below, their efforts, beyond providing compensation payments to workers, were largely unsuccessful.

Following the closing, OBES geared its efforts toward meeting the needs of the mass unemployed in several ways. First, a satellite office of OBES was established at a local union hall so that workers could receive services in convenient, familiar surroundings. Job counselors and TAA representatives were assigned to work only with laid-off steelworkers. Second, OBES advertised its services extensively in the mass media, with posters and brochures, at public meetings, and so on. Officials worked closely with union leaders to gain maximum worker compensation. Third, the agency's top administrators contacted many businesses for leads on available jobs in an effort to reemploy workers. Some close working relationships between OBES and local firms were developed. Fourth, OBES administrators participated in citizen action groups, human service agency provider groups (as described in Chatper 6), and consortia made up of political and community leadership.

Evaluating the Employment Services Response

The Ohio Bureau of Employment services accomplished only part of its services mission toward laid-off steelworkers. Its success was as a conduit for passing public funds from state and federal sources (i.e., unemployment compensation and TAA benefits) to workers applying for them. The other part of its mission, which was to help workers find jobs by assisting in the job search, establishing or funding retraining programs, and providing relocation subsidies, remained unaccomplished (see especially Thompson, 1965: 214; Foltman, 1968: 111-2; Wilcock and Franke, 1963).

The compensation disbursement function of the bureau was easily carried out since administrators were required to pay those who qualified for compensation. The failure of the reemployment mission, by contrast, was a function of a complex interaction between several fundamental shortcomings of employment service delivery systems, which it should be noted are not peculiar to the Youngstown area. Reasons for the failure will be discussed in the sections that follow. Chapter 7 will use this evaluation to draw out the policy implications for employment services and reemployment generally.

Absence of Local Labor Market Information

In order for a public (or private) employment service to operate effectively in a community, it must have accurate, detailed and timely labor market information (see Thompson, 1965: 224-228). At a minimum, this information must include rough estimates of the current and future manpower needs of community businesses and industries. And it must include information on the labor pool which is available, or could, through retraining, become available for work. Only when both kinds of information are known can the unemployed be matched by the employment service with available jobs.

Labor market information required by the public employment services is generally *not* available (e.g., Holt, 1980). Many reasons may account for this. The private sector, where most jobs are to be found, is a poor source of information about its own manpower needs. Managers may believe that by revealing manpower needs, especially about the future, they may be aiding their competition. Others feel that they have no difficulty in locating qualified workers, since many have extensive waiting lists of job applicants with new applicants being added all of the time. As a result, the additional time and expense of keeping the public sector informed is not perceived to be cost-beneficial. Still others do not know what their future manpower needs might be, especially in turbulent economic times. And finally, some are not pleased with the quality of workers they receive from local bureaus. These managers prefer to rely on private agencies or on their own personnel departments. Regardless of the reason, the effect is that the private sector does not keep the public sector informed.

Also important is the fact that other public sector agencies that might be able to supply even limited manpower information to employment services apparently have a disincentive to do so. In the Mahoning Valley, as noted in Chapter 2, several public economic development organizations competed with one another to expand or save existing industry and to attract new industry. These organizations continued to be funded by local, state, and federal sources, depending on their success in development activities. By informing an employment service bureau about these activities, each perceived that this would tip off other public competitors and jeopardize development plans. This situation is compounded by secrecy requirements which some industries may impose on these organizations as a necessary condition for participating in development activities. Again, employment services exist in an information-poor environment.

To make matters worse, local employment services do not have the manpower or resources to produce labor market information, even by means of surveys of the general public. The expense of such ventures is initially prohibitive in most cases, but certainly prohibitive on a continuing basis.

The second component of labor market information, data on workers who would like to work, is also problematic to produce and maintain. Once workers exhaust unemployment compensation benefits, they do not, in most cases, maintain an updated file with the bureau concerning their employment status. Consequently, the bureau may be able to produce a portrait of the labor surplus pool based on compensation payments and the limited active files of unemployed workers who remain registered with the bureau, but this picture will be highly distorted because much of the potential work force is not accounted for.

Again, even where scraps of public sector manpower information are known it may not be shared among organizations. For example, in the Youngstown area, there exists a Bureau of Vocational Rehabilitation (BVR), an agency mandated by the State of Ohio to work with the disabled in order to return them to employment in the labor force. Many laid-off steelworkers visited this agency after the closing for treatment of mental and physical disabilities. BVR has clients who, for the most part, are able to work at all skill levels in a wide variety of jobs. Yet OBES refused to share information on available jobs with BVR. Consequently, a valuable pool of workers who are qualified and want to work is systematically being excluded from participation in the labor market (Thompson, 1965: 237)

It is not surprising, therefore, that local employment services cannot adequately serve the needs of the mass unemployed, the hard-to-employ, or the unemployed generally. In this environment,

—jobs available in the community are not known;
—retraining is funded without evidence for demand for skills being developed; and
—relocation is encouraged without knowledge of job availability.

Jobs for Displaced Workers

One of the reasons why the reemployment mission of OBES failed was that workers did not use the service to any great extent and when they did use the service, many were not satisfied with the help they received. A major question becomes, then, were the workers behaving irrationally in ignoring an information source of jobs in the community?

In order for workers to profit from a visit to OBES, the bureau must have timely information on preferred jobs which correspond to workers' preferences. In addition, this information must be accurate; that is, the jobs must exist. And information must be disseminated without lengthy delays and red tape.

Employment service bureaus cannot, especially from the workers' perspective, deliver services in this fashion. According to workers and job counselors in the bureau, job information about the local labor market is poor—job openings either are unknown to the bureau or are filled before workers apply for them. To receive this service of dubious quality, workers

Thomas Smith
Employed by Youngstown Sheet and Tube Company: 1977–1978
Age: 22
Spouse: single
Education: vocational school

Tom and his fiancee arrived at OBES early in the morning to begin gathering information on job opportunities. They waited about one hour to have their turn examining the video scan machine which contains OBES job listings. Once on the scan machine, they spent several hours searching OBES files for job possibilities. Tom and his fiancee decided on several jobs which looked promising. Toward the end of their perusal of the job file, a counselor happened to approach them. He examined their list of job possibilities. He pointed out that these jobs were not available since they had been taken by others much earlier. Tom and his fiancee decided to search for jobs on their own.

Tom Cinelli
Employed by Youngstown Sheet and Tube Company: 1971–1977
Age: 26
Spouse: Betty, divorced January 1980
Children: son, 4
Education: high school diploma

Tom was enrolled in a drafting design course at a local trade school in 1978. When Tom was laid off, he completed the application forms for training programs available under provisions of the Trade Readjustment Act. He wanted to retrain and learn a new skill immediately rather than waiting for the maximum six-month extension period following his first year of trade readjustment allowances. However, through unexplained delays, his application was not processed until almost six months later.

Tom was angry about this situation, too. He felt that had his application been handled properly, his training would have been completed quickly and he would have found a job. Despite the delays, Tom obtained his industrial drafting certificate in April 1979.

must endure long waiting and much red tape before they are sent to apply or interview for jobs. Retraining programs are also plagued by lack of current information on employers' needs. The bureau cannot adequately identify what sorts of retraining will be required to enhance worker qualifications for jobs (Ferman, 1980). Delays and red tape also accompany these programs.

Since many workers appear to be able to search for, qualify for, and find jobs on their own initiative in ways which are more viable than those offered by the bureau, it appears that the bureau constitutes only a poor substitute for the individual job search. The failure of the bureau, then, is that it cannot offer workers a better alternative. At present, employment services can play only a minor role in reemployment activities. One way the bureau might pursue its mission more productively is by enhancing the individual's job search skills, rather than trying to replace them.

Relocation Subsidy Programs

Ferman (1971; 1980) concludes that relocation subsidies do little good and perhaps a great deal of harm to workers unless subsidies are governed by the following criteria: (1) workers must have a definite job commitment in another community, (2) both the "sending" community and "receiving" community must be aware of each other's activities in relocation, (3) the receiving community must have adequate and appropriate social support facilities to assist workers, (4) the sending community must monitor or track the displaced worker to the receiving community, and (5) where possible, social service agencies should work with each other in the worker's behalf. Provision of relocation allowances, although perhaps a necessary condition for relocation, is not considered sufficient for successful implementation.

If the criteria above are not applied, it is very likely that workers will simply be trading one place of unemployment for another. However, unemployment away from familiar and supportive surroundings may be much less desirable. In the Youngstown case, for example, some workers reported that friends had sold everything and left the community only to return with less than when they left. Others who could not afford to return to Youngstown were left stranded.

OBES dispensed relocation funds without considering any of the above criteria. It is difficult, moreover, to see how a program of this sort might be locally administered, since OBES would be required to be in contact with perhaps hundreds of communities in complex and expensive ways which appear to be beyond their capability. Consequently, based on this evidence, relocation policies appear to require careful reconsideration.

Dealing with Workers Under Stress

As observed in Chapter 3, many workers are under stress following termination, especially those who are unable to find new jobs. Stress may manifest itself in two ways that are relevant here. First, workers may absorb little of the information disseminated to them concerning everything from the filling out of forms to their benefits under TAA programs. Second, workers may show little tolerance for the bureaucracy which will process their benefits and compensation claims or help them find jobs. This is especially true for workers whose "bureaucratic competency" (see Taber, Walsh, and Cooke, 1980) is not well developed in the first place. These manifestations may make service delivery to workers difficult.

In the Youngstown case, no programs to train job counselors in dealing with this stressful class of people were developed. Either it was assumed that this training would not be required or the need for such a program remained unrecognized. Similarly, programs intended to enhance the bureaucratic competency of workers were not offered. It appears that in Youngstown there is reason to believe that workers and counselors were under stress and that this may well have caused some workers to drop out of the employment services system (see Lipsky, 1980). The training of counselors and clients may help to avert problems of interaction between the two groups.

Discrimination Against Workers

Confidential interviews in the public sector suggest that a great deal of discrimination may occur in providing services to workers. This discrimination is not necessarily based on age, sex, race, or ethnicity. Instead, some workers are not helped because they are perceived by job counselors as being "undesirable" for employment by businesses which do employ workers sent to them by the bureau. For example, a worker under great stress seeks help from a mental health agency. If this worker is having great difficulty coping with job loss, he may not be sent out on job interviews, because the bureau fears that businesses will not wish to hire this worker. Business desires "high quality" workers. Therefore, the bureau, in order to preserve working relationships with some businesses, may not diligently assist some workers. This process, often referred to as "creaming" is considered a common practice in employment services (see Lipsky, 1980; Blau, 1964: 36–56)

The irony of this situation is that many of these workers are those most in need of jobs and are those who may perform their duties on the job quite well. By lowering their priority in the job search, the bureau may in some cases exacerbate mental and emotional problems.

Discrimination might also occur in other ways. In any community, there are many unemployed persons who would like to work. As previously noted, a substantial number of these workers are the hard-to-employ, who have few skills and little work experience or are unwanted for other reasons, including racial discrimination. When a major industry shuts down, local labor markets are glutted with experienced skilled workers. Assuming that in distressed communities there will be large labor surpluses, public employment services are faced with a major dilemma: which clientele—mass unemployed or the hard-to-employ—will be given priority?

In the case of Youngstown, this question appears to have been resolved, de facto, in favor of the mass unemployed. The dilemma concerning priorities still remains, however, increased competition for jobs may further discourage the hard-to-employ from bothering to search for jobs. Ultimately, this group must appear as recipients of transfer payments in compensation for the lack of work or as low-paid workers in the hidden economy which is characterized by "illegal" jobs (see Ferman, et al., 1978).

Employment Services Self-Evaluation

The Ohio Bureau of Employment Services doles out millions of dollars to displaced workers in the form of unemployment compensation, retraining benefits, and relocation subsidies. The local bureau, as well as the state-level agency, has not yet evaluated the impact of its programs in helping workers. For example, state TAA administrators have filed TAA client records in such a manner that they cannot be retrieved by year for an individual company which may have shut down. As a result, the bureau has no way of knowing how effective their services were in meeting the needs of the mass unemployed.

Conclusion

Most workers in the wake of the Youngstown Sheet and Tube plant closing appeared able to search for, locate, and obtain jobs on their own initiative. They did this by applying for jobs at plants where they wanted to work or by discovering leads through an extensive grapevine of informal personal contacts.

Nonsteel jobs found in the Youngstown area were bound to be less desirable than those lost. Steelworkers, perhaps the highest-paid workers in manufacturing, could only do worse in new jobs obtained outside the steel-making sector. As a result, some adjustment in life style, standard of living, and/or life expectations may have been necessary; but this adjustment appeared not to have precipitated severe mental and emotional problems.

One potential problem not related to accepting lower-paying jobs is that workers appeared to switch jobs periodically in order to better themselves. Others lost new jobs after a short time because of cutbacks resulting from local or national economic trends. There is no evidence that this job instability has yet had severe effects. Over the long term, however, workers who had become accustomed to job security, high wages, and handsome fringe benefits may begin to experience emotional and financial problems.

Retraining programs available to workers appeared not to lead to jobs to any great extent, but may have prolonged the financial security of participants. These programs, which may in some cases delay the inevitable, may also account for an absence of more severe emotional problems.

Most workers do not consider out-migration from a community to be a viable option. Many doubt that they would get a stable or satisfactory job in another community. Relocation would also remove workers from a strong social support network. Our studies offer compelling evidence that the informal social support network composed of families and friends in often predominantly ethnic neighborhoods may have lessened the burden of mass unemployment for many workers. Even those apparently not well integrated in a network may have had the personal resources to respond in positive ways to their unemployment dilemma.

The public employment services appeared not to be successful in supplementing individual worker initiatives in seeking employment. Workers did not use available job-search and counseling services to any great extent. When these services were used, they were perceived by workers to be inadequate for their needs.

Employment services cannot assist workers in part because they lack information on the local labor market, both from the standpoint of who is available to work and where jobs might be available. This results both from a dearth of information from the private sector and from a lack of cooperation within the public sector.

Employment services delivery also raises major policy questions concerning which workers should have priority in obtaining jobs, the mass unemployed or the hard-to-employ less-qualified workers.

In Chapter 7, the evidence presented here is used as a basis for considering employment policies appropriate to communities experiencing mass unemployment. First, however, it is necessary to complete the portrait of crisis responses by describing other ways in which workers coped with termination and how the various human services agencies in the community attempted to deal with an anticipated increase in service needs following the closing.

6. Other Responses: Individuals and Agencies

Most individuals were able to deal more or less successfully with the emotional stresses produced by sudden job loss. This much was established in Chapter 3 by the analysis of the closing's psychological impact. Chapter 5 has shown one reason for this: that many steelworkers, without the assistance of formal agencies, made a fairly rapid transition to new permanent jobs. Success in finding new work greatly reduces the impact of job loss. However, both for those who are quickly reemployed and others, coping with this or any personal crisis also involves various other changes from past behavior.

This chapter first describes some of those other ways in which workers and their families typically responded to the shutdown. It then examines the responses of human services agencies intended to help workers and others affected to deal with the presumed effects of sudden job loss. Considering the needs generated by the crisis and applying the definition of positive mental health offered in Chapter 3, it is possible to judge the appropriateness and effectiveness of the local human service system's response to the crisis.

Other Coping Processes

In the crisis of mass unemployment, most workers do not experience a need for life-sustaining necessities. Unemployment compensation, pensions, or finding a job reduce the threat to physical well-being. Nevertheless, many face emotional stresses beyond their previous experience. It is not apparent how one is to cope in many cases. A worker may have worked all his life in the mills. Perhaps he cannot retire, or his skills are not transferable to other jobs, or he is in poor health because of conditions

118

where he has been working. He may have children in college or parochial schools and a mortgage on his home. Most of his life he has had a middle-class income. There may be little in his personal experience that would guide him to an appropriate response.

Aside from what was, for most workers, the central task—finding or preparing for new jobs—how did most respond? We can begin by noting what they did not do. First, very few workers engaged in collective action, either through the unions or other political organizations. Despite substantial and prolonged efforts by a coalition of community leaders to engage them in the campaign to reopen the mills under community-worker ownership, a majority took no part in rallies, letterwriting, or other political action to influence federal and state decisions on subsidies for this purpose.[1]

Second, only a small minority of terminated workers made any use of formal human services, including those established under a state emergency grant to the community mental health program. For instance, of the over 4,000 affected workers, less than 2 percent had contact with the community mental health centers during the year following the closing. A "drop-in" mental health counseling center in the union hall, operated throughout 1978, was visited by only 22 workers. Although terminated workers were significantly more likely than nonterminated workers to report contacts with any of 46 principal local human services agencies, the

Juan Fernandez
Employed by Youngstown Sheet and Tube Company, 1951–1978
Age: 53
Spouse: Maria, married 1950
Children: six sons, four daughters

Juan could not believe he had been laid off after years of secure employment. Then, less than two months later, he was recalled to work; but he developed painful spinal arthritis. Since that time, the family has managed to live on gradually declining sick leave benefits and Maria's modest salary as a nutritional aide. Juan's application for Social Security disability benefits was denied. He is bitter toward the company, especially since they refused to rehire him in a less physically demanding job. He has watched many of his dreams "go down the drain." Recently, Juan's skill with the guitar has given him much comfort; he says that without this, he would be in a mental hospital. Both Juan and Maria also say their religion has been a great source of strength.

overall level of contact is surprisingly low—less than one contact per individual, when visits to the employment service for unemployment checks are excluded. This lack of agency use must be considered in light of major worker-targeted efforts at outreach conducted by local human services agencies.

To the extent that workers relied on others for help in handling their personal crises, they turned to informal networks of social support for extra help. (Both terminated and nonterminated workers were asked whether, in the last six months, they had "asked for extra help" from any of these sources.) However, when their use of such supports as friends, immediate family, close relatives, coworkers, union, doctor, neighbors, lawyers, and former employers is compared with that of non-terminated workers, the results are surprising.

Terminated workers were less likely than nonterminated workers to have asked for extra help from friends, neighbors, and coworkers. In fact, the lending agency was the only potential helper from which the terminated workers sought assistance more frequently than the nonterminated workers. To the extent that they sought extra help during this period, both

---

Averill Cristman
Employed by Youngstown Sheet and Tube Company, 1965–1978
Age: 42
Spouse: Jayne, married 1965
Children: two daughters, one son

After 13 years as an ironworkers rigger in the mill, Averill was laid off, then recalled and injured; by the time he recovered, his former position had been eliminated. After the first layoff, and following bitter arguments, Averill acquiesced in his wife's return to work at a health spa. Sometime after his second layoff, he develped diabetes, which his doctor attributed partly to tension. Averill jokes about becoming a "housewife" and says he now understands better his wife's frustration at being "homebound" by three growing, demanding children. Nevertheless, during this period, he and Jayne argued almost constantly about money problems and about the amount of her free time she was spending away from the house; they discussed separation but remained together. In late 1978, Averill found part-time, temporary work as a shoe salesman; a year later, he was hired by a local Jones & Laughlin specialty steel plant at a job paying less than he once earned. In July 1980, Averill and Jayne reported they were "saving more and spending less."

groups of workers placed greatest reliance on their immediate families and other close relatives. Under stress, workers did not see the need for or were reluctant to ask for help from others—especially from those they knew best.

Such evidence suggests that most workers coped with the crisis individually rather than collectively and often withdrew from social contact rather than reaching out to others. Here is an example from one mental health worker attempting to organize a self-help group among the laid-off workers.

> I met with neighbors of mine who are unemployed but who do part-time work out of their homes. They had skills such as carpentry and they're doing home improvements, etc. One guy did everything he could to fix up his home and now he's working for relatives. It's hard to get a profile of the individual we want to help or to start a self-help group. They're very independent, many don't want to help or won't admit they're scared. I talked to a group of four unemployed steel-workers, sort of an informal get-together in my house, and one neighbor still gets called out to work every so often. His friends told him since he's close to retirement age, he should transfer to Indiana Harbor. But he isn't about to transfer; he has a lawnmower shop set up in his garage—it's handy—that way he picks up some extra money.

Individual efforts to cope independently with a personal crisis are not necessarily less functional than efforts that involve reliance or dependence on others. Still, there are many examples of how unemployed or prematurely retired persons can benefit by turning to others for counsel or emotional support.

A retired person can be helped to cope with sudden enforced idleness through contacts with other retired workers who have made or are making similar adjustments. The anger and resentment many terminated workers feel can find expression through constructive political action. Workers who maintain contact with one another after termination can share information on events and alternatives while enjoying each other's company. However, the evidence is that most workers did not cope in this fashion and that many either were or became isolated from such sources of support.

Human Services Response

A major potential resource for helping workers find such ways of coping more effectively with the stresses of job loss was the complex of formal human services agencies in the community. Their leaders were not

Jim Sedlowski
Employed by Youngstown Sheet and Tube Company, 1955–1977
Age: 66
Spouse: Alice, marrried 1939
Children: one son, one daughter

Jim was employed for 22 years in the company's management. Preparing to leave for a one-week vacation in October 1977, Jim was called into his supervisor's office and asked for his thoughts about retiring. He said he had thought about it but wasn't ready yet. When he returned from his vacation, Jim was told he had one week left to work. Thirteen months shy of age 65, he was forced to retire early at a much-reduced pension.

The first several months of retirement were difficult. Although depressed, he put his handyman skills to good use by building a dining room table and chairs and enclosing a patio. His wife, Alice, has been very patient and understanding. The couple has more recently reported they are "very happy."

only willing but anxious to respond to needs generated by massive unemployment. Yet, as will be shown, their efforts were unsuccessful, whether the standard of judgment is the evidence of needs presented so far, the goals set by the professional leadership of the agencies, themselves, or the response of workers to their offers of help.

There is no established body of knowledge which suggests how the individual and collective social and psychological reactions to mass unemployment will manifest themselves or how to treat them. When over 4,000 workers lost their jobs with little warning, Youngstown's human service delivery system was caught by surprise. Subsequent responses demonstrated it was ill-prepared to respond to the crisis of mass unemployment.

The literature on human services, organization theory, systems theory, and so on provide some models by which human services agencies might come together in a coordinated response to economic crises (see Delbecq and Van de Ven, 1971). However, there are very few cases in which these models are applied in practice. Agencies searching for guidance will have few examples from which to choose.

One model has been constructed and tested by Thomas Taber, Jeffrey Walsh, and Robert Cooke (1979). The Taber model combines James Thompson's (1967) notion of a *synthetic organization* with A.K. Rice's (1970) *interorganizational systems* theory. Thompson (1967) suggests that synthetic organizations often emerge as ad hoc responses to a community crisis.[2] Taber, for example, describes the formation of a "community services council" following a plant closing, combining the efforts of community decision-makers, experts in the affected industry, human service agency administrators, University of Michigan social scientists, and United Auto Workers Union leadership (Taber, Walsh, and Cooke, 1979). This council accepted responsibility for coordinating human service delivery following the shutdown.

To build a synthetic organization and have it operate successsfully requires a concern for complementary resource commitments, interdependencies, communication, and authority relationships among the participants. In the Taber example, manpower, education, finance, health, and recreation agencies all cooperated. Each functional responsibility was connected organizationally with every other; and a liaison group comprised of representatives from each group dealt directly with laid-off workers to assess their needs, marshall resources, and make referrals. Taber reports that the effort was effective in meeting some needs of affected workers. However, the model's utility is somewhat restricted by the lack of participation by community mental health agencies.

Emergency Mental Health Grant

The Youngstown community's effort to mount a comparable response took two directions. The first responses were precipitated by a state grant to the community mental health agency serving eastern Mahoning County, the area most affected by the closing.[3] The mental health center received about $150,000 to provide "emergency" service to terminated workers and their families. This grant allowed the center to add two social workers, one psychologist, and three new clerical workers. With this new capacity, the center established new programs aimed at the terminated workers. In addition, small portions of the grant were passed through to a credit counseling agency and an emergency telephone information and referral service to meet anticipated increases in demands for service due to the crisis. The center's new programs included the following:

Drop-in center. A drop-in center was established in one local union hall. In addition to a mental health worker, staffing included CETA (Comprehensive Employment Training Act) workers and employees of a consumer credit counseling service. The principal objectives of the center were: to act as a referral point for persons who needed assistance and might otherwise not enter the services system, and to provide advocates to assist workers in obtaining needed services.

Community mental health liaison. A full-time mental health staff worker, based at the drop-in center, was assigned to provide "outreach" contact with union leaders and maintain communications among all

124   Shutdown at Youngstown

service providers. The staff worker worked with the union's counselors and other human service agency workers attempting to construct a coordinated response.

Community outreach/organization. This effort brought together experts and interested persons in the community in attempts to lessen the problems produced by the steel crisis. Objectives of this program were to: organize community groups of unemployed persons at various sites (preferably making the site as "natural" a setting as possible), and to provide each group with a trained team leader or observer.

Community education. This effort would inform and attract potential clients to the center and gain and maintain community support. Objectives included: insuring mass media coverage of programs; creating agency programs which would provide group presentations as needed by community groups; and coordinating community workshops which would reach a large number of persons and inform them of available services.

Agency coordination/in-service training. Since many staff workers in local service agencies would have no special experience with the mental and emotional problems of the unemployed, in-service training to upgrade professional skills of staff workers was developed.

In addition, the center's hours of operation were extended to 70 hours a week. Agencies expected substantial increases in service demand due to the economic changes occurring in the community.

Despite high visibility and varied outreach efforts, there was little worker response to this, as to other formal helping efforts. During the first year after the emergency grant, 49 former Youngstown Sheet and Tube workers or their spouses, and 34 men and women from families who had a member still working at Youngstown Sheet and Tube used the agency's services. The agency's figures indicate that, of 4,100 workers who were laid off, less than 2 percent visited the agency. In fact, families associated with other mills in the area (Republic Steel Corporation and U.S. Steel) used the services almost as much as those from Youngstown Sheet and Tube. No deluge of potential clients, directly or indirectly associated with the layoffs, was forthcoming.

It is unlikely that the union hall was a good location for contacting many workers, independent of whatever social stigma was attached to mental health service. As one mental health staff worker whose father was laid off from the mills during an earlier economic crisis period, explained:

> The last place my dad would go when he was laid off was, very
> simply, the union hall 'cause those were the people who didn't
> protect his job and he had paid them $20 a month to do that. He
> wanted no part of that. When he went back to work, they were
> great people.

Administrators were frustrated by the unexpected lack of response and offered various explanations:

> I met with a mental health administrator last week about that informal support idea and she brought me up to date on what they have been doing. It's really amazing. They started off with a consumer counseling session and advertised it through the union and the local churches in Campbell and Struthers. Nobody showed up. Then they had one on problems of alcohol. Same thing, they advertised and nobody showed up. She says one of the major problems has been that the union has more or less been in the way: you cannot really form an informal network without angering the union because the union sees itself as official. She said that she went around and around with the union on sending a letter mailed out that would explain the services available. I saw the letter—it was never mailed.

> I think we have to keep trying, but there's another factor that enters in. I'll use the parallel of working with unwed mothers. One of the first problems you have to do is get the girl to admit that she's pregnant. Sometimes she's in her ninth month and sometimes she's in the process of delivering and if you tell her that she's pregnant, she's going to be very angry with you and she probably isn't even going to talk with you until she's ready to say, "Yeah, I'm pregnant." I think with the laid-off steelworkers, if we go to them and we say, "This is a program for laid-off steelworkers," and they're not ready to admit they're laid-off steelworkers yet, they're not only going to not come—they're going to be mad at you 'cause they don't want to hear that. At the point where they're ready to say, "OK, I'm ready to hear this, I have to deal with it now," that's when you have to be ready to deal.

Views that people hold of formal helping systems may inhibit them from approaching service agencies. Seventy percent of the terminated and nonterminated workers said they found it "hard to ask others for help." More than 60 percent believe "grown people should stand on their own two feet," rather than "depending on someone else sometimes." More terminated workers (33%) were bothered by seeing the government spend tax dollars on the unemployed than were the nonterminated (23%). Likewise, more nonterminated workers said it was easy to ask for help (32%) and sometimes be dependent (37%) than terminated workers (26% and 30%). A comparison of the attitudes held by the two groups suggests that job loss may reinforce, rather than diminish, the desire to be self-reliant.

Community Planning Process:

Simultaneously, a second direction was taken by the community in developing a systemwide human services response. Youngstown State University's Center for Urban Studies, supported by a grant from the Ohio Board of Regents, brought together most of the involved community human services planners and administrators and assisted them, over a year-long period, in thinking through the nature of the community's need and the kinds of human services programs appropriate for this crisis.[4] From that process, there emerged a consensus on goals for action to meet the needs generated by the crisis. These 20 goals—set by leaders of the human services system itself—provide one comprehensive, concrete set of standards against which to judge the system's performance. Here are some examples.

A. *Outreach*
   1. There should be a central, noninstitutional, accessible place at which there is a staff capable of providing appropriate information, referral, follow-up, and linkage to service agencies and other helpers.
   2. Existing naturally-occurring networks of association— friendships, such as kinship—will be used for information and referral wherever possible.
B. *Services*
   1. *Goal. A Stabilization Training Package Will Be Developed. Subgoals:*
      a. To assist unemployed persons to meet their financial obligations.
      b. To assist unemployed persons to have and follow a personal/family financial plan.
      c. To assist unemployed persons to have the necessary legal knowledge to cope with unemployment and job search.
      d. To help insure that unemployed persons will act within the law.
   2. *Goal. A Unique Preventive Family Counseling Program Will Be Developed. Subgoals.*
      a. To help unemployed persons recognize predictable social stress indicators.
      b. To help unemployed persons to use peer support groups, local community groups, as well as social service agencies, to cope with symptoms of social stress.

      c. To help unemployed persons to identify and practice ways to anticipate and counteract damaging consequences of social stress.

      d. To help unemployed persons to avoid serious social stress consequences.

  3. *Goal. Human Service Knowledge Will Affect the Private Sector to Prevent Future Employment Crises.*
     Subgoals:

      a. A pre-retirement program will be made available to private-sector companies.

      b. A prelayoff program will be developed and available to each company.

      c. All employed persons should know what benefits are available in the event of layoff or retirement.

      d. Company management, community leaders, and other decision-makers should act consistently with knowledge of the effects of closings/layoffs on the total economic/social picture.

C. *Financial Needs*

  1. *Goal.* There will be a health insurance alternative for the over 1,700 unemployed steelworkers who have lost their group coverage.

  2. *Goal.* A social service deferred payment system for both short- and long-term credit will be devised and implemented.

  3. *Goal.* A program to protect mortgages will be developed in cooperation with banking institutions.

D. *Administration*

  1. *Goal.* *A representative human service providers' council should be formed and meet regularly.*

  2. *Goal.* The providers' council should monitor a coordinated response to crisis.

  3. *Goal.* The providers' council should oversee evaluation of the coordinated effort.

Six months after these goals were set—and more than a year after the layoffs began—the group who had set these goals and subsequently worked to implement some of them was asked whether each was "already accomplished," "badly needed," "possibly useful," or "not necessary." *None* of the 20 was seen by a majority as having been accomplished. Our own review of progress through 1980 showed that still virtually nothing had been done to achieve these human services goals—or to meet similar needs created by the wave of new mill closings in 1980 which terminated an additional 5,000 jobs.

Assessing the Human Services Response

To evaluate the community's human services response through its array of formal helping agencies it is necessary both to assess the appropriateness and effectiveness of what *was* done and to note what was *not* done to meet the needs of affected workers. Both must be compared to some standard of appropriate response, given the needs of workers and others affected.

A standard of appropriate human services response can be derived from the definition of positive mental health and evidence of personal stress presented in Chapter 3 as well as from the information on worker responses presented in this and the preceding chapter. On the one hand, there is little evidence of trauma or breakdown of the type typically treated by crisis-oriented mental health and other social services agencies. On the other hand, it is apparent that workers had widely varying experiences and demonstrated varying levels of ability of cope. Some managed the stresses of job loss and unemployment gracefully or even creatively, discovering the opportunities inherent in crisis. Others, either from bad luck or a lack of personal capacity, handled stress in ways that were destructive or at least unhelpful. Those who were unemployed for long periods appeared to have the most difficulty, although the direction of causality is far from clear. If the objective is to help workers manage their personal crises in ways that are beneficial rather than destructive, then helping efforts that build personal and group self-help coping skills and resources are the most appropriate. Many of the helping strategies appropriate to the workers' needs fall into the category of "primary prevention," as defined by community mental health professionals (Catalano and Dooley, 1980).

The steel crisis response illustrates the difficulty of developing effective programs of prevention and in reaching people with problems less severe than those generally classified as pathologies or "break-downs." In-depth discussions with local mental health administrators produced a portrait of administrators frustrated and floundering. They were surprised by the lack of response to their efforts to reach workers through media publicity, mass meetings, the union hall walk-in center, and other means. And they were unable to identify preexisting models for successful outreach to such groups or for services appropriate to recently terminated workers.

Our own investigation indicates why this was likely to be the case. What little academic research exists on plant closings and their social and psychological effects is virtually silent on the design of outreach or human services programs of this sort (Catalano and Dooley, 1980). It is reasonable, therefore, to conclude that existing theory and practice are not sufficiently developed to allow for dissemination of specific information to community services agencies on how to respond to such crises. Until various outreach and preventive services approaches are thought through and tested, community human services agencies will be forced to develop ad hoc responses to massive unemployment. Here and in the following chapters we have begun the process of thinking through what alternative human services responses to such events are possible and useful.

Options Not Taken: The local human services system failed to find or develop on its own a primary prevention approach to the mental health needs created by the steel crisis. In the absence of preexisting models, the local agencies faced the practical task of spending an emergency grant in a way that was consistent with their general continuing mandate and with the specific mandate of the grant to meet the mental health needs of workers.[5] The following examples give some idea of the range of options open to them as to other local services agencies:

1. To reduce stress, the agencies might have used the limited funds to provide small emergency grants to steelworkers with unusual expenses, such as uninsured illness or injury expenses. The short-term financial needs of most workers were met by unemployment insurance and other benefits; however, some suffered severe income losses or built up heavy debts.

2. To reduce stress, the agencies might have enhanced or supplemented existing support groups and informal helping networks among the workers. To do this, they would have had to avoid any institutional stigma, gain much more than verbal, passive support from the union, churches, and voluntary associations in the community, and work intensively "on the street" to build interpersonal networks providing two-way communication with most of the workers. The feasibility of such networking strategies is suggested by the remarkable stability of this labor force after the closing and the ability of individual workers, up to two years later, to locate and describe job histories of several dozen of their former coworkers. In these circumstances, gaining the trust and active assistance of a handful of workers in each area of the mill would put the mental health staff at only one remove from personal contact with every worker in the plant.

3. To reduce stress, human services professionals might have helped to organize collective political or social action by the workers. Opportunities

were present to support such action initiated by the unions and others. Any role that a public agency plays in such actions is likely to be controversial. Nevertheless, the Federal Community Action program of the 1960's provides examples of how organized collective responses can produce both material and psychological benefits—especially where powerlessness threatens to produce despair.

4. To increase competence and coping skills, the mental health centers might have developed and conducted education and training programs for the workers. This was among the action goals set by the group of human services administrators and planners participating in the university-led planning process. Catalano and Dooley (1980: 33) believe that "employer-sponsored 'stress inoculation' programs offer an ideal setting for reactive primary prevention among those workers likely to be affected by a company's economic fortunes." Such programs would include: (1) *education,* giving workers awareness of the social and psychological as well as the economic consequences of job loss and knowledge of reemployment prospects and available human services; (2) *cognitive restructuring* to destigmatize job loss and protect self-esteem; and (3) *behavior training,* providing such coping skills as relaxation, stress avoidance, and skills needed for active efforts to overcome the effects of job loss, including job search skills and new job skills. A virtually identical list of needs was generated in the community of planning process but not acted on. To deliver any such training to a large proportion of the workers, the system would first have to solve the problem of outreach, and then identify the specific skills needed to cope with this crisis as well as an appropriate training model.

These four examples illustrate the realistic range of options open to the local human services system. The community's failure was not specifically a failure to implement these specific programs or any others. Rather, it was a failure to evolve a coherent conception of how to aid workers in coping more successfully with their varied situations. Although community mental health workers and others understood, in a general way, the need for targeted primary prevention, they evolved no practical program to meet this need.

When we examine what *was* done by the agencies to meet the perceived needs of workers, we find no clear-cut strategy. Most effort was devoted to outreach and education designed to draw workers into existing services programs. In nearly all cases, these programs are not oriented toward primary prevention or development of new coping abilities in relatively healthy individuals but toward treatment of individuals who have already demonstrated either temporary or chronic inability to manage problems without professional assistance.[6] Moreover, many of the programs have eligibility limits or fee structures that pose barriers to their use by recently unemployed workers. The inappropriateness of the existing array of human services programs is highlighted by the fact that they could not be used or tailored to meet any of the service goals set in the community planning process. Finally, this abstract judgment is confirmed by the workers' indifference to available services.

A good deal of evidence suggests that it is difficult to construct human services appropriate to economic crisis. A major obstacle is the lack of knowledge and experience, not only at the local level where services are delivered, but at higher levels of government where programs are designed, funded, and sometimes coordinated. A second set of barriers is posed by the existing structure of services, priorities, eligibility, and financing—which does not recognize the particular needs of recently unemployed workers. Despite these obstacles[7] and the failure in Youngstown to overcome them, effective human services policies—including employment and training policies—can be developed to meet the needs created by major plant closings. These are the subject of the following two chapters.

PART 4

SOCIAL POLICIES FOR MASS UNEMPLOYMENT

Based on the evidence of impact and responses presented so far, the final three chapters discuss social policies appropriate to the needs generated by local economic crisis. Limited theory, and experience and environmental constraints are identified as major obstacles to the design of effective intervention strategies.

Social welfare functions or programs have been categorized in various ways. For our purposes, the most useful distinctions are between: (1) *developmental* programs, which produce lasting improvements in the capacities and resources of individuals and groups; (2) *maintenance* programs, which are designed to sustain people during periods when they lack the material resources to provide themselves or their dependents a satisfactory existence; (3) *crisis interventions,* to help individuals or groups whose previous capacities have been temporarily but severely weakened and who, therefore, cannot adequately care for themselves or who present an apparent danger to others; and (4) *custodial* programs to care for chronically incapacitated persons.

Examples of the first group include: (1) education, skills training, and related "human resources investments;" (2) those venture capital, technical assistance, and research/technology development programs designed to promote lasting gains in economic self-reliance and material well-being for individual entrepreneurs or collectives; and (3) an analogous group of "political development" programs that build organizational and community capacities to meet a broad range of social needs and achieve a greater degree of community autonomy. Therefore, some but not all so-called economic development and area assistance programs can be classified as developmental social programs.

The second group of social welfare programs is what the Reagan Administration has called the "social safety net" programs, including income or in-kind transfers to dependent populations such as children or low-income families, the elderly, the disabled, and the unemployed. Such programs do little to increase individual or group capacities, and there is some evidence that they may even push some people toward chronic dependency.

The third group of programs is designed to restore the normal or previous capacities of individuals or groups or to control dangerous deviance by means of corrective interventions. These include emergency medical and psychological assistance, police crisis intervention and protective services, refuge for victims of violence or natural disaster, alcohol and drug "dry out" and rehabilitation, and many other stabilizing and rehabilitating programs to deal with particular symptoms or dysfunctions. Most are focused on individuals and most are devoted to treating people whose deviance or dysfunction is so severe that either they or others see that professional intervention is needed. Some are treated involuntarily.

Finally, a fourth group of programs includes nursing and custody of the chronically ill or disabled and other special populations.

All but the fourth group of social welfare programs are of interest here. Social interventions to help unemployed workers, their families, and others in the community include *developmental, maintenance,* as well as *crisis intervention* programs. (See Figure 5.1.) "Primary prevention" strategies in community mental health encompass both developmental and maintenance efforts. On the other hand, many local social services programs, including those offered by community mental health agencies, are primarily oriented toward crisis intervention. The reasons for this are several: (1) a widely shared sense that the highest priority use of limited resources is to meet the needs of people whose dysfunction presently threatens their well-being and that of others; (2) the relative bias of program authority, funding, and professional orientation toward treatment of illness or dysfunction rather than toward personal development or prevention of future dysfunction; (3) the lack of experience and theory related to developmental programs for adults; and (4) the symptoms of personal crisis that are difficult to ignore, in contrast to the difficulty of identifying and reaching out to people at risk but not in immediate crisis— such as those experiencing stress due to job loss.

The evidence presented in previous chapters sheds light on the relative need, in the wake of major plant closings, for each broad category of services. The needs of workers are best met by maintenance programs and developmental services. There is little evidence of trauma or debilitation among the workers calling for crisis interventions; and they do not respond to outreach efforts that carry the implication of such a need.

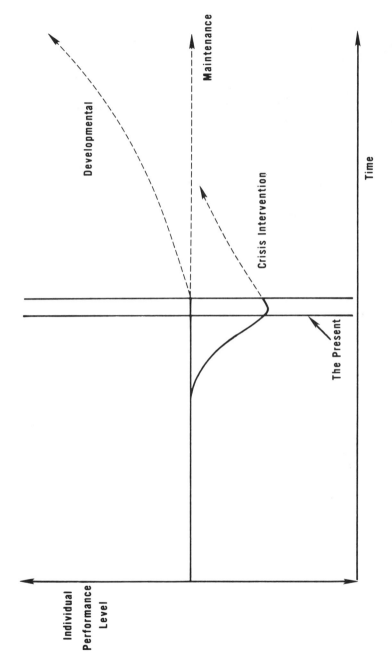

Figure 5.1 Intended Effects of Three Types of Social Intervention Programs on Individual Performance

The evidence concerning agency responses presented in Chapters 5 and 6 confirms the difficulty of designing an intervention strategy combining appropriate developmental and maintenance services for the workers directly affected. We also have noted the lack of attention to the delayed secondary wave of impacts on others in the community and the absence of efforts to identify and directly aid those in this group, many of whom have fewer resources and less skill or work experience than the industrial work force first affected.

Based on a consideration of the evidence of need and response and on a review of experience and theory concerning appropriate intervention strategies, Chapers 7 and 8 offer a partial intellectual basis for designing social policies more likely to meet the needs flowing from sudden and massive economic contraction. Chapter 9 presents a more speculative analysis of the longer-term needs of such communities.

7. Employment Policy

Massive, localized unemployment caused by a major plant closing or similar event is a distinct class of unemployment. It differs, on one hand, from *cyclical* job losses associated with national recession and characterized by widespread short-term layoffs across a wide range of employment categories; it differs, on the other hand, from what is traditionally recognized as *structural* unemployment, the chronic unemployment or underemployment of the least-qualified fraction of the labor force. Aside from a few path-breaking studies of technologically-displaced workers in the 1960s (e.g., Schultz and Weber, 1966; Wilcock and Franke, 1968), published analyses about employment policy have largely ignored the distinct problem of permanent job loss affecting those with skills, experience, and stable work histories, and have failed to prescribe for this group.

Chapter 5 examined the experiences of terminated workers with regard to reemployment, retraining, and relocation; and it described the responses of employment services agencies, training and educational institutions, and related programs to workers' needs. This chapter uses that evidence and other information about the effects of a plant closing on the local economy to derive the basic elements of an employment services policy specifically for communities experiencing this distinct type of unemployment.

Toward an Employment Policy for Mass Unemployment

To develop an employment policy addressing the effects of a major plant closing means confronting three analytical problems:

—First, a basic choice must be made about where to apply limited resources: to the needs of recently unemployed industrial workers or to less-experienced, less-skilled groups, such as minority youth.

—Second, with regard to the redundant industrial worker, a strategy must be developed that maximizes his or her chances of secure reemployment while addressing other policy objectives, such as the reinforcement of family and social relationships.

—Finally, certain technical and organizational problems that hamper the operations of employment services and training programs must be corrected.

These analytical problems are discussed, in turn, below.

Priorities. As we have noted, analysts of employment and training policy have distinguished between efforts aimed at structural unemployment and those aimed at cyclical unemployment. The former category of unemployment is either due to a mismatch between the job needs of employers and the qualifications of the labor force or to chronic failure of the national economy to produce enough paid work. The latter is due to temporary labor surpluses associated with national recessions. The recent wave of major plant closings and the continuing decline of manufacturing call our attention to a new type of structural unemployment resulting from the decline of major industrial sectors. In 1980 and 1981, the national recession, the new structural unemployment, and chronic structural unemployment of those with minimal job qualifications combined to produce unemployment rates of between 10 and 20 percent in the older industrial centers of the Great Lakes states. Even so, discussions of employment policy typically ignored the important distinctions among these three classes of unemployed persons.

In communities with large numbers of unemployed of all classes, policy-makers and agencies must consider difficult choices about whom to serve. In doing so, they are constrained by the priorities set at higher levels of government. The Federal Comprehensive Employment and Training Act (CETA) programs generally serve only the least qualified potential workers. In contrast, the training and mobility programs offered under the Trade Adjustment Assistance Act (TAA) serve only experienced workers. The job search help provided by state employment services is potentially more flexible, but priorities may be established at the state rather than the local level. These constraints leave community policy-makers and administrators with control over only a fraction of the resources devoted to employment and training, making the choices they do make still more difficult.

In our view, given a choice between serving the relatively experienced, skilled fraction of recently unemployed or the large groups of less competitive job-seekers, communities should concentrate scarce resources on the latter. This can be argued from several perspectives, including the higher percentage of this group whose unemployment places them in poverty and the greater cost in social disorder and public income maintenance in failing to employ them.

A Strategy for Redundant Workers: However, if resources are to be targeted on the new group of structurally unemployed, what mix of job search, training or education, and mobility programs would best meet their needs and the needs of the community? Here, the distinctions offered in the introduction to this section between *developmental, maintenance,* and *crisis intervention* services are helpful.

Few, if any, employment services programs fall into the category of *crisis intervention.* However, contact with these agencies can facilitate early diagnosis and referral of people presenting symptoms of severe, unmanageable stress. It was noted in Chapter 6 that terminated workers have far more contact with the employment service than with any other human services agency; however, the employment counselors of this agency were instructed *not* to pursue counseling unrelated to employment. If it were administratively feasible to expand the role of these professional counselors, they could be the first point of access to help for people in need of other services.

Aside from this limited role in crisis intervention, employment and training programs can be classified as either *developmental* or *maintenance* in function. Developmental programs, in this context, are those which increase workers' job-seeking efficiency and/or increase their long-term employment and income-earning capacities.[1] Maintenance programs, on the other hand, offer only temporary substitute employment or income. For instance, training that moves workers from declining industries to high-growth sectors by augmenting their obsolete or limited job skills can be considered developmental. However, training or education undertaken as a source of extended unemployment benefits and providing job skills already in oversupply can only be classified as maintenance. Obviously, programs that develop new capacities not only for workers but for the communities in which they live are more desirable. This is why reemployment, retraining, and relocation policy should be tied into a general strategy of local economic revitalization.

Areas affected by major plant closings can anticipate having chronic labor surpluses. The decline of manufacturing reduces work opportunities for both the skilled and the unskilled. However, the major part of the burden is rather quickly transferred to the less-skilled and -experienced fraction of the work force. Skills training for these potential workers, in the absence of any new job creation, merely increases their competitiveness with more experienced workers for stable or shrinking numbers of skilled jobs. There is no net gain in local economic welfare.

This, too, suggests that the better use of training is in conjunction with an area economic redevelopment strategy. Viewed this way, training or education is a human resources investment. It is designed to produce precisely those skills needed by expanding local firms and by firms likely to locate new operations in the area. Preferably, such training will be linked to the long-term needs of particular firms, being developed and carried out with their cooperation. Such highly targeted human resources investments, if successful in facilitating new job creation, can produce net gains in community economic welfare.

Although the advantage of using training as a development lever is theoretically appealing, experience suggests it is hard to put into practice. Before training can become part of an overall development strategy, various technical problems in the operation of employment services programs and their relationship to potential employers must be addressed.

Technical Barriers: A lack of reliable information on job needs of employers, difficulties in compiling useable information on aggregate labor force characteristics, and the lack of articulation between economic development and employment services constitute a formidable set of barriers to an effective strategy for reemploying the surplus labor of areas experiencing the new structural unemployment produced by industrial decline (see Chapter 5).

Given the problems of setting priorities between the newly unem- ployed and the chronically unemployed, the need to evolve reemployment strategies that meet the needs of both groups of workers, and the just- mentioned technical barriers to an effective reemployment strategy, we next consider the roles of the private and public sector. Particular attention is given to the private sector for three reasons: (1) corporations closing plants have frequently miscalculated their own interest in working to reemploy their terminated employees; (2) the public sector, as noted above, is not in a position to solve these problems without private-sector cooperation; and (3) the corporations have resources and expertise that allow them to perform this role effectively.

What the Private Sector Can Do

As noted in Chapter 2 the Lykes Corporation did little or nothing to help workers find jobs or to aid them in any way. Instead, it simply closed up shop, and left the community and workers to fend for themselves. Although easily accomplished, this strategy may have cost the corporation more than it realized. Plant closings can be exceedingly costly to corporations as well as communities. The closing of the Campbell Works, for example, is estimated to have cost the Lykes Corporation approximately $183 million ("S & T Shutdown Expense Is High," 1978). Also, the 1979 closing of U.S. Steel's New Haven Works, which employed 12,000 workers, is said to have cost $808.6 million in payments to laid-off workers (Barks, 1980). In both cases, workers used considerable proportions of their company-financed severance benefits following the closings. In the short term, then, it appears to be in the interest of corporations to insure that workers are reemployed elsewhere.

Thanks to the cut-and-run tactics of firms like Lykes, other long-term costs may be on the horizon for firms closing plants. These would result from the increasing number of "industrial hostage" laws currently being proposed in the states and at the federal level, which would greatly restrict corporate options and add to their costs.

By mid-1981, at least 11 states had considered legislative proposals intended to accomplish the dual goals of discouraging relocation and ameliorating its effects. Even more stringent legislation had been proposed at the federal level. A brief overview of bills proposed in the Congress will serve to illustrate the gravity of the burdens they might impose on corporations. Taken together, they would: (1) require at least one year's prenotification of the closing; (2) require additional compensation and severance payments for displaced workers, usually up to but not more than a worker's preclosing salary; (3) necessitate the filing of an economic and social impact statement; (4) require continued health and welfare benefits coverage for at least one year; (5) guarantee workers' rights to transfer to other facilities owned by the corporation; (6) establish a new federal agency to deal with plant closings; (7) require continued payment of tax revenues to the community for at least one year; and (8) impose monetary penalties to be paid to the community.

Public concern over plant closings is one reason why corporations may want to rethink the ways they implement decisions to close facilities and terminate workers (Buss and Redburn, 1981). Assuming that corporate decision-makers wish to avoid further legal restrictions on their future flexibility in reallocating capital and minimize the costs of closings, how should a company go about shutting down a major facility?

1. Preparing for a Closing

When Lykes Corporation shut down the Campbell Works, there were no agreements in force with workers concerning company obligations for prenotification of a closing, reemployment assistance, retraining relocation, or health and human services provision. The corporation did have an agreement with the USW to supplement unemployment compensation benefits.

In order to meet the needs of the corporation and the workers, both parties should negotiate in advance the rights and obligations of each before, during, and after a plant closing (Mick, 1975). Perhaps the best known effort at this was accomplished by Armour Company in the establishment of its Automation Fund Committee (Schultz and Weber, 1966; Wilcock and Franke, 1968). The committee, established through collective bargaining, was mandated to study the problems of displacement, to promote transfers within the company by providing retraining and relocation allowances, and to consider other employment opportunities. The committee was supported by $500,000 from the company.

2. Early Warning of a Closing

Most observers advocate that corporations inform workers well in advance of a plant shutdown. Many recommend at least a year's lead time for workers. The intent of this warning is to encourage workers to find new jobs and restructure their lives. Very early warnings to workers are probably counterproductive from the corporation's, if not the workers', point of view. First, corporate decision-makers often make decisions which must be kept from the public and from the competition. Also, a corporation merely contemplating closing as an option, and yet forced to make this public, might be forced to follow through because the announcement scared away potential customers and investors. Second, productivity is very likely to decrease in plants which are perceived by workers to have a low probability of remaining open. This occurs in part because sick leave or vacation time is used as a way to search for a job without losing income. Many workers may fail to report for work regardless of income loss. A few vengeful workers may resort to sabotage. The longer the advance notice and the sharper the drop in productivity, the less profitable the enterprise. Third, evidence in the steel industry suggests that workers in hazardous jobs who are experiencing stress as a result of a closing announcement may become more vulnerable to accidents (see Chapter 3). The longer workers are under stress created by an imminent loss of work, the more likely they are to be injured. This, of course, will lead not only to workdays lost but also to increased compensation claims. If early warning to workers is not particularly helpful to workers, and may harm the company, management must seek other ways to offset this problem.

2. Reemployment Responsibilities

Corporations closing plants should assist workers in seeking reemployment. Corporations may help their workers in a variety of ways.

Perhaps one of the most important is to provide skills necessary in finding and applying for jobs, including filling out job applications, preparing resumes, interviewing, and so on. Union Carbide (Judson, 1976) and Jones & Laughlin Steel Corporation (Barks, 1980) both prepared workers in this fashion and reported that these programs appeared effective. Union Carbide accomplished this with its own personnel department, while Jones & Laughlin contracted with a private firm to deliver the service at a cost of $100 per person trained.

Another way that corporations can help is through interplant transfers. In practice, many transfer programs yield few takers among workers. In the Armour Plant shutdowns (Schultz and Weber, 1966: 57), for example, only four workers, among 1,200 who were offered a transfer, accepted. In the case of the closing of the Brier Hill Works, only 15 out of 1,400 accepted. Corporations can easily offer this option to workers, since it costs very little, is seldom used, and retains mainly experienced, skilled workers.

Finally, corporate executives should conduct their own canvass of other firms to locate job opportunities which might exist for large numbers of laid-off workers and which might not come to the attention of workers through public employment services. Many executives have good working relationships with managers of other firms, so that information can be shared privately and confidentially.

4. Retraining Responsibilities

Accumulating knowledge about retraining workers to assume other jobs after a plant closing suggests that most retraining programs have been either ineffective or otherwise undesirable (Ferman, 1980; Stern, 1973; Foltman, 1968; Schultz and Weber, 1966). As previously noted, training programs are often operated without knowledge about what skills are required by local businesses or by firms, which might locate in the community in the future. From the worker's perspective they are also undesirable because many workers are reluctant to change occupations. Designers of training for workers whose skills have become obsolete must confront this reality: experienced workers either cannot or will not adjust quickly and easily to new occupations.

Even so, corporations can accomplish several things which might help to reemploy workers. First, corporate personnel officers can provide private and public employment services agencies with detailed information on the skills and occupational experience of workers. This will help these agencies to identify the groups of workers most easily retrained and the retraining programs most likely to lead to reemployment. Second, where cost is not prohibitive or with public funding, corporations should implement their own retraining programs. This suggestion encompasses several alternatives. Union Carbide (Judson, 1976), for example, continued apprenticeship training for workers even though the plant employing the workers had been shut down. This provided a large number of workers with skills which would make them more readily employable. Other industries (see Schultz and Weber, 1966: 44-45), have provided retraining in jobs related to those lost or, in some cases, in different jobs altogether. Still other corporations have canvassed local companies in an effort to reach retraining agreements to supply them with workers.

5. Information Dissemination

The workers' informal communication network, also known as the "rumor mill," is the major conduit through which information about the corporation is funneled. This network usually exaggerates information either positively or negatively as it is passed from worker to worker. As information flows through the work place, a worker's hopes, plans, and expectations are broken and reformed in a continuing process. During the period before, during, and after the closing, workers feel stress because they cannot obtain accurate information upon which to base their decisions. For example, on one day, they hear a plant will reopen only to hear in the following week that not only will the plant close but they will also lose their retirement benefits.

Much of the information possessed by corporate decision-makers is not so restricted or confidential that it cannot be shared with workers in a timely fashion. All too often, however, corporations simply restrict all information during the shutdown of operations. But overcontrol of information may be counterproductive. Workers who are under stress in part because of an information-poor environment may direct their frustration and anger toward the corporation. Work stoppages, plant takeovers, and even violence may be precipitated in part by worker uncertainty under stress.

A prudent strategy is to hold frequent meetings with workers, if only to inform them that the status quo prevails. Although union leaders should also be kept informed, executives should make every effort to deal with workers directly. This is because unions do not or cannot reach all of their members even if they want to, and because information disseminated by unions may be modified as it is relayed to workers.

What the Community Can Do

1. What should communities do to prepare for the unemployment resulting from sudden loss of a large number of jobs?

Communities should develop "early warning systems" to anticipate plant closings, as well as contingency plans for dealing with them once a closing occurs. Abstractly, the utility of early warning systems is found in their ability to provide the capacity to detect or intercept signals from the environment in sufficient time to apply appropriate interventions. In an environment of interdependency and instability, communities must develop mechanisms which anticipate major plant closings. State (see Buss and Waldron, 1982) and federal (Nathanson, 1980) initiatives to assist communities in providing this capability are currently under way, but formal mechanisms have yet to be implemented and tested. As a minimum, communities must develop techniques for: identifying industries which have a high probability of shutting down, keeping high-risk industries from shutting down where possible, and better targeting their efforts to attract industry and aid expansion of existing firms. Computerized information systems that centralize and analyze data on trends in industry, manpower needs, and labor force status are useful for these purposes.

Because of the potential harm associated with major plant closings, communities should have well-developed contingency plans for dealing with their impacts. A council composed of labor, private-sector management, public administrators, and other community leaders can predefine the steps to be taken once a closing is announced. The outcome of this process should be a set of formal agreements among major community institutions on how they will respond in the whole of a major closing. The community-wide labor/management committees formed by Mayor Stanley Lundine in Jamestown, New York (Council for Northeast Economic Action, 1977) are examples of this type of cooperative planning.

2. What kinds of training and employment services are most appropriate for the new structural unemployment?

The appropriate focus of reemployment and retraining for experienced workers remaining in the community after a major closing is very different from that appropriate for entry-level, unskilled workers. Consequently, the typical CETA-sponsored training programs and many other public and private employment and training programs will be of little value to these workers. As said earlier, we do not endorse changing the priorities of these programs at a time when increased competition from more experienced workers further reduces the job opportunities available to the less qualified. If other resources are available, however, they should be used in two ways: (1) to give the terminated industrial worker a much wider range of employment choices than is available to most at present; and (2) to develop new pools of work skills that match as closely as possible the likely long-term needs of area employers.

The range of employment options brought within reach of the terminated worker is limited, first, by how much useful information about job opportunities is received and, second, by the job-seeking skills in his or her possession. We have already indicated the need for properly maintained computer-based information systems as an aid to reemployment. Training in job search skills should be provided to workers prior to actual termination or as soon afterwards as possible.

To make most efficient use of limited retraining resources, training offered under TAA or similar programs should not be wholly at the discretion of the individual workers. Rather, it should be targeted to well-documented needs of existing employers or to the needs of employers with definite plans to relocate in the area. Such training for high-skill positions reduces competition between terminated, experienced workers and less-qualified workers for low-skill and entry-level jobs. We do not recommend, however, that training be limited to industries with high growth prospects nationally, partly because such forecasts are not sufficiently reliable and partly because area and national sectoral growth patterns often differ significantly (Bendick and Ledebur, 1981). Some analysts, for instance, advocate emphasis on high-technology industries in distressed areas. Although many New England communities have pursued this strategy successfully, it is not likely to work as well in the heavy industry belt now experiencing most of the new structural unemployment. One way communities can gradually reduce labor surpluses is by increasing the share of new jobs taken by local residents; it is ironic, indeed, that new jobs in distressed communities are often filled by highly skilled people recruited from other areas.

3. What is the place of publicly sponsored relocation in a strategy for reemployment and community revitalization?

Consideration of mobility programs must begin with the recognition that interests of redundant workers and distressed communities do not coincide. Workers with transferable skills can benefit financially by migrating to areas where these skills are in short supply, and many, especially younger workers, will do so even if they must themselves finance the move. Less-skilled, less-experienced workers also may benefit from migration but are less likely to move for various reasons and will be ineligible for government mobility assistance. Consequently, mobility programs may accelerate the loss of a declining area's pool of skilled, younger, but experienced manpower. The loss of these human assets may discourage potential new employers from locating in the area. Thus mobility programs designed to reduce labor surpluses can have a perverse effect on the balance between labor force and employment opportunities.

Mobility programs also may be undesirable for both workers and communities because of the disruption they cause in family and other social relationships. The separation of people from established networks of social support combined with the stresses produced by adjustment to a new job in a strange environment puts them at risk; it also weakens the social fabric of the communities left behind. More research on the potential social costs of mobility programs is needed before they are pursued on a large scale.

Recent evidence suggests that, whatever their value for workers, publicly sponsored relocation efforts may be difficult to implement. Although job-search and moving expenses were available to Youngstown's workers under TAA, very few used this option. Nationally, of 500,000 workers eligible for this program between 1974 and 1979, only 2,700 took job-search expenses and only 1,700 actually relocated (Samuelson, 1980). The mobility of the total U.S. population had declined gradually since the 1950s, in spite of increasing proportions of younger, better-educated people. Publicly sponsored mobility programs may, therefore, prove to be an impractical means of correcting regional labor force imbalances.

Conclusion

The impact of even well-designed employment and training policies is limited by their small scale relative to other forces shaping labor opportunities. Eli Ginzberg (1980:10) estimates that national "manpower policies and programs have had only a modest impact relative to the far-reaching effects of the underlying forces propelling the economy and the society." Prospective reductions in federal spending for such programs further reduce their potential as developmental tools for distressed communities. They, therefore, do not constitute a short-term solution to the compound problems of chronic labor surpluses, high unemployment, depressed income, and consequent drain of talented youth and skilled workers from distressed communities. This is one major reason why reemployment policies should be tied into a longer-term strategy of economic revitalization. The nature of an appropriate long-term revitalization strategy is discussed further in Chapter 9.

Despite its limitations, a properly designed and administered employment policy can improve the reemployment prospects of terminated workers without taking employment opportunities from less qualified workers. It can also support a comprehensive strategy for community economic revitalization. The key element is close articulation between the training needs and job-seeking of redundant workers and the prospective needs of employers. Publicly funded mobility programs, on the other hand, should be approached skeptically, since they may have perverse consequences for some workers who use them and for the communities they leave behind.

8. Human Services Policies

Employment policies must be a central focus of the public response to economic crisis. However, efforts to reemploy workers and to expand the job base of the community are only part of an appropriate response. A comprehensive services strategy will involve a range of innovative programs requiring cooperative action by a variety of public and private human services agencies, volunteers, business, and labor. This strategy should be aimed at reducing the incidence and severity of financial and emotional stresses experienced by affected workers, their families, and others indirectly harmed by economic contractions.

Toward a Human Services Policy for Mass Unemployment

The design of a human services strategy for massive localized unemployment is constrained by three sets of circumstances:

—First, the nature of economic crisis makes it especially difficult both to design and to implement an effective response to the human stress produced.

—Second, there is virtually no body of theory of clinical practice to guide communities in designing successful interventions.

—And, finally, the prevailing pattern of fragmented, uncoordinated, and underfunded services provides an unpromising organizational and resource base from which to launch appropriate actions.

These barriers to a successful human services strategy are elaborated, in turn, below.

The Crisis: A review of evidence on the impact of economic crisis suggests the following:

1. the harmful effects develop slowly and are spread out, but gradually accumulate, over many months or years;

2. the people most harmed are not necessarily those experienced workers whose jobs are first eliminated;

3. the people directly affected are, for the most part, emotionally healthy and resourceful people whose service needs are limited and are distinct from the clientele normally seen by mental health centers and many other service agencies;

4. because the shock, shame, or stigma experienced by many people due to job loss, unemployment, reduced income, or dependency may cause them to conceal the true extent of their problems from others, and for other reasons, those affected will show little interest in formal human services.

One consequence of these facts is that human service agencies will not experience a surge of demand for services in the weeks or months following a major plant closing. Nor will social indicators of distress show a sharp rise from the preceding period. The lack of visible evidence of immediate suffering may cause communities to misjudge the true extent and nature of stresses produced. They may fail to react. On the other hand, because many effects of an economic crisis are delayed, there is usually adequate time for local leadership to plan and organize an effective postcrisis response—even when job losses occur without warning.

Current Theory and Practice: Dooley and Catalano (1980: 463) have noted that each linkage in the causal time sequence beginning with economic change and ending with the onset of behavioral disorder (see Figure 3.1) "suggests a public intervention with the goal of reducing the negative consequences of economic change." The earliest and most problematic intervention would be an effort to prevent economic changes that are likely to cause widespread harm. On an individual level, it is possible to intervene at any time prior to job loss to "inoculate" someone against the harmful effects of such an event. The community may intervene after an economic shock either to bolster social support or to provide coping skills. Still later, the community may intervene to treat manifest symptoms of individual psychological or financial stress. And ultimately the community may be called upon to treat those individuals who sooner or later suffer severe emotional or other harm and to pay a large part of the social and economic costs of the loss of a productive individual. In part, the choice of an appropriate intervention strategy depends on a complex analysis of the public costs and benefits associated with early or late interventions of one kind or another.[1]

More research is needed to determine the relative value of various intervention strategies. On the benefit side of this decision analysis, it will be necessary to determine which interventions are most powerful under varying environmental circumstances and for various kinds of individuals. For human services, benefits are typically coproduced in an intimate collaboration of client and professional helper.[2] If active, voluntary cooperation of the person is essential to productive intervention yet evidently very difficult to achieve, then a major initial task is to develop and test service strategies that dissolve this barrier to effective treatment. Also, because older workers have different problems and responses than younger workers, because workers themselves have different problems and responses than their spouses, because individuals vary in their abilities to tolerate and cope with economic change, it will be necessary to devise interventions that are either highly flexible or varied in their basic elements, i.e., tailor-made not only for the particular crisis but also for the needs and receptivity of various groups of affected individuals.

On the cost side, the decision analysis is similarly complex.[3] Here the time dimension is again relevant. Early intervention, if effective, may avoid very substantial social and economic costs, e.g., by avoiding prolonged income loss, suicide, hospitalization, or development of chronic disability or disorder. On the other hand, early interventions cannot be so easily targeted on the small group likely to suffer such severe effects; thus, they will be more difficult to design and possibly more expensive to administer. Also, because so little is known about primary prevention and developmental services, the action research process required to develop effective early intervention techniques is likely to prove time-consuming and costly.

Moreover, it is important to recognize that economic change cuts in complex ways—benefiting some and hurting others. Thus, public interventions to reduce economic hardships for one group may add to the burden on others. Major plant closings exacerbate preexisting hard choices about where to place scarce community resources. For instance, decisions must be made about the relative developmental needs of unskilled youth and those of experienced, skilled workers. The decision analysis regarding human service interventions must be both comprehensive, in its specification of benefits and costs, and extensive, both geographically and in time—so as to capture the major opportunity costs of each contemplated policy.

Resources and Organization: Although many agencies may have potential capacity to assist with the problems created by economic crisis, their actual capacity is limited in two ways: (1) their existing case loads are nearly always sufficient to absorb most or all of the funding and staff time of the agencies; and (2) their programs and outreach-in-take procedures give priority to those who are easiest to serve because they have problems which are readily identifiable; these typically include those with more severe problems. As noted in the introduction of this section, there are several reasons for this crisis orientation; these include: the belief that problems posing a more immediate threat to well-being deserve priority; the bias of professional training, funding, and theory toward crisis intervention and away from departmental services; and more obvious symptoms of personal crisis in contrast to the difficulty of identifying those merely at risk.

In times of economic crisis, it is unlikely that local service agencies will experience net gains in funds or program capacity. The absence of federal and state human service programs aimed toward localized economic crisis means that any augmentation of services' budgets from these levels typically will be ad hoc and small-scale. Furthermore such grants may be offset by declines in local support due to the economic pressure on government budgets. For example in 1981 and 1982, funding for local community mental health programs in Detroit, then experiencing the nation's most severe unemployment, was reduced to such an extent that most programs were targeted toward recently deinstitutionalized mental health patients, rather than to the unemployed or underemployed. In such circumstances, it is appropriate to ask whether service needs that would not ordinarily come to the attention of existing agencies should be addressed. This again raises the problem of equity, because there are individuals in the community with similar levels of need who would not be served by a program that is targeted to a newly terminated group of workers.

Our view is that service resources should be allocated on the basis of relative needs, as assessed by the community. However, this is not a useful guide to action unless some reasonable way of assessing relative need is available. A systematic needs assessment is, therefore, appropriate.

Aside from the problem of resources and priorities, there are bound to be major organizational barriers to effective action. In most if not all U.S. communities, the human services system is characterized by diversity and fragmentation of services' programs, reflecting a diversity and fragmentation of funding sources, authority and accountability, geographic jurisdictions, and professional orientations (Redburn, 1977). Despite federal and state reorganization demonstrations, the pattern prevailing in most places bewilders even the professionals who work within it, not to mention persons seeking help with a problem (Polivka, et al., 1981).

Despite its complexity, the local services system does not necessarily offer an array of programs appropriate to the needs of terminated workers and their families. Many services, outreach efforts, and eligibility criteria should be reoriented if the system is to efficiently meet needs flowing from an economic crisis. However, it will be very difficult for providers and their funding/supervising agencies to reach agreement on who should take responsibility for financing, administering, and delivering the nontraditional services called for at such times. Moreover, agencies will lack experience with administration and delivery of these nontraditional services. This will require start-up costs for training, new procedures, and the sorting out of roles and relationships. Recognition of these costs by already heavily burdened services providers does not make the task of achieving consensus on service strategy any easier.

An Effective Human Services Response

An effective human services response will be one that:

—Recognizes the distinctive needs produced by sudden, massive layoffs of experienced workers;
—Devises new outreach techniques to provide early identification and intervention to prevent severe personal crisis; and
—Consistent with local priorities and funding limits, develops innovative service programs that lie outside the normal responsibilities (although not the capacities) of local service providers and require a reorientation of staff and administrative procedures.

Given the needs of affected workers and their families, it is likely that greatest benefits will flow from actions that protect self-esteem, provide coping skills, and give access to resources. For instance, training of unemployed workers for roles as information-givers and network-builders—work for which they could be paid and which builds both their capacities and those of former colleagues *without* implying dependency—may prove a valid, cost-effective technique. Many and diverse agencies and actors can be part of a human service strategy to aid those under temporary stress. However, the state of theory and practice compel an experimental nondogmatic approach to designing and implementing a response. More specific recommendations follow.

Prelayoff Interventions: The days or weeks before layoffs begin are a critical time for two reasons: first, because this is a period of considerable stress and anxiety, complicated by contradictory rumors; and second, because it is the last time when the whole group of workers can be reached easily and without expense. Catalano and Dooley (1980: 33) believe that "employer-sponsored 'stress inoculation' programs offer an ideal setting for reactive primary prevention among those workers likely to be affected by a company's economic fortunes." Such programs would include: (1)

education, giving workers awareness of the social and psychological as well as the economic consequences of job loss, and knowledge of reemployment prospects and available human services; (2) *cognitive restructuring* to destigmatize job loss and protect self-esteem; and (3) *behavior training,* providing such coping skills as relaxation, stress avoidance, and skills needed for active efforts to overcome the effects of job loss, including job-search skills and new job skills.

Few U.S. companies or unions have given much attention to preparing workers for termination.[4] In contrast, prior to the closing of a national British Steel Corporation mill in North Wales, workers received careful individual counseling on reemployment, training, and how best to protect and invest their sizeable severance payments. At that time, also, the workers were given written information on social services and arrangements were made for later follow-up contacts by a team of counselors (Buss and Redburn, 1981).

Needs Assessment: As noted above, communities may misjudge the true extent and nature of stresses produced by massive job losses. Therefore, a formal needs assessment should be undertaken to: (1) monitor developing and spreading impacts, (2) identify needs for human services, and (3) determine the local human services system's capacity to meet present and projected needs generated by economic crisis.

Communities without the capacity to undertake a formal, continuing needs assessment may refer to previous research concerning the impacts of mass unemployment or seek the help of local researchers and planners in carrying out an appropriate impact assessment. There is likely to be enough variation among communities and jobless situations to make total reliance on studies of past plant closings unwise. For example, this study has concerned laid-off steel workers who were almost entirely male, highly skilled in specialized occupations, typically older, and married. The 1981 closing of the Robertshaw Controls Corporation, in western Pennsylvania, affected several thousand workers who were mainly female, semiskilled, younger, and single. Probably, the needs of the two groups of workers and the abilities of their communities to help them are very different. Any effort to develop a human services response is likely to benefit greatly from accurate data on the true extent and nature of the economic crisis and an objective assessment of the local human services system's strengths and weaknesses.

Planning Process: The sense of emergency produced by a major plant closing or similar event creates an unusual opportunity for coordinated planning at the local level. Community leaders should move quickly to use this relatively brief interval during which people are focused on the economic problem, more willing than usual to subordinate parochial interests, and willing to devote substantial energy to problem-solving through analysis and discussion. At this time, the best persons to convene and lead the human services planning processes are likely to be top officials of general purpose local government. Because these officials' responsibilities span a range of services and because they have the authority and visibility needed to start up a serious effort of this type, their early involvement is probably essential. Although they may not participate in the detailed design of a services strategy, they must ultimately make the decisions that will put that strategy into action. For example, a mayor or county exceexecutive may be called upon to clarify agency responsibilities, approve funding for new programs, or negotiate with higher levels of government over the benefits and services available to terminated workers.

A planning group composed of persons representing various local government and voluntary sector human services agencies may oversee the detailed planning of a services strategy. This will vary depending on local jurisdictional patterns and the nature of existing provider councils. Where an active comprehensive human services provider council exists prior to the crisis, it may serve as the vehicle for planning a response; if such a council does not exist, the crisis may bring it into existence, as similar crises have in the past (Taber, Walsh, and Cooke, 1979). Since authority is typically fragmented and responsibility for organizing and delivering the needed services is unclear, only voluntary and determined efforts to construct a comprehensive workable services strategy can produce effective action; no one can impose an effective strategy.

Whom and When to Help: Basic choices must be made about where to apply limited resources. We have already emphasized that those first affected by economic crisis are not necessarily those who experience greatest hardship. They may quickly find new work or they may pursue training, education, or other nonwork options while receiving temporary insurance payments. The unemployment problem, meanwhile, is rapidly passed along to others. And within the group of terminated workers, again as noted previously, there will be wide variations in the degree and type of services needed. Given the limited ability to generalize about who needs help, the community's own needs assessment, plus outreach efforts that keep track of and reach out to those most predisposed to harm, are the best means of insuring that services are appropriately targeted.

Although the issue of when to intervene is complicated, our current hypothesis is that early intervention, if effective, may prevent substantial social and monetary costs. For instance, if workers can be moved quickly into training and alternate employment, stresses may be minimized and long-term income prospects improved. But, as noted, early interventions cannot be so easily targeted toward the relatively small number of workers likely to suffer severe effects.

Once layoffs have begun, the initiative must rest mainly with the worker to seek help if needed. Yet, despite the stresses produced by job loss, very few will voluntarily turn for assistance to a formal agency. Consequently, the lack of timely knowledge about developing problems by agencies in a position to help is a serious obstacle to service delivery. As is often true even apart from economic crisis, persons needing help will typically come to the attention of someone in the human services system only when a disastrous personal crisis has already occurred. This paradox is addressed below.

Reaching Those Who Need Help: Solving this problem requires dealing with two barriers: the aversion to or distance from formal helping agencies of most of those who may need help, and the incoherent structure of the local services system. To state these two problems succinctly, those workers who need help may not seek it, and those who seek it may not find it.

To solve this problem, the local services system should present to those it wants to help a clearly labeled single point of entry. Beyond this, it must go to great lengths to communicate with workers and their families. And it must establish the usefulness of its services. Finally, there must be a payment mechanism that allows workers to use services as needed without stigmatizing them as dependent. Accomplishing all of these things, is, to say the least, difficult. The following steps are suggested.

1. A central, noninstitutional access point staffed by professionals with assistance from laid-off workers should be created through which workers can be referred to *all* community services. Its noninstitutional character is important, given the reluctance of workers to approach formal agencies. Union sponsorship is one possibility.

2. Some individuals should be responsible for maintaining contact with each affected household after the closing. This could be a union counselor, a professional outreach worker not working for a single agency, or a laid-off worker working for pay or as a volunteer. This intervention should be as unobtrusive as possible, since considerations of privacy may in many cases outweigh the desirability of maintaining contact with the unemployed.

3. Existing, naturally occurring networks of association such as friendships and kinship—should be used for information and referral whenever possible. Recent research has confirmed the importance, in neighborhoods and communities, of an informal network of self-help practices (Silverman, 1980; Froland, et al., 1981; Warren, 1981). This network operates in the shadow of the formal system to provide support for individuals and families in time of need. For instance, for several months

following the Youngstown closing, a group of terminated workers met regularly for breakfast. Further research is needed to evaluate various methods by which the formal services system can support and use, and not supplant, these informal helping networks.

4. Because all nonretired workers are required to visit state employment services offices regularly in order to receive unemployment compensation, employment services counselors should be mandated to make referrals for obvious problems not directly related to employment. Although employment services agencies are otherwise not well-equipped to perform a centralized access and referral role, their regular contact with workers is an advantage that should not be neglected.

5. Finally, companies responsible for massive layoffs should be strongly urged, and probably required by law, to provide information needed by public agencies in order to contact affected workers, and to do so as soon as plans for layoffs are final. Ideally, detailed information on every worker's employment experience and skills, interest in further training and education, medical and other personal and household characteristics should be placed—*with the worker's informed consent*—in a computer file where it can be analyzed to develop an individualized package of diagnostic services and other assistance appropriate to the needs of that worker and his dependents. Such information can be most readily assembled prior to termination, with the cooperation of both management and unions. The resulting personal data file must be safeguarded to prevent abuse; however, its existence is, on balance, a benefit to workers since it so greatly facilitates all subsequent efforts by service providers to contact workers. It also aids in integrating agency service efforts, supports an adequate system of monitoring and accountability, and, finally, permits research to evaluate human services responses to the crisis.

Because of concerns of privacy, there may be great resistance to the sharing of information about workers with formal agencies. Some unions, for example, have by law provisions forbidding the release of personal information on members. The concern for privacy may not be so prevalent outside the United States. In Sweden, for example, *all* laid-off workers are continually accounted for by a highly sophisticated nationwide computer system (see Harrison and Bluestone, 1981). Evaluations of this system have suggested that it is very efficient and effective, although perhaps expensive.

Financial Aid: Continuing income-maintenance programs are an important component of any intervention strategy aimed at reducing stress. Beyond the fairly standard compensation payments provided to workers in most plant closings, there are unfulfilled needs for special kinds of financial help. For instance, most terminated workers will soon lose their group health insurance coverage. The community must act quickly if workers are to be provided with relatively inexpensive alternate group coverage. At a later time, continuing loss of income may cause workers to miss home mortgage payments. If these homeowners' investments are to be protected, alternate payment terms must be worked out in cooperation with community leaders. In smaller communities, a substantial permanent layoff of workers can threaten property values and business incomes on a large scale throughout the community. In these instances, continuing income-maintenance programs may be essential to the stability and viability of those places. Similarly, special state or federal aid may be needed to fill the revenue gap created in the public sector, so that essential services are maintained and government can function effectively as the community's agent for eventual revitalization.

Beyond these financial aids, consideration should be given to how best to support those special human services required by affected workers and their families. Since this should not be done at the expense of others eligible for and in need of such services, the best mechanism may be a deferred-payment plan or emergency revolving loan pool. This would allow workers to pay for present services while minimizing any stigma associated with financial dependency.

A program of the Detroit–Downtown Community Conference Economic Readjustment Program illustrates one way in which human services can be inexpensively delivered to those who need them. In 1981, a group of local public officials, health and human services providers, health insurance agencies (Blue Cross and Blue Shield), labor union leaders, local merchants, and industrialists formed a "health care referral network." A staff of trained health care professionals was established in a highly visible centralized location. Unemployed workers with health problems were screened there, and those with health problems were referred to one of several hospitals or clinics where physicians and other health care professionals donated their time and facilities to provide to workers free or inexpensive services, including physical examinations.

Unemployed workers with health problems may not be hired by firms conducting their own preemployment physicals. To avoid this problem, the Downtown Community Conference provides laid-off workers with free preemployment physicals in order to discover and treat problems before workers are sent to job interviews.

Creating Personal Development Options: Job losses reduce options for many in the community. Forced unemployment also encourages or requires people to consider new possibilities: new careers or more education, for instance. Employment-related services can help to make some of these possibilities real. However, other human services can play an important and complementary role in helping people to think through the choices available to them and to design personal strategies for development. These developmental services programs may be already present in the community, but often they must be tailored to the particular needs of experienced blue-collar workers. An especially important example of such programs is counseling for workers forced into early retirement (Stone and Kieffer, [1981]).

Another kind of developmental service that creates options for the unemployed is community organization. For instance, some agencies might identify and facilitate the activity of naturally occurring support groups and informal helping networks among the unemployed. To do this, they would have to avoid any institutional stigma, gain much more than passive support from unions, churches, or voluntary associations, and work intensively "on the street" to communicate with these groups. The feasibility of such strategies is enhanced by the stability that is characteristic of an experienced industrial labor force after a plant closing. Such community organization not only provides short-term psychological support to workers but may lead to lasting gains in collective capacity in the form of new businesses, political action groups, and so on.[5] Specific kinds of informal helping networks, too numerous for review here, have been examined in the following works: Silverman (1980), Froland, et al. (1980) and Warren (1981).

Conclusion

The circumstances of communities in economic crisis do not make it easy to construct an effective human services response. The probable lack of federal and state assistance, the uniqueness of each situation and community, the limited resources and knowledge from which to build a response, and the ambiguous long-term nature of the battle that must be fought all make this a major challenge. Therefore, communities must depend primarily on themselves to make appropriate decisions and create needed new capacity, must plan carefully for the use of scarce resources, must be innovative, and must be persistent. The state and federal governments could be supportive of such communities to the extent that they would provide timely information on what other communities have done and encourage or require the participation of companies and unions in joint planning for the closing and its after math. Companies, unions, and associations of human services professionals also could help by identifying past successful community efforts to meet such crises and offering their technical assistance in replicating these successes.

9. The Longer Run

At the conclusion of Chapter 4, it was suggested that the full impact of a major plant closing can only be gauged over a period of many years. Because analogies are often drawn between economic crisis and natural disaster, it is useful to contrast the timing of their impacts, as suggested by the abstract figure below.

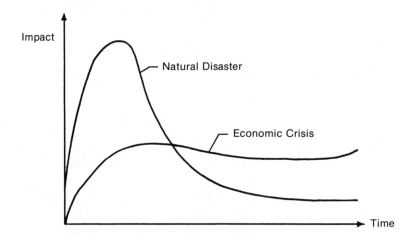

Figure 9.1 Impact over Time of Natural and Economic Disasters

In a natural disaster, most of the severe impacts are confined to a relatively brief period. *Crisis intervention* services are most appropriate to such crises. The nature of the damage—both physical and emotional—is such that repairs and healing can take place rather quickly. A return visit to the community several years later would, in many cases, discover no significant lasting effects.

In an economic crisis, the short-term stresses are measurable but less severe, seldom constituting trauma. *Maintenance* and *developmental* services are more appropriate. The nature of the damage, however is insidious. There is evidence that much, and perhaps most, of the economic costs of a plant closing will eventually be transferred to less-skilled, less-experienced workers and their dependents. Moreover, much of the damage is cumulative, a gradual buildup of both financial and emotional indebtedness that is hard to trace directly back to the original loss of work and income.

A major closing signals to other investors the need to reconsider plans for local expansion. A reversal of economic fortunes may cause the community's people with talent and ambition to seek opportunities elsewhere. Fiscal stress pressures local government to maintain or increase tax rates, yet they still may be forced to cut back services. Such challenges may attract talented political leadership; however, they may also repel potential leaders. In Youngstown, there is no evidence to indicate that the quality of political leadership or local administration was strengthened by economic crisis.

Nongrowing Areas: Social and Institutional Effects

Edgar Rust (1975) has examined the experience of all U.S. metropolitan areas that failed to grow between 1900 to 1970. The following analysis draws heavily on his investigation and insights:

Demographic Lags: Nongrowing communities quickly develop a surplus dependent population. This is due to the population age structure and the dynamics of migration. Although net out-migration is typical of such areas, the natural increase due to an excess of births over deaths may cause continued increases in total population for a period of time after job growth has ceased. Declining birth rates and continuing out-migration may eventually lead to net population declines but are unlikely to eliminate the surplus of unneeded or underused labor. As the highly mobile fraction is skimmed off, the remaining population is characterized by low mobility and strong local attachments.

Institutional Isolation, Rigidity, and Dependency: Nongrowing areas typically experience a relative weakening of communication and transportation links to the outside world. Their major remaining enterprises and financial institutions are less likely to be under local ownership and control. Their governments are weaker relative to other power centers in and out of the community and more fiscally dependent on other levels of government and on institutional debt-holders. Due to this dependency, to smaller inflows of new personnel, and to declining chances for talented personnel to move up, risk-avoiding styles of management become predominant. Institutions lose their flexibility and capacity to innovate, even as the challenges facing them multiply.

Economic Imbalances: As highly mobile factors of production— especially capital—drain away to growing areas, declining regions are left with surplus capacity in nonmobile infrastructure, land (often scarred, poisoned, and unusable), and the immobile section of the work force. A large proportion of the community's educational investment in its youth also leaks away through migration and is not replaced. The resulting shortages of capital and of educated, flexible labor make the area progressively less attractive to firms in high-growth, high-technology sectors. Instead, Rust predicts such areas will specialize in low-wage, low-growth industries.

Opportunity and Quality of Life: The depression of per capita income and the declining job opportunities begin a process of declining opportunity and life quality that continues over many years. The effects of cutbacks in infrastructure maintenance and public services are painful in the short run but more destructive in the longer run.

Speculation on the Long-Term Effects of Economic Decline

What might happen to a community if, over a period of years, it experienced chronic underemployment of its population, a decline in personal income, and little in the way of economic opportunity for its young people? Changes in personal experience and attitudes might trigger a social dynamic that affected long-term prospects for redeveloping community political autonomy and employment opportunities.

We may put this speculation in the form of a model relating initial economic changes (job losses) to immediate psychological changes (such as lowered expectations) which in turn produce behaviors that probably contribute to further economic losses and deterioration of the community's self-governing capacity. This is a model in which psychological variables play a key role, due in part to their relative volatility and in part to their influence on behaviors that are keys to economic development and effective government.

A vital economy requires entrepreneurial activity that combines creativity, hard work, and risk taking. A locality must generate a large share of its entrepreneurial action. Otherwise, outsiders control the new uses of its human and physical resources, and its rate of economic growth may slow or become negative.

A vital political system requires a leadership responsive to the needs of major groups of citizens, and supported by them. A declining economy strains the relationship between leaders and followers, and makes government appear less effective as it tries to meet greater needs with declining public resources. If deteriorating government performance reduces public support for leadership, it may be still harder for leaders to put together coalitions in support of programs for economic and social reconstruction.

Massive unemployment may trigger psychological and behavioral responses that themselves become a self-reinforcing engine of decline. The effects of such dynamics are illustrated in Figure 9.2. Once a distress psychology is established, it becomes an independent source of further economic and political system deterioration. Outside intervention may be required to reverse this self-feeding process.

At some point, attitudes and behavior that were initially pragmatic adaptations to changing conditions become normative. That is, the changes alter the pattern of human relationships and the socialization experiences of children to the point that the new pattern becomes a distinct culture. In fact, depressed area cultures are familiar to historians and social scientists. They have appeared after a relatively few years in former frontier areas such as Appalachia and in former industrial-era mining or manufacturing boom towns such as those of Pennsylvania and South Wales. Harry Caudill's description of eastern Kentucky in the 1950s and 1960s captures the essence of one such culture:

> Out of this background has grown a mass melancholia of
> ominous and ever-deepening proportions. To escape its grip, some
> commit suicide while others...find surcease in the cheap product
> of tiny household stills.... The old fierce pride and sensitive spirit
> of independence have died from the continuing social trauma of a
> half-century. In countless instances, people who grew up in clean
> cabins, and whose parents would have starved before they would
> have asked for charity, now in their old age shamelessly plot to
> "get by" on public assistance.... With the demise of their
> traditional values has come a curious reverse pride, a pride in not
> having pride.

Whether this speculative model of decline applies to Youngstown and other currently declining industrial areas is uncertain. These are complex systems from which may emerge at any time new entrepreneurs and new political coalitions and leaders capable of reversing the process of decay. Moreover, these are open systems. Private firms or public investment may fill the vacuum of idle skilled labor and vacant facilities, bringing new jobs.

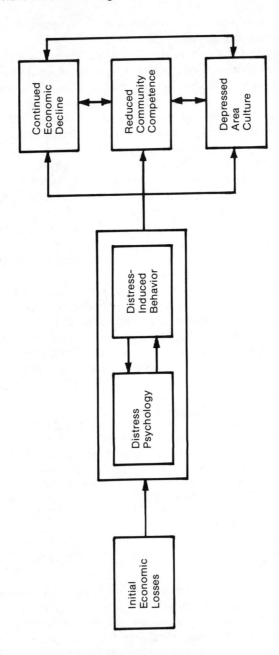

Figure 9.2 A Model of Regional Decline

Decline is not inevitable. It may, however, take on a momentum that is increasingly difficult to overcome. If the effects of initial economic reverses tend to multiply, the most effective, and by far the least expensive, public interventions may be those that occur soon after the first major economic losses.

Toward a Longer-Term Social Policy for Distressed Communities

Sometimes the closing of a plant is an isolated event that has little to do with a community's long-term economic prospects. Today, however, many mature industrial communities experience shutdowns as part of a generalized process of decline. Once a series of economic losses becomes, and is perceived by the community to be, a broader process of disinvestment and decay, the problem becomes more than how to replace lost jobs. These communities risk falling into a self-reinforcing process of decline, as described above. Because of this risk, public policies to strengthen these communities and preserve their attractiveness and value as places to live should pursue economic revitalization as part of a more general effort to strengthen local institutional capacities.

Just as *developmental* human services are appropriate for individuals making the adjustment to new economic roles following job loss, specially designed *community development* programs are needed as a response to economic distress. If the model of self-reinforcing decline suggested above is at least partly correct, then the most-needed interventions are those which encourage rapid development of new institutional capacity and leadership in both public and private sectors.

Creating New Political Capacity

Political capacity is the community's ability to get its act together: to reach a consensus broad enough to synthesize special interests and reflective enough of the long-term public interest, to organize and implement actions competently and quickly, and to protect the community's interest from decisions reached elsewhere that threaten it. Some of the important components of political capacity are the quality of people selected to lead, the quality of relations between leaders and other citizens, the efficiency of administrative machinery, and the ability and willingness of public and private sectors to work together on a basis of mutual respect and equality. The major threats to political capacity posed by economic decline are limited fiscal capacity, increasing citizen alienation, loss of first-rate leadership talent, and the increasing rigidity of all local institutions. To these threats must be added the high degree of geographic and functional fragmentation of public authority that afflicts so many urbanized areas. In the face of these weakening influences, a principal goal of social policy for distressed communities should be to create new political capacity.

Reversing Economic Fortunes

Not every distressed community can expect to reverse its economic fortunes. Moreover, it can be argued that, from a national perspective, it is wasteful to pour public resources into distressed communities dominated by declining industries. For the moment, however, we deliberately adopt the perspective of the affected locality. Every community has a majority in favor of continuing economic prosperity; it therefore seeks to stimulate new investment. However, some development strategies that produce jobs may not help the community in other ways. Alternative economic development strategies should be evaluated in relation to the need of a distressed community for new institutional capacity.

By this standard, a poor economic development strategy is one that creates jobs at unnecessarily high cost to the community's long-run ability to control its destiny. The repeated exploitation of the people and resources of Appalachia by outsiders (Caudill, 1963) shows just such a pattern. Most communities can avoid such exploitation at the outset, provided they are sensitive to the potential for harm.

Economic development can simultaneously increase local political capacity and efficiently create new jobs. To do so, it should give priority to helping new ventures that emerge from local innovation and are controlled by local entrepreneurs. There is evidence that emerging small firms are highly efficient job-generators (Birch, 1979). However, young enterprises are chronically short of capital. Today, states and communities are developing new financing mechanisms to aid these struggling firms (Litvak and Daniels, 1979).

The big business emphasis of recent economic development policy has meant that governments and local financial institutions were subsidizing corporations whose net income from the subsidized investment was mainly spent outside the community and reinvested elsewhere. It makes sense, instead, to redirect economic development policy toward assistance to smaller, locally controlled firms. Such a shift in economic development policy is consistent with the objectives of attacking institutional rigidity and restoring community autonomy and power.

Roger Vaughan (1980) notes that this kind of community-based economic development is distinguished not by where it occurs but by how it occurs, i.e., with active participation by community groups which have displayed competence in the area of economic development. Moreover, he believes, we do not know how to implement a local economic development strategy that has this emphasis.

Yet Vaughan argues that community groups are the appropriate vehicle for successful economic development. Using their sensitivity to the needs of local firms and entrepreneurs, community-based economic development groups can provide effective technical assistance, finance packaging, and job placement in a more efficient and representative manner than other organizations. Equally important from the perspective of distressed communities, the resulting growth of smaller, locally controlled firms and the buildup of community competence help to restore local autonomy and self-esteem.

Community-based development also implies increasing and improving human resources investments through education and retraining. In Chapter 7, these policies were discussed as ways of meeting the short-run needs of terminated workers or those losing work due to a secondary round of economic losses. However, these policies also are supportive of these communities' longer-run need to strengthen their public and private institutions.

Nongrowing areas, experiencing net outflows of talent, need to steadily replace these lost human resources. Only by making heavy and productive investments in their youth and in the underemployed fraction of the adult population can they both offset current losses and eventually restore their communities as places that can retain their share of entrepreneurial, technical, scientific, and public leadership talent.

The need for greater investment in developmental programs applies not only to workers directly affected by industrial decline. It is the best available means to achieve gains across the whole range of public and private initiatives required to maintain and improve the quality of community life.

If such places need new enterprises whose services and products can be exported, then what better way to foster such innovation than to develop the scientific, technical, and business expertise of the population? If these rapidly growing firms require unusual technical specialties, why not provide these by retraining experienced workers who possess some of the basic work skills? If such places need to retain talented youth, what more constructive way than to create opportunities for self-development through early identification of their leadership potential, accelerated training, and rapid advancement to successively broader responsibilities?

The nation, as a whole, has recently neglected this aspect of investment. It has permitted its educational systems to deteriorate to the point where this generation of high school graduates is the first in our history to be less well prepared than its parents. The nation has not yet recognized the waste that occurs when the continuing development needs of adults are underserved. Declining industrial communities have the greatest needs for improvements in this area of social policy. Either the communities themselves or higher levels of government should acknowledge these needs by making such communities centers of intensified human resources investment.

Industrial vs. Area Revitalization: The Context for Changes in National Policy

It is a mistake for higher levels of government to ignore the localized consequences of massive changes in the national economy. Conversely, area redevelopment policies cannot be in direct conflict with the goals of national economic policy.

The context in which new area development policies might be developed can be summarized as follows:

1. Area development aid by the federal government has been limited in scale and impact; in fact, it is dwarfed by the largely unintended regional effects of other federal investments for defense, transportation, and other public works.

2. State governments have competed with one another for new business investment, with little net result other than a general subsidizing of private development.

3. There is no political consensus in favor of area development programs (Kasarda, 1980; Redburn and Buss, 1981); and the major federal economic development programs are being curtailed.

4. A rising international challenge to the nation's competitive position has brought proposals for a national industrial revitalization policy, the goals of which may conflict with those of programs to maintain the economic vitality of our older industrial centers (Buss, Redburn, and Ledebur, 1982).

Such observations suggest the severe political constraints on developing a national policy to deal with local concentrations of unemployment and declining economic opportunity. There are a range of possible actions that would actually prevent plant closings or—what amounts to the same thing—substantially increase the costs to private industry of shifting investment from one site to another. Such a course assumes that the goal of industrial revitalization should be subordinate to the preservation of a fixed regional pattern of development. A more optimistic and pragmatic view is that the goals of promoting industrial revitalization and facilitating local adjustment to economic change can to some extent be reconciled.

The apparent conflict between policies for national economic revitalization and for regional redevelopment largely disappears when the long-term costs of unmanaged regional decline are considered. The findings of this and similar research should help to persuade national policy-makers that the waste associated with mass unemployment is not primarily due to short-term stress and idleness. Rather, it would appear that the larger social and economic costs are in the continuing underuse of skilled labor and the long-term deterioration of community-based social relationships and institutions. The policy direction implied by such findings is toward area redevelopment that facilitates in-place reorientation of human resources and institutional structure. Thus, a national policy to deal with massive unemployment should aim at preserving particular communities while reorienting their economies and labor force toward new functions.

All of the more specific policy and program recommendations of this and the preceding two chapters are consistent with this goal of community preservation and reorientation. Such public policies would not only address the short-run problems created by economic crisis, they would also contribute to each community's longer-run capacity to revitalize and regain control over its own economy; to help those who are economically dependent; to redefine its purposes and identity; and to restore its self-esteem.

> From the city square, on nights when production is up and the mills are roaring, the horizon is painted with an uncertain light where the stack-flung ceiling of smoke gives back the glare of the mill fires. And when production is down and only a few furnaces carry "heat," the forlornness of the squat and silent mills seeps out into the whole city. ("Youngstown," *The Ohio Guide,* 1940).

Appendix A. Methodology

Participants in the Study

The central findings concerning the impact of the Campbell Works closing are based upon personal interviews with steelworkers and their spouses. Steelworkers whose jobs were terminated constituted the major "treatment" group for study. Spouses of these laid-off workers constituted another major "treatment" group. Steelworkers from the same company whose jobs were secure at the time of the study comprised one "control" group. Their spouses comprised another "control" group. A group of autoworkers from the same community as the steelworkers, but who were unaffected by the steel mill closing were included as an additional control group.

Interviews were completed one and two years after the steel mill closing. This allowed for a longitudinal investigation of mental health effects. By comparing responses from the above groups on the same survey questionnaire, it was hoped that a clear picture of the impact of the steel mill closing would emerge. An overview of the data sets produced and an analysis of the above samples is presented below.

Personal interviews were conducted with 284 steelworkers from the Youngstown Sheet and Tube Company, Youngstown, Ohio, and 220 of their spouses during July and August 1978. This was the first wave of the study. Some 85 autoworkers from the General Motors plant in Lordstown also were interviewed for control group purposes.

Data from the samples were also collected by administering paper and pencil questionnaires at appropriate times during interviews. Steelworkers included in the study were drawn from a probability sample designed to represent all "basic steel" employees at Youngstown Sheet and Tube Company. Secretarial workers were not included in this sample. Autoworkers were drawn from a probability sample produced by the United

Autoworkers local from a computer-based union membership list. Interviews were conducted in steelworker's homes by specially trained staff from the Center for Urban Studies,[1] Youngstown State University. The interviews took 150 minutes. Data were also obtained by paper and pencil questionnaires administered after the interviews. Approximately 700 different observations were collected for each respondent.

United Steel Workers Union locals representing Youngstown Sheet and Tube Company publicly supported the project. Respondents were sent a letter of intent by the authors explaining the purpose of the study and requesting permission for the interview. The letters of intent were then followed by telephone calls to set the time and place of the interview. Steelworkers and their spouses were interviewed separately. Less than 15 percent of those contacted refused to participate.

Follow-up personal interviews were conducted with 155 of the 284 steelworkers and 120 of their spouses who had been initially interviewed. Only 20 autoworkers were interviewed so it was decided to not include more autoworkers in this second analysis.[2] Interviews were conducted during July and August 1979. No attempt was made to substitute respondents for those who could not be located or interviewed in the second wave of the study. Data was collected from respondents by the same staff in a manner similar to that described above. Interviews took about 90 mintutes to complete. Including paper and pencil measures, approximately 500 different observations were collected for each respondent.

The Steelworker Sample

The First Wave

Steelworkers in the sample [3] were stratified into several groups for purposes of analysis. Steelworkers were initially divided into workers whose jobs were permanently terminated (51.4%, N = 146) at Youngstown Sheet and Tube Company, and workers who remained *employed* at the steel mill (48.6%, N = 138). Workers in the *unemployed* groups were further divided into those who *retired* (24.7%, N = 36), those who were *rehired* in any other full-time job (34.2%, N = 50) and those who remained *unemployed* (41.1%, N = 60).

Analyses of variance (ANOVA) were conducted with the four steelworker subsamples described above using three social characteristics: education, age, and income.[4] The subsamples were significantly different with regard to education [$F(3,280) = 3.96, p < .001$], age [$F(3,279) = 32.67, p < .001$] and income [$F(3,279) = 5.96, p < .001$]. Mean values for ANOVA in Waves I and II for each sample are presented in Table A.1.[5]

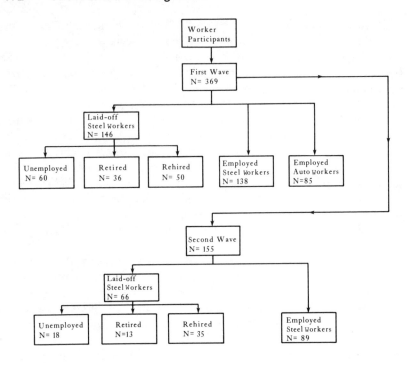

Figure A.1 Steelworker Sample Breakdown

Analysis revealed that the unemployed had a higher level of education. They were much younger than any other group, except the rehired, and earned less than any other group. Age appears to be important in explaining unemployment. Two distinct age groups were identified: very young workers (early twenties) and middle-aged workers (forty or more). Results of the ANOVA suggested that although the younger unemployed were formally educated, they had not yet developed either saleable skills or an extensive job record. Hence, they had difficulty finding a job. It also suggested that older workers had less formal education, more job experience, but were not highly skilled. Once they lost their unemployment compensation benefits and could find no job, both young and old unemployed workers reported having less income from any source.

Employed workers—those who still work for Youngstown Sheet and Tube Company—were demographically the opposite of the unemployed workers. They were less educated, older, and had the highest income of any group. Apparently, this generation of workers had not received or aspired

Table A.1 Mean Values of Steelworkers, Spouses and Auto Workers for Selected Demographic Characteristics According to Employment Status 1978 and 1979 First and Second Waves

Demographic Characteristic	Steelworker				Autoworker	Spouse[f]			
	Unemployed	Retired	Rehired	Employed		Unemployed	Retired	Rehired	Employed
First Wave, 1978									
Education[a]	3.10	2.36	2.97	2.86	3.58	3.19	3.09	2.96	2.96
Race[b]	1.21	1.13	1.20	1.18	1.22	1.17	1.06	1.19	1.17
Age[c]	3.00	6.63	2.69	4.49	---	4.25	5.35	3.00	3.31
Income[d]	2.43	2.61	2.65	2.80	2.87	2.82	2.76	2.70	2.57
Marital Status[e]	1.19	1.09	.87	1.12	1.00	---	---	---	---
Second Wave, 1979									
Education[a]	3.72	3.75	2.96	3.65	---	3.58	4.41	3.11	3.56
Race[b]	1.94	1.92	1.89	1.96	---	1.16	1.07	1.09	1.17
Age[c]	4.94	6.85	2.15	3.41	---	4.36	5.45	3.00	3.30
Income[d]	2.55	2.53	2.33	2.78	---	2.66	2.64	2.38	2.86
Marital Status[e]	1.11	1.23	1.21	1.16	---	---	---	---	---

[a] Education: grade school = 1, some high school = 2, high school, trade school, and other secondary schools = 3, some college = 4, college = 5, grad/professional school = 6
[b] Race: white = 1, black = 2, Asian = 3, Spanish = 4.
[c] Age: 1953 through 1958 = 1, 1947 through 1952 = 2, 1940 through 1946 = 3, 1934 through 1939 = 4, 1928 through 1933 = 5, 1922 through 1927 = 6, 1901 through 1921 = 7.
[d] Income: $1,000 through $8,999 = 1, $9,000 through $14,999 = 2, $15,000 = 3.
[e] Marital status: 1 = married, 0 = single.
[f] Employment status is that of the steelworker.

to higher educational attainment. They were able to earn a high income by developing skills or gaining seniority.

Those workers who were rehired—employed at other than Sheet and Tube—were younger than any other group. They earned less wages than the employed, but more than the retired. Clearly, these workers were highly skilled and jobs to suit their skills were available. But since they were beginning a new career, they were forced to take lower wages. In some cases, they were underpaid given their experience and skills.

Retired workers began working before higher levels of educational achievement were common in the labor force. They earned less on a pension than any of the other groups with an income.

Differences between the steelworker samples provided the *expected* kind of demographic impact due to a plant closing. The steelworker sub-samples showed us that since the steel crisis affected different groups in various ways, the subsamples would reveal different effects.

T-tests were conducted between similarly defined samples of steel-workers and autoworkers. Results of these analyses are presented in Table A.2.

Autoworkers were significantly older than their unemployed counter-parts and slightly older than the rehired and employed steelworkers. Autoworkers were, however, much younger than retired steelworkers. Age differences across various samples support the notion that those steel-workers who are younger tend to be laid off first and those who are very young and inexperienced tend not to be readily rehired. But, since those rehired were somewhat younger than rehired autoworkers, reemployment may not be offered to those workers who are getting older, but are too young to retire (Wilcock and Franke, 1968; Foltman, 1958; Sheppard, Ferman, and Farber, 1959).

A review of means in Table A.2 indicates that each group of steelworkers differed more from one another than they did from the autoworkers. This provides some evidence that autoworkers comprise a reasonably representative sociological control group against which the effects of mass unemployment can be gauged.

The Second Wave

Some 155 steelworkers in the four subsamples—unemployed, retired, rehired, and employed—were reinterviewed in the second wave. Analyses attempted to discover how a worker's employment status had changed over the past year. Results of this analysis are presented in Table A.3.

Results in Table A.3 show a wide variety of movement in employment status from the first wave to the second. Of the 155 interviewed in the

Table A.2   *T*-Test Comparisons with Autoworkers and Steelworkers According to Employment Status for Selected Demographic Characteristics[a] 1978

Demographic Characteristics[b]	Unemployed Steel- & Autoworkers		Retired Steel- & Autoworkers		Rehired Steel- & Autoworkers		Employed Steel- & Autoworkers	
	t	*p*	*t*	*p*	*t*	*p*	*t*	*p*
Education	1.57	NS	.50	NS	.14	NS	.98	NS
Age	7.64	.01	5.75	.01	4.38	.01	10.75	.01
Income	1.41	NS	1.24	NS	.01	NS	.18	NS

a Mean values reported in Appendix A text.
b See Table A.1 for scoring of characteristics.
NS = not significant at $p < .05$ or less.

Table A.3 Steelworker Changes in Employment Status by Percentage Distribution in First Wave, 1978, According to Second Wave Distribution, 1979

Employment Status: Second Wave, 1979	**Employment Status: First Wave, 1978**				
	Unemployed %	**Retired** %	**Rehired**[b] %	**Employed**[c] %	**Total** %
Unemployed	3.2	0.0	1.9	3.9	9.0
Retired	3.2	5.2	0.6	2.6	11.6
Rehired	7.7	0.6	3.9	7.1	19.4
Employed	16.8	6.5	12.9	23.9	60.0
Total	31.0	12.3	19.4	37.4	100.0

a Percentages based upon total sample of 155 workers.
b Rehired other than at Youngstown Sheet and Tube.
c Currently employed at Youngstown Sheet and Tube.

second wave, about 9 percent were unemployed (N = 14). This figure matches Ohio Bureau of Employment Services (OBES) statistics which estimated that between 10 percent and 15 percent of the laid-off workers remain unemployed (see Bagshaw and Schnorbus, 1980). In our sample, only 3.2 percent of the workers were continuously unemployed since the mill closing in September 1977. The mill closing did not have as great an effect on unemployment rates as might have been expected (Bagshaw and Schnorbus, 1980; see also Chapter 4).

Even though many workers were laid off during the closing, many more were called back at least once by Youngstown Sheet and Tube Company. Most were called back to assist others in closing down the works. Others were rehired in company departments which were kept open. Results showed that about 60 percent (N = 93) of the workers in the sample experienced this reemployment. This also is consistent with OBES statistics. For example, OBES reports that even though 5,000 workers were laid off and about 10,000 workers were believed to be employed by the company, over 11,000 former Youngstown Sheet and Tube Company workers applied for and received unemployment compensation.[6] Interestingly, 12.9 percent of the sample gave up a job in order to be rehired temporarily at Youngstown Sheet and Tube Company.

Only about 19.4 percent (N = 30) of the sample were rehired in jobs other than at Youngstown Sheet and Tube Company. This group was primarily made up of the unemployed (N = 12) and those who initially were not laid off at Sheet and Tube (N = 11).

A rather large group of workers chose to retire (11.6%, N = 18). The composition of this group continued to change as more and more retirement applications were processed by the company. In addition, some workers waited several more months in order to qualify for special retirement plans (see Hayes, 1979).

The 155 respondents in the second wave were assigned to groups based upon their current employment status: unemployed (N = 18), retired (N = 13), rehired (N = 29), and employed (N = 89). An ANOVA was conducted using three social characteristics—education, age, and income. Unlike Wave I, age [$F(4,142) = .46$ $p > .05$] was not significantly different. The subsamples were significantly different with respect to education [$F(4,140) = 7.97$, $p < .001$] and income [$F(3,142) = 5.08$, $p < .002$].

Analyses revealed that the unemployed were the most educated, followed in turn by the employed, rehired, and retired. This supports the finding in Wave I which led to the suggestion that workers with an education, but without accompanying skills, might not be readily employable.

With regard to income, the four subsamples yielded results which were unexpected. Employed workers earned more than any other group. This makes sense since steelworkers are among the highest paid industrial workers in this country. However, the unemployed earned slightly less than this group and more than either the retired or rehired groups. In an effort to explain this anomaly, employment data for employed respondents were examined. Results of this analysis showed the mean income was elevated by those workers who were called back to work at Youngstown Sheet and Tube and were subsequently laid off a second time, and by those workers who found high-paying jobs but could not hold onto them. The retired workers earned less than either the employed or unemployed, but more than the rehired. Apparently, the rehired workers were able to find jobs, but these jobs were not as lucrative as their previous employment. Retired workers were able to earn more than the rehired.

In addition to examining the 155 respondents who were interviewed in both the first and second waves, it is important to examine the remaining 127 respondents who were interviewed only in the first wave. About 15.7 percent (N = 20) of these respondents were known to have left the Youngstown area, presumably in search of employment opportunities elsewhere. This proportion of the sample who left the area is consistent with previous studies (e.g., Foltman, 1968; Aiken, Ferman, and Sheppard, 1968) and data gathered by the Ohio Bureau of Employment Services. Apparently, most of the workers did not perceive employment opportunities as any better outside their immediate community. In addition, most of these people had family obligations, a sense of community, ties with close relatives, and perhaps mortgaged or fully-owned homes. These things precluded their mobility. Those who moved were single, young workers.

Two respondents passed away during the time period of the study. Both were at or near retirement age. It was impossible to determine to what extent (if any) the termination of their jobs and forced retirement contributed to their deaths (e.g., Brenner, 1977).

Many workers were able to find jobs in the area once they were permanently laid off. Some 23.6 percent (N = 30) found jobs which required a good deal of commuting time. Many of these jobs were located 15 to 20 miles north of Youngstown in Warren, Ohio, where Republic Steel Corporation hired some workers from Youngstown Sheet and Tube. Because of work schedules and commuting time, these respondents could not be contacted during the period of the study. Many of the ex-steelworkers also were hired at the Lordstown General Motors plant located about 20 r. .es from Youngstown. Commuting time, swing shifts, and overtime made these workers difficult to locate.

A relatively large (27.6%, N = 35) group of respondents who were not interviewed in the second wave refused to participate but were willing to report reasons for their refusals. Almost to a person, respondents stated that the results of their participation during the first wave had not produced any change in the public policy for the area. They reported that governmental agencies charged with helping them during the steel crisis had not done so. Many grouped local, state, and federal government, Youngstown Sheet and Tube, and Youngstown State University in this perception. Our impression was that many classic symptoms of alienation were observed in their comments, although systematic study of their responses was obviously prohibited. No significant differences were observed in employment status and the propensity to respond in this fashion. Clearly, these repondents may well represent one of the groups most severely affected by the closing. Unfortunately, in spite of letters of appeal and telephone pleas, we were unable to convince them to participate.

The Spouse Sample

The First Wave

In our sample, spouses of steelworkers were included as follows. If a steelworker selected in our probability sample who consented to an interview was married, his spouse was interviewed, too. Only five spouses whose husbands were interviewed refused.

Spouses were stratified into the same four groups as the steelworkers, *based upon the employment status of the steelworker.* First wave results showed that 24.6 percent (N = 44) of the spouses were married to *unemployed* steelworkers, 16.8 percent (N = 30) to *retired* steelworkers, 24.6 percent (N = 44) to *rehired* steelworkers, and 34.6 percent (N = 62) to *employed* steelworkers.

ANOVA's were conducted for the four subsamples described above. Dependent variables were: education, age, and income. Results of these analyses were similar to those conducted on the steelworker sample. No significant differences were observed for education [$F(3,178) = .816, p = .49$] or income [$F(3,175) = .939, p = .42$]. Only age was significant [$F(3,174) = 3.10, p < .05$].

ANOVAs for spouse data seem to be consistent with the findings for the steelworker sample. The exception was on income. Spouses were not significantly different with regard to employment status, while steelworkers were. One possible explanation for this is that spouses may have

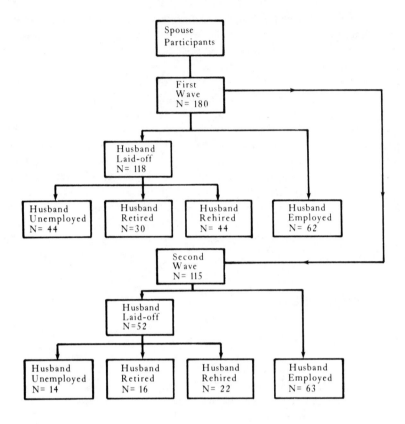

Figure A.2   Steelworker Spouse Sample Breakdown

systematically erred in reporting their husband's income, thereby sup-
pressing variation in the data. Another might be that steelworkers, for a
variety of reasons (e.g., suspicion, embarrassment, confusion, etc.), may
have misrepresented their incomes in their own responses. This would
create more variation in the data (e.g., Lucas and Adams, 1977: 25–32).

The Second Wave

Some 114 spouses (63.7%) were reinterviewed in the second wave of
the study. Spouses were classified into the following categories, based upon
their husbands' current employment status: *unemployed,* 12.3 percent (N =
14); *retired,* 14.0 percent (N = 16); *rehired,* 19.3 percent (N = 22); and
employed, 55.3 percent (N = 63).

As before, no significant differences were observed for education [$F(3,110) = .001, p > .05$] or income [$F(3,111) = 1.018, p = .389$]. Age was again significantly different [$F(3,110) = 3.110, p < .05$].

Appendix B. Politics of a Plant Closing

The War between Development Corporations: MVEDC, WREDA, and CASTLO

The challenge of a major steel facility shutdown also led to various independent, separately funded economic development efforts. Each of these pursued the goals of industrial revitalization and retention, as well as attraction of new industry.

The Mahoning Valley Economic Development Corporation (MVEDC) was established in October 1977 by former Congressman Charles Carney. MVEDC was funded by an Economic Development Administration $1 million grant to be used primarily to develop a Comprehensive Economic Development Strategy (CEDS) plan for the area. MVEDC is also funded by private sector contributions. The organization is composed of representatives from local government, business, and labor, plus private citizens. From 1977 to 1979, MVEDC was directed by the Mayor of Youngstown, Philip Richley.

The Western Reserve Economic Development Agency (WREDA) was established in December 1972 by William Sullivan, a local attorney. WREDA was funded by grants from the Economic Development Administration and the private sector, notably the steel industry. WREDA was mostly represented by public officials, although some members of the organization were drawn from industry and labor. William Sullivan directed the organization.

From the beginning of the local steel crisis, WREDA and MVEDC pursued their independent strategies for solving the problems of the mill closing. Through MVEDC, Mayor Richley pursued two strategies for "Saving the Valley." The first was a program of industrial diversification. According to Richley "Steel is a thing of the past. . . ." The future of the city lies in "total and complete diversification" (Petzinger, 1978b). The second was a plan for developing a national steel research and development center. It would conduct needed research on steel-making for the domestic steel industry. The steel research and development center would cost between $10 million and $500 million, depending upon the extent of the activities to be financed. MVEDC sought funding for these projects from the Economic Development Administration of the U.S. Commerce Department. Richley also was able to interest Robert Strauss, a trade policy advisor to the President, in the projects.

At first, Sullivan of WREDA had sponsored the community/worker ownership plan with the Ecumenical Coalition. He then elected to sponsor two other plans. One was Father William Hogan's plan for the joint blast furnace center to be shared by the steel industry in the region. The blast furnace would utilize proven technology, establish new markets and constitute a solution for regional unemployment problems. Unfortunately, the enterprise would cost in excess of $1 billion. The center would be financed in part by HUD and private investment (see Industrial Economics Research Institute, 1978). The other Sullivan proposal was initiated by the Steel Communities Coalition, of which he is president. Sullivan lobbied with many federal agencies to fund the Mahoning Steel Company, which would establish a coke plant in the Campbell Works.

Internal problems plagued MVEDC in its revitalization efforts (Garland, 1980). After a nationwide search for a director of the corporation, one was finally found. Almost immediately, disagreements on the Comprehensive Economic Development Strategy (CEDS)—required to secure EDA funding—developed. The executive board, embroiled in controversy, fired the director. The CEDS plan was permanently shelved and another version of the plan would await the initiative of a new director. This failure to produce a viable plan caused the withholding of EDA funds and also left the region without a blueprint for redevelopment.

A new director was appointed and eventually produced another version of the CEDS plan. The new version, in an effort to avoid controversy and to save time, amounted to a summary of public works projects *already* underway in the community. From start to finish, the plan, which was to take four months to produce, took 18 months to finalize, led to extensive delays in receipt of federal funds, was not of any use in planning for the region and was expensively produced.

This failure to produce a plan may have greatly affected the ability of the community to recover economically. Without a plan, efforts at revitalization were not coordinated and often contradictory or counter-productive.

CASTLO was established as an alternative to federal assistance. The citizens of Struthers, Campbell, and Lowellville became concerned that their direct interests in the closing of the steel mills were being overlooked by the Youngstown-dominated MVEDC and Ecumenical Coalition. The three cities contacted Governor Rhodes for assistance. In February 1978, Governor James Rhodes appointed George Wilson, former Director of the Ohio Department of Economic and Community Development, to establish an office for self-help in the three communities. The office would be referred to as CASTLO, an acronym for the three communities. The Ohio Legislature granted $2 million to fund the office. Grants also were obtained from the Economic Development Administration of the U.S. Commerce Department and HUD.

CASTLO planners rejected schemes which would reopen the mills. They believed that the mills were finished and a diversified industrial base for their communities should be established. CASTLO focused its attention on converting the Struthers portion of Youngstown Sheet and Tube into an industrial park. Through patient effort, they were able to attract a new speciality steel company to the park. A May 1980 grant from HUD for $10 million assured that this company will be able to employ several hundred workers. More than two years after the closing, CASTLO had been the only successful redevelopment effort in the Youngstown area.

Labor and Business Considerations

Labor and business clashed over proposals for "Saving the Valley." The United Steel Workers of America lobbied heavily through the Department of Labor to counteract the steel industry's attempts to close plants indiscriminantly across the country. The steel industry countered with lobbying efforts in the Department of Commerce.

Two private industry proposals were made. One proposal came from a computer software development firm. It indicated that it wished to build a $150 million aircraft manufacturing factory in the Youngstown area. The firm, to be called ICX Aviation, was headed by Dale Lewis. He claimed already to have raised $50 million for the enterprise. Lewis attempted to secure federal loan guarantees from the Economic Development Administration for $100 million.

The second proposal was offered by a retired engineer, Karl Fetters. He once was an employee at Youngstown Sheet and Tube. The Fetters plan called for $125 million to build three electric arc furnaces at the Campbell Works. The furnaces would supply steel rounds to a profitable seamless pipe facility in the Campbell Works. The proposal was submitted to the Economic Development Administration. It was supported by many local business interests in Youngstown.

Ohio Congressional Delegation and the Steel Caucus

Congressman Charles Carney was the Congressional Representative for the 19th District when the steel mill closing occurred. Carney had served in that capacity for many years and was a powerful Democratic member in the House. As part of his efforts to help the 19th District during the crisis, Carney established the Congressional Steel Caucus. Its members were congressmen primarily from Ohio, Pennsylvania, Indiana, Illinois, Alabama, and New York. The purpose of the steel caucus was to pressure Congress and the President into acting in the best interest of states that depended heavily on the steel industry. Carney was elected chairman of the caucus.

The caucus was largely unsuccessful in its efforts to develop or influence public policy for the steel industry or communities suffering because of the steel industry. No major legislation was initiated. No large federal funding was raised.

During the 13 months following the closing, it became clear that Carney's inability to obtain massive federal assistance for the area would harm his chances for reelection. Since Carney held what was considered a "safe seat" in Congress, having repeatedly won in a district having a vast majority of registered Democratic voters, the Democrats in Washington, D.C., did not wish to see Carney lose. In an effort to bolster Carney's electoral chances, Vice President Walter Mondale and Secretary of Housing and Urban Development (HUD) Patricia Harris, both visited Youngstown and strongly endorsed his reelection.

Despite this show of concern and support, in November 1978, Republican Lyle Williams defeated Carney, giving Youngstown its first Republican representative in Congress since 1934. Many political observers credit Carney's defeat with his inability to help Youngstown after the mill closing (Peterson, 1978). The defeat also was interpreted by many to be a signal to the Carter Administration. They could not ignore the Youngstown area and still receive the traditional Democratic votes.

Failure to Save the Valley

Without exception, *all* of the "schemes" to save the steel industry—especially the Campbell Works—have failed, at least up to the time of this writing (June 1980). The portion of the Campbell Works that once employed 5,000 steelworkers still remains vacant. Even the small coke plant, which was kept open and employed 400 steelworkers, announced that it was shutting down as of June 1980. Since the closing of the Campbell Works, the Brier Hill Works of the former Youngstown Sheet and Tube

Company, now a Jones & Laughlin subsidiary, closed down in January 1980, idling 1,400 more steelworkers. And during the same month U.S. Steel closed down, laying off another 3,500 steelworkers. At present, only one steel-maker remains in Youngstown—Republic Steel. But Republic Steel appears to be heading north to its more modern facility in Warren, Ohio.

A major question is, why did the efforts of so many groups fail to produce even one plan which could salvage the jobs of the thousands of workers who were affected by the closings?

One way to answer the question is to chart the various groups involved in proposing plans, and the federal agencies that these groups approached for federal assistance. Patterns of influence are presented in Figure B.1 (see Peskin, 1978b, 1978c, 1979).

The federal agencies could not fund all of the schemes, not only because of the large sums of money involved, but because of the incompatibility of implementing several plans simultaneously. The Campbell Works simply was not that large a facility to accommodate more than one revitalization effort. Therefore, only one plan could possibly be implemented. The others would not succeed.

The federal agencies approached for funding tend to be very competitive. Commerce and Labor typically compete with one another over differences in business-labor disputes. The Economic Development Administration of Commerce often is at odds with its counterparts in Community Planning at HUD, especially with regard to urban and industrial revitalization. The presidential advisors who provided presidential links with Commerce, HUD and Labor have a different orientation concerning urban and industrial problems than do presidential advisors and groups like the Solomon Task Force on Steel. It appears unlikely that a consensus about which plan to adopt could have been reached in this particular situation. The result was a stalemate at the federal level. The maintenance of the status quo constituted the decision.

In like manner, the groups vying for the revitalization of the steel industry in Youngstown also were competitive. Each group, especially the group leadership, desired credit for "Saving the Valley." Many leaders apparently felt that the individual responsible for solving the problems of Youngstown would gain national prominence. Ambitions for political, social, and economic power began to emerge from each group.

The competition to get credit for solving the valley's problems may have destroyed any hope for federal aid for several reasons. First, each group inevitably offered credible reasons for the infeasibility of its competitors' plans. At the federal agencies involved, this caused serious doubts as to the viability of any of the plans, as well as in the private sector,

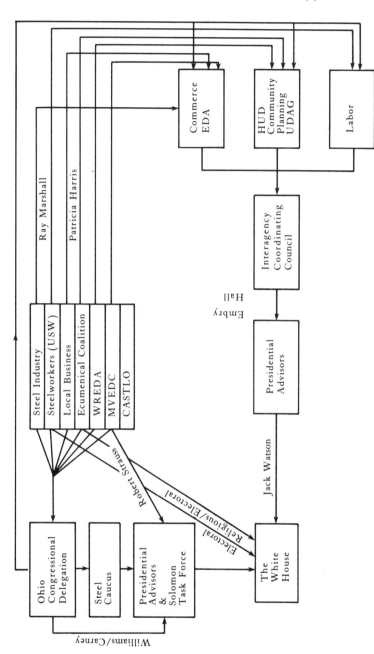

B.1 Major Actors and Channels of Influence in the Youngstown Steel Mill Closing

which would be required to underwrite any of the plans for hundreds of millions of dollars. Second, each group represented only a consensus of opinion for members of its group. No one group was able to obtain much support from the others. Even more important, they were unable to gain the support of the general public in the community. This placed potential funding sources in the peculiar position of coming out on the losing end no matter which group they supported. Third, the competition between groups indicated to outside observers that the community had no dominant leader. As a result, the federal government did not wish to determine which politician would emerge as the winner. The following column provides one indication of the problem of competition:

If the member communities of CASTLO—an acronym for Campbell, Struthers, and Lowellville—aren't celebrating their share of a likely grant to the Mahoning Valley Economic Development Committee, it's because they feel they're being used.

CASTLO project director George Wilson huddled with state Sen. Harry Meshel, D-33, last week over whether the group should accept $60,000 of a $600,000 U.S. Economic Development Administration grant to MVEDC. Wilson believes MVEDC is capitalizing on the economic plight of the three cities that were hardhit by last year's layoffs at Youngstown Sheet and Tube. His feeling is that the impact of the layoffs are centered in the CASTLO cities, but federal assistance may be distributed throughout the two-county region.

"We've got some problems with the MVEDC's community development strategy," Wilson acknowledged. "We believe the effort should be directed at us."

What has got Wilson and city officials from Campbell, Struthers and Lowellville so upset is that MVEDC needs the CASTLO cities to qualify for the EDA grant, but that only 10 percent of the grant has been designated to the cities over the next two years.

"The figure is completely arbitrary," Wilson said. "They (the MVEDC officials) never asked us how much we needed."

Besides, Wilson told his executive committee, CASTLO would receive $70,000, not $60,000. "I don't like to look like I don't know what I'm talking about," he explained.

Wilson expects to do more talking—this time with Youngstown Mayor Philip J. Richley, the MVEDC chairman—this week. (Dale Peskin, "Business Beat" column, *Youngstown Vindicator,* September 17, 1978)

In the final analysis, the competing schemes simply cancelled each other out. More important, the lack of consensus made it easy for the federal agencies to turn their backs on the problem.

There were other important reasons for the failure to "Save the Valley" which deserve mention. The Youngstown efforts were billed as a model for community recovery after the disaster of mass unemployment. The federal agencies were looking at the area in terms of creating a public policy to help other communities in similar situations. Other communities with equivalent or worse economic problems were anxiously awaiting the results of Youngstown's activities. If Youngstown, in its precedent-setting role, was able to obtain hundreds of millions of dollars from the federal government, then these communities also would have valid claims for similar bailout funding. This was significant, because most observers did not realize that so much capital would be required to aid similar problem communities across the country. It appears that the federal government may have found it cheaper to pay workers unemployment compensation than to pour hundreds of millions of dollars into questionable ventures.

A final point is that the community misperceived the amount of "clout" it had in Washington, D.C. Various efforts at mobilizing nation-wide religious groups, labor unions, the general public, and politicians in order to pressure decision-makers either in Washington or in industry failed. Efforts at threatening electoral or moral sanctions were ineffectual. When discussing this situation with federal officials and industrialists, Youngstown promoters may have left a very bad impression among decision-makers.

Appendix C. Measurement of Mental Health

Scale Construction

Psychological impact on workers was measured by constructing a series of indices which concerned alcohol abuse, drug abuse, victimization, apprehensive avoidance, stunned immobility, aggression, acute dependency, helplessness, family relations, anxiety, trust, and hypochondriasis. These indices were constructed from 130 separate items.* In general, each index was constructed from six or more items such as: "I am bothered by pains over my heart or in my chest." Both "positively" and "negatively" worded items were included. For positively worded items, *agreement* was coded as a "1." For negatively worded items, *disagreement* was coded as "1." All other responses were coded as "0." Indices were constructed by summing responses to each item in an index. Possible scores ranged from 0 up the the total number of items in the index. The items composing each scale are presented in Table C.1.

Responses to items were obtained using self-administered paper and pencil questionnaires. The format of the questionnaire and the administration procedure were similar to standard personality inventory instruments such as the *Minnesota Multiphasic Personality Inventory.*

Further Methodological Considerations

Analysis of mental health data is extremely complex and difficult to report with brevity. A complete description of the many analyses

---

*The mental health instrumentation was developed by and used with the permission of David Cliness.

performed is, therefore, presented in another study (see Buss, Redburn, and Waldron, forthcoming). This supplemental study contains methods and results of the correlational and dimensional analyses performed, reliability testing, validity indicators, bias in mental health scale scoring, and other technical considerations.

Table C.1
Mental Health Scale Items

Alcohol Abuse

1. I often take a drink or two to get started.
2. I drink when ever I have a chance.
3. I drink to forget my troubles.
4. I find that I need a drink in order to relax.
5. I drink to ease the pain.
6. I have good reasons for getting drunk.

Drug Abuse

1. Except by a doctor's orders, I never take drugs or sleeping pills.
2. I am having to take medication to calm my nerves.
3. I find that I must take drugs in order to feel good.
4. I am unable to sleep unless I take sleeping pills or powders.
5. My friends often supply me with drugs that make me feel better.

Aggressiveness/Irritability

1. I easily become impatient with people
2. I get angry easily.
3. I feel like swearing all the time.
4. I am often cross and grouchy.
5. I am so touchy on some subjects that I can't talk about them.
6. I find that I ususally get what I want most quickly by demanding it.
7. At times, I feel like smashing things.
8. At times, I feel like picking a fist fight with someone.
9. Others say that I am hotheaded.
10. I become easily annoyed when I am arguing.

Acute Dependency

1. People often disappoint me.
2. It seems to me that most people think about themselves and tend to forget others.
3. If I let my work go, someone else will usually help me finish it.
4. As a rule, I prefer having people do things for me rather than do them myself.
5. I often think, "I wish I were a small child again."
6. I often feel I am being neglected.
7. I have a strong need for someone to love me.
8. I often pity myself.
9. People don't seem to understand me.

Poor Family and Marital Relations

1. I have a strong desire to leave my home/family
2. There is very little love and companionship in my family.
3. I am unable to trust my spouse.
4. Our family is constantly in the midst of quarrels.
5. My wife/husband and I are having trouble agreeing on family priorities and goals.
6. I feel hate toward members of my family whom I usually love.
7. My spouse and I seem to have nothing in common.
8. Our marriage is in trouble because of money problems.
9. My home life is as happy as it should be.
10. My home is a very pleasant place.

High Anxiety

1. I have a difficult time sleeping.
2. I have a habit of biting my fingernails.
3. I find it hard to sit still for long.
4. I find if difficult to relax and take things easy.
5. I have nightmares every few nights.
6. My sleep is fitful and disturbed.
7. Almost every day something happens to frighten me.
8. I am a high-strung person.
9. I often feel all wound up.
10. I feel tense and anxious most of the time.

Apprehensive Avoidance

1. I dislike having people about me.
2. I find myself crossing the street to avoid meeting people I know.
3. I shrink from things which might prove difficult for me to handle.
4. I dislike social affairs.
5. Whenever possible, I avoid being in a crowd.
6. I avoid people when it is possible.
7. It is difficult for me to get acquainted with people.
8. I don't like carrying on a conversation at group gatherings.
9. I prefer to be alone most of the time.
10. I usually choose to do things which I know I can do rather than try things I'm not sure I can handle.

Depression Immobility

1. I'm having difficulty in starting to do things.
2. I seem to have given up.
3. I've stopped trying because all that I do seems to end in failure.
4. I find it difficult to get out of bed in the morning and get started on some things.
5. I am so confused by things that I don't know which way to turn.
6. I have periods of days, weeks, even months when I can't take care of things because I can't "get going."
7. I feel as though I am paralyzed.
8. It is as though I feel numb all over.
9. I seem to be in a state of shock.
10. I can't seem to do anything about my situation.

Helplessness/Depression

1. Most of the time I feel blue.
2. I feel like giving up quickly when things go wrong.
3. Things are so bad that I feel as though life is hardly worth living.
4. I am often worried about possible dangers that I cannot control.
5. I am often tempted to give up trying to solve my problems.
6. I certainly feel useless at times.
7. I don't seem to care what happens to me.
8. I shrink from facing a crisis or difficulty.
9. My difficulties are piling up so high that I cannot overcome them.
10. I feel like giving up when things go wrong.

Victimization

1. I am sure I get a raw deal from life.
2. My conduct is largely controlled by the customs of those around me.
3. I feel as though I am a condemned person.
4. It seems like people are always taking advantage of me.
5. I feel that I am a victim of circumstances.
6. I seem to have very little control over what happens to me.
7. It appears as if I am often blamed for what others do.
8. I am being made to suffer for the actions of others.
9. It people had not had it in for me, I would be much more successful now.
10. I feel as though I have been betrayed.

Trust/Suspicion

1. I believe that I am being plotted against.
2. I often feel that people are looking at me critically.
3. I tend to be on guard with people who are somewhat more friendly than I had expected.
4. I find that I have lost my faith and trust in the future.
5. I do not believe that people will do right by me.
6. I am troubled with the idea that people are watching me on the street.
7. I do not trust certain members of my family.
8. Someone has it in for me.
9. I feel that it is certainly best to keep my mouth shut.
10. My way of doing things is apt to be misunderstood by others.

Hypochondriasis

1. Much of the time my head seems to hurt all over.
2. I am bothered by pains over my heart or in my chest.
3. I have dizzy spells.
4. My heart sometimes pounds as if it were coming out of my chest.
5. I am troubled by attacks of nausea and vomiting.
6. I frequently notice my hands shaking when I try to do something.
7. I feel weak all over much of the time.
8. I am bothered by a great deal of gas in my stomach.
9. I feel very tired most of the time.

Appendix D. Eulogy to a Shutdown Steelmill

It took us a long time to get here; it took decades. Decades, which have been thrilling—dangerous, wonderful, frustrating, and, for those of us in retirement, filled with vivid memories.

Memories of places like the McDonald Mills, especially the 17-Inch mill. It is easy to be sad as we see the old mill closing. She has been good to us. To our families, our community, and our nation.

She has labored mightily over the decades—taking in the materials which by themselves are nothing. Taking them, and with your help turning them into products which turned America into what it is today, a modern nation of spreading highways, and massive cities. That is what she meant to the nation but her care was more tender, more personal to those of us who meet here tonight.

How many families worked in the mills.

How many of us has she kept fed and kept warm?

How many homes did she build and pay for?

How many of our children did she educate in the winters and provide jobs for in the summer?

She gave of herself during World War II, she gave her production to help arm a nation and its allies.

She froze us in the winter, and she cooked us in the summer. She screamed and thundered at times beyond our tolerance. She showered us with sparks and grime, and made us sweat as if preparing for hell itself.

And she often seemed not to need us. As we left at the end of our shift, we could look back and see her ceaseless smoke stacks arrogant with flame, as if saying we were her tools—tools she used and then replaced every eight hours, three times a day, 365 days a year. But she was always there—still spitting fire when we returned.

195

And how many ways did we curse her? Misuse her, mistreat her, or simply ignore her as the years went by?

We only fully realize now—as she stands finally still and quiet, cool and defeated—only now do we realize what she meant to us, and how much apart of us she was. I know the loss; over 40 years of my life was spent in that old drafty mill. I knew her when she was younger and newer and still in need of training. We both were young then. I gave her all my working days as did all of you. She wasn't always a pleasant friend.

I knew times when she cobbled the steel and balked at modern ideas and I know of times when she set records producing more and better steel than we believed possible. She was a demanding friend.

Some would say I am wrong to say a mill has personality. They would say that the steel sidings and girders rusting away is an old eyesore, look at the layers of scale, paper cups, lids and junk. Many are probably happy that it is gone.

But they did not work there with good friends like I did. She is old, as will all of us; time has taken its toll. Even I must admit she is not the mill she used to be. She was a good mill, my mill, a steelworker's mill. I am proud of the work she let me do, and when an old but great mill becomes worn and rusty and cannot be fixed one more time, she must be put away.

But that doesn't change the fact that for a lot of years, you and that mill spent a lot of time together.

When the day comes to put it away, you pause—and think and remember the good results. You laugh quietly about the silliness of your younger years, and think soberly of the wisdom gained. And you remember the stories that mill could tell if it could talk.

This is our feeling as we prepare to put away a Grand Lady. Remember it once was. Remember what we did together over the years. Think of the rewards and wisdom we gained and then finally think of all the friends we made.

We have traveled a long and difficult road together—you, me and our old mill. Now many of us are retired and 17 Mill has rolled its last round of steel.

Our younger friends will move on to new livelihoods while we older workers take our rest and talk of old times—the way it used to be. But somewhere tonight a newer mill is operating, and young men are cursing her and training her—beginning decades of work rolling steel—building families—and making memories which we will never know. But we envy them.

Paul Hadu's
Letter to the Editor
Youngstown Vindicator
July 13, 1980

Notes

1. Introduction

1. From "Youngstown," *The Ohio Guide,* compiled by workers of the Writer's Program of the Works Progress administration in the State of Ohio. The summary of Youngstown's history in this chapter is based largely on this reference.

2. A major exception was the farsighted preservation of Mill Creek Park, a deep, natural gorge and forest, winding for miles through the southwest part of the city—as beautiful a city park as exists anywhere.

3. The Department of Labor's Employment and Training Administration collects available information from local and state employment service offices on major layoffs. Cf., *Sharpening Government's Response to Plant Closings* (1979).

4. See Roger W. Schmenner, *The Location Decisions of Large, Multiplant Companies* (1980). These corporations operated an average of 36 domestic plants each and together employed over 7,000,000 people in the latter part of the 1970s.

5. In 1979, the U.S. Justice Department approved the controversial merger of Lykes with LTV Corporation, headquartered in Houston, which meant the combination of Youngstown Sheet and Tube and LTV's steel subsidiary, Jones & Laughlin. The new steel company took the latter name, thus obliterating the remaining symbolic connection between company and community.

6. In Chapter 2, the effects of the Lykes takeover and its subsequent management of the steel company are examined.

7. One exception is the emerging body of research and literature on mental health impact of unemployment and economic change (cf., Ferman and Gordus, 1980). However, only a small portion of this writing focuses on unemployment related to plant closings.

2. Black Monday

1. Overall, the failure of Youngstown's efforts to revitalize its steel industry or to restore lost jobs may also be explained using a sociological model of community

structure that characterizes communities on three dimensions: *structural differentiation,* referring to the extent of division of labor for complex tasks and the extent of specialized interests thus developed (Clark, 1968; Zisk, 1972; Hawkins, et al., 1975); *social integration,* referring to the degree of individual attachment to a community, especially with regard to consensus on norms, values, and goals (Coleman, 1957; Danielson, 1976); and *centralization of authority,* referring to the distribution of community leadership or authority among a few in a hierarchial arrangement or among the many in a highly pluralized arrangement (Crain, Katz, and Rosenthal, 1969; Banfield and Wilson, 1963). Using these dimensions as applied to the Youngstown case, one might have predicted (see Smith, 1979) that an apparently high level of structural differentration and low level of social integration and centralization of authority would inevitably lead to a failure to adopt any particular policy or plan for revitalizing the area.

　　2. The issue of "trigger pricing" is highly complex, yet important in understanding the "steel crisis." The Carter Administration attempted to tow the line in keeping our trading partners happy while at the same time protecting the steel industry. The steel industry, however, felt that the TPM was never really adequately enforced primarily because the Carter Administration intended it as an artificial mechanism for holding down rising domestic steel prices in an inflationary economy. See Bowers (1980).

　　3. The following account is based upon personal interviews with approximately 50 white collar employees at Youngstown Sheet and Tube. See also Beck-Rex (1978) and Peskin (1979).

　　4. One of the many ironies of the steel crisis was that the Japanese, who have been blamed by American steel producers for many of the problems in the steel industry, experienced a permanent steel mill closing four months after the closing of the Campbell Works. Nippon Steel located in Kamaishi, Japan, displaced 8,000 workers in a community of only 68,000. The mills accounted for 80 percent of the local economy. A further irony was that the corporation blamed foreign imports for the closing ("Japan Has Own 'Steel Valley'," 1978).

　　5. By Machiavellian, we mean acting exclusively out of self-interest. According to Machiavelli, "A prudent ruler ought not to keep faith when by so doing, it would be against his interest, and when the reasons which made him lend himself no longer exist." (*The Prince:* Chapter 18)

　　6. These conclusions are based on personal interviews with white collar workers and steelworker local union officials, who were assured of confidentiality.

　　7. The authors have no direct means for determining the motivation of high level corporate executives. Most of our impressions were gleaned from interviews with middle level managers, union leaders and public officials.

　　8. Many observers have noted the parallel between the political/social activist movements of the 1960s and the Ecumenical Coalition's efforts (e.g., Peskin, 1978d). The organization of religious groups, the use of corporate stock holdings as leverage for social action, the pressure tactics against the political "system" and the "establishment" all have many precedents. The Coalition even had a protest song. See, for example, Saul Alinsky's book *Reveille for Radicals* (1969) and Robert Bailey, *Radicals in Urban Politics: The Alinsky Approach* (1974).

9. The amount requested is similar in magnitude to the Chrysler Corporation's bailout which involves almost 100,000 autoworker jobs. See Pasztor (1980).

10. A major misconception about the closing of Youngstown Sheet and Tube is that the steel mills are located in Youngstown. Actually, the steel mills reside primarily in two municipalities which are situated southeast of Youngstown—Campbell and Struthers. The three cities share common municipal boundaries—it is impossible to tell when you are leaving one and arriving in another. A possible cause for the misconception is the activities of Youngstown community leaders attempting to save the steel mills. The impression has been given that Youngstown is in trouble. However, after the closing, Youngstown's unemployment rate was 6.9 percent, while those of Campbell and Struthers jumped to 30 percent (Peterson, 1978).

3. The Psychological Impact

1. Empirical research confirms the expectation that mental strain—including that induced by economic problems—is highly correlated with increased coping behavior. For instance, Caplovitz (1979) finds those under emotional pressure are much more likely than others to engage in efforts to raise income, curtail consumption, increase economic self-reliance, hunt for bargains, and share with others.

2. For a detailed sociological portrait of the work and community life of steelworkers see Kornblum (1974).

3. See Buss, Hofstetter, and Redburn, (1980) for an examination of the political response of workers to the closing.

4. The case studies of affected workers and their families summarized in Chapter 5 provide additional evidence of individual variation. See Dooley and Catalano (1980: 462) for reference to the literature on interaction between economic change and the individual's circumstances and personality.

5. A related book by Slote (1969) contains case studies of the managers and workers of the closed plant before and after shutdown. These personal portraits are in many respects more revealing of both the intensity and the variety of personal responses than are the parallel statistical analyses of Cobb and Kasl (1977).

6. Marshall and Funch (1979), in a replication of Brenner's analysis, raise methodological criticisms, but their analysis supports his basic findings.

7. First interviews were conducted in Summer 1978, when most workers had been unemployed for three to six months.

8. It should be noted that the second wave unemployed group includes many who were still employed, rehired in new jobs, or retired when first interviewed and that many of those unemployed at first interview were among the rehired when reinterviewed. (Only nine workers were unemployed on both the first and second waves). This pattern of discontinuous, intermittent unemployment is a continuing effect of the initial job loss that can, by itself, produce longer-term financial and emotional stress. The study design is not adequate to fully address this aspect of job loss.

9. Other respondents' scores changed more between the two testing periods. One way to determine the degree to which changes were occurring would be to collapse the mental health scale scores into fewer categories and then recompute the correlations. So, for example, a scale whose values ranged from 0 to 10 was collapsed as follows: 0–1=0; 2–3=1; 4–5=2; 6–7=3; 8–9=4; 10=5. Results of this analysis substantially increased correlations, suggesting that changes in scoring from one period to the next were minimal.

10. Results of the analysis of variance were not reported here because of spatial considerations.

11. The marriage relationship is generally viewed as a major clue to understanding the mental health of either partner; and employment status of either spouse has been found to greatly affect the marriage.

12. For a comprehensive analysis of this topic see Boggs and Buss (1980).

4. The Community Impact

1. These data, in contrast to personal interviews, are "unobtrusively" gathered, that is, not biased by respondent/investigator interactions (see Webb, et al., 1966).

2. These studies assumed a "multiplier effect" of 1 or more. That is, they assumed that for every worker laid off at the mill, one or more workers would also be laid off in related industries which supported the mill.

3. Mean values for the t–test were "before" = 80 and "after" = 80. The t statistic was not significant.

4. Data were analyzed by two- and, where available, four-digit standard industrial classifications.

5. An a priori assumption here is the trend in employment in any sector in the year preceding the Campbell Works demise would hold for the following year. While heroic, this assumption would not appear outrageous, particularly with respect to total manufacturing employment. For example, U.S. manufacturing jobs increased by 2.6 percent from September 1976 to August 1977 and by 3.4 percent from September 1977 to August 1978. In the case of durable goods employment, which dominates Youngstown-Warren area manufacturing, U.S. jobs grew by 3.4 percent between August 1976 and September 1977 and 4.7 percent between August 1977 and September 1978. It is not unreasonable to argue that the Youngstown-Warren SMSA would have shared in these national gains in jobs over the two-year period, albeit at more modest rates of growth. Data was computed from *Economic Indicators,* various issues, p. 14.

6. Fabricated metal products and transportation equipment were manufacturing sectors in which actual employment consistently exceeded trend or share-of-state estimates in the year following the Campbell Works job losses.

7. Mean values for the t–test were "before" = 206 and "after" = 210. The t statistic was significant at the .05 level.

8. United States data from *Economic Indicators,* various issues, p. 14. Ohio data from Ohio Bureau of Employment Services, *Ohio Labor Market Information,* various issues.

9. Computed from data in Table 4.2.

10. It is of interest to note here that in another study of the Campbell Works closure, Bagshaw and Schnorbus used a trend analysis technique known as intervention analysis. They estimated the loss of jobs at 4,000 by the end of 1977 (Bagshaw and Schnorbus, 1980: 22). Their study concluded that area unemployment rose by 3,200 from September through December 1977. They estimated 1,400 workers left the local labor force over these four months. For the month of December 1977, our trend analysis places the job loss at 2,500, while the share-of-state method yields a loss of 4,000.

11. Data were not uniformly available for each desired indicator. Reporting agencies gather data to suit only their specific needs. Some data were obtained on a monthly basis, others annually. In a few cases, changes in reporting procedures or format as well as special programs or circumstances made data incompatible from one year to the next. In some instances, data were gathered for the City of Youngstown, but in other cases, only county-level data exist. Finally, some desirable data were simply not gathered or accessible for purposes of this study.

12. The pairwise t-test was used to test significance.

13. Telephone interviews were conducted with 302 adults in the Youngstown area. Respondents were selected at random from the Youngstown area municipal telephone directory which includes residents of the City of Youngstown and of the rest of Mahoning County, including Campbell, Struthers, and Lowellville. Each city contributed an appropriate proportion to the sample.

Pairwise t-tests were conducted on the sample comparing responses from residents in each city. Only a few statistically significant differences were observed. These were not consistent across all subsamples. Since this was the case, we elected to treat the sample as representative of the Youngstown area, rather than separating out our findings city by city.

In order to verify that the sample was representative, standard demographic information (see Verba and Nie, 1972) was gathered. The information concerned education, age, occupation, employment, union membership, marital status, race, income, and sex for 1960 and 1970 from U.S. Census reports. These were compared with characteristics of the telephone survey sample.

14. Letter to the Editor, *Youngstown Vindicator*, December 31, 1979.

15. *Youngstown Vindicator*, March 27, 1979.

5. Reemployment, Retraining, and Relocation

1. The workers' former employer, the Lykes Corporation, as mentioned earlier, did not help workers in any way.

2. In order to discover how these three groups differed not only among themselves, but also with workers employed at other Youngstown Sheet and Tube facilities, analyses of variance (ANOVA) were conducted using three social characteristics: education, age, and income. The subsamples were significantly different with regard to education [$F(3,280) = 3.96$, $p < .001$], age [$F(3,279) = 32.67$, $p < .001$] and income [$F(3,279) = 5.96$, $p < .001$]. Tabular data is contained in Appendix A.

3. This also is consistent with OBES statistics. For example, OBES reports that even though 5,000 workers were laid off and about 10,000 workers were believed to be employed by the company, over 11,000 former Youngstown Sheet and Tube Company workers applied for and received unemployment compensation. Laid-off workers ironically do not qualify for CETA programs. This is because they are targeted toward low-income or minority workers (see Hallman, 1980). In November 1980, the U.S. Labor Department authorized the Youngstown area to relax CETA eligibility requirements so that steelworkers could be eligible to receive education and retraining benefits. This step had yet to be implemented as of June 1980.

4. See Hallman (1980) for a description of the CETA program.

5. The study was based on a telephone survey of adults in the Youngstown area who were asked questions identical to those asked of steelworkers during July–August 1978.

6. Preliminary Census results for the Youngstown-Warren Standard Metropolitan Statistical Area (SMSA) showed that the area had remained fairly stable in population over the decade, but the City of Youngstown had lost seven percent of its population.

7. See Terry F. Buss, "Out-migration for a Distressed Community," Research Monograph, Center for Urban Studies, Youngstown State University, 1980.

8. Based upon preliminary conclusions of an ongoing study by the authors for the National Institute of Mental Health.

6. Other Responses

1. See Buss and Hofstetter (1981) for a discussion of political involvement by the laid-off steelworkers.

2. An effective synthetic organization is characterized by the following: first, it has potentially greater freedom to develop and distribute community resources; second, it has reached consensus among its members as to what the problems facing the community are; third, it has reached agreement about which members will deal with problems in which service areas; fourth, members successfully defend the integrity of their own resources, programs, and personnel; fifth, it has developed its organizational structure while it simultaneously begins to provide services; sixth, it is able to accomplish the above without well-developed channels of communication (Thompson, 1967).

3. The mental health center consists of one main and seven branch offices serving one-half of Mahoning County's population. Prior to special funding, the center employed eight full time and one part-time professionals. Each staff worker treated patients during an average 52-hour workweek. In addition, the center employed a psychiatrist and a physician part-time. Prior to the steel crisis, during any given month, approximately 60 potential clients were placed on waiting lists. Staffing was insufficient to provide all the services requested.

4. The process followed was modeled on Harold Lasswell's "decision seminar," as first operationalized by the staff of the Mershon Center, Ohio State University. For more information on the seminar and its outcome, see Buss and Redburn (1980).

5. See Catalano and Dooley (1980: 34–36) for additional recommendations.

6. Local credit counseling services and efforts to inform workers about available services, training, and employment constitute exceptions to this general statement.

7. Another line of inquiry that might be useful in explaining of the community failure is the notion that community organizations each developed a different context to organize their response to the closing. Consequently, organizations may have pursued strategies which appeared to be rational to them as individual actors, but which turned out to be irrational when viewed on the community level. An excellent example of this kind of analysis is illustrated in Nigg and Cuthbertson (1982).

7. Employment Policy

1. Education that improves capacities not related to work but enabling people to gain more from leisure or enhancing the quality of their lives in other ways is also developmental.

8. Human Services Policies

1. The issues relating to costs and benefits are reviewed by Sclar (1981).

2. Although the production functions for benefits from human services programs are hardly understood, there is an interesting new literature on coproduction that stresses the need for active, voluntary cooperation of clients in the production of greater individual welfare (Parks, et al., 1980).

3. Cost here is used to encompass both the financial costs of programmed intervention and the partly financial but less easily measured economic and social costs to the worker, family, and community of untreated stress and disorder.

4. Researchers describing responses to a Michigan plant closing reported successful implementation of an in-plant counseling program developed with the cooperation of company, union, and United Way community services (Taber, Walsh, and Cooke, 1980: 144). There, management representatives counseled salaried employees. UAW local officials were released full-time by the company to counsel wage employees. The United Way provided these counselors with three days of training. "The purpose of the in-plant counseling program was not to provide professional psychological guidance to employees. Instead, the counselors served primarily to diagnose problems, get their clients in contact with the appropriate agency, and follow up to insure the client had in fact taken corrective actions."

A manual designed to aid communities in developing pre-layoff programs has been developed by Judson Stone and Charles Kieffer [1981] of the Six Area Coalition Community Mental Health Center, near Detroit.

5. A different viewpoint on the relative value of community organization and other practical help is expressed by Josefina Figueira-McDonough (1978).

Appendix A. Methodology

1. Interviewers were research associates at the Center for Urban Studies. Interviewers all had extensive experience in interviewing by telephone and in person. Interviewers attended an 8-hour training session geared specifically to this study. A training manual was developed which outlines our operating procedures.

2. Rather than weigh the data set for autoworkers, we elected to exclude them from the analysis on the second wave. The autoworkers appeared to be much more mobile in their jobs and place of residence than steelworkers; hence, the low response rate for the second wave.

3. Estimates of the number of workers employed at Youngstown Sheet and Tube were not available from the corporation. The Ohio Bureau of Employment Services estimated that perhaps 10,000 workers were employed at all of the corporation's facilities. The sample was initially stratified into two groups: the employed who were working primarily in the Brier Hill Works and the unemployed who were mostly from the Campbell Works. Since approximately 5,000 workers were affected in the initial closing of the Campbell Works, approximately equal numbers of employed (N = 138) and unemployed (N = 144) were interviewed.

4. Question wording followed that of Verba and Nie (1972). See Table A.1 for coding format. The demographics, race, and marital status were initially included in the analysis; but since no statistically significant differences were observed, they are not reported here.

5. Mean scores and standard deviations are available but were not reproduced here due to consideration of space.

6. The political nature of unemployment rates is clearly revealed in this explanation by an administrator at the Ohio Bureau of Employment Services:

> I still see the same picture I saw after "Black Monday." I talked to the company the other day, I just sent the new report to the federal government that's going to shock everybody. They wanted a cumulative figure of unemployment. (This means we had to count a worker who was laid off, called back, laid off again, and so on, as separate individuals.) Each time these "on-again, off-again Charlies" come into the office, we had to count them because that's what the federal government wanted. Nobody in their right mind is going to let me believe that I had more people on unemployment from Youngstown Sheet and Tube, this is the Sheet and Tube report only, than actually worked at Youngstown Sheet and Tube. Total figure is 11,039 people who collected unemployment benefits since last September. (Confidential interview, Employment Service)

7. Few steelworkers in the steel mills were women. Results of sample design yielded only male representation.

References

Adams, Leonard P. and Robert L. Aronson. *Workers and Industrial Change.* Ithaca: Cornell University Press, 1957

Aiken, Michael, Louis A. Ferman, and Harold L. Sheppard. *Economic Failure, Alienation and Extremism.* Ann Arbor: University of Michigan, 1968.

Alinsky, Saul D. *Reveille for Radicals.* New York: Vintage Books, 1969.

American Iron and Steel Institute. *Steel at the Crossroads: The American Steel Industry in the 1980s.* Washington, D.C.: American Iron and Steel Institute, 1980.

Aronson, Robert L. and Robert B. McKersie. *Economic Consequences of Plant Shutdowns in New York State.* Ithaca, New York: New York State School of Industrial and Labor Relations, 1980.

Arthur Andersen and Company. *U.S. Automotive Industry Trends for the 1980s.* Chicago: Arthur Andersen, 1980.

Bagshaw, Michael and Robert H. Schnorbus. The Local-Market Response to a Plant Shutdown. *Economic Review:* Federal Bank of Cleveland, January, 1980, 16–24.

Bailey, Robert. *Radicals in Urban Politics: The Alinsky Approach.* Chicago: University of Chicago Press, 1974.

Bakke, E.W. *Citizens Without Work.* New Haven: Yale University Press, 1944.

Banfield, Edward C. and James Q. Wilson. *City Politics.* New York: Vintage, 1963.

Barks, Joseph V. It Can Pay Off to Help the Laid Off. *Iron Age,* April 28, 1980.

Barling, P. and P. Handel. Incidence of Utilization of Public Mental Health Facilities as a Function of Short-Term Economic Decline. *American Journal of Community Psychology,* 8 (1980), 31–40.

Bateson, Gregory. *Mind and Nature: A Necessary Unity.* New York: Dutton, 1979.

Beck-Rex, Marguerite. Youngstown: Can This Steel City Forge a Comeback? *Planning,* January 1978, 12–14.

Beetle, George. *New Steel at Campbell.* Youngstown, Ohio: Western Reserve Economic Development Agency, December 16, 1977.

Bendick, Marc and Larry Ledebur. National Industries Policy and Economically-

Distressed Communities. In Redburn and Buss, eds. *Public Policies for Distressed Communities,* 1981, pp. 3–14.

Birch, David. *The Job Generation Process.* Cambridge, Massachusetts: M.I.T. Program on Neighborhood and Regional Change, 1979.

Blau, Peter. *The Dynamics of Bureaucracy,* rev. ed. Chicago: University of Chicago Press, 1964.

Bluestone, Barry and Bennett Harrison. *Capital Mobility and Economic Dislocation.* Washington, D.C.: The Progressive Alliance, 1980.

Boggs, David L. and Terry F. Buss. Effects of Massive Unemployment on Opting for Education and Training to Prepare for New Careers. *Proceedings of the 1980 Annual Meeting of the Adult Education Research Conference,* Vancouver, Canada: Adult Education Research Society, 1980.

Bowers, Edwin W. How Commerce Pulled the Trigger on Steel. *Iron Age,* April 21, 1980, 20–21.

Brenner, Harvey. Personal Stability and Economic Security. *Social Policy,* May/June 1977, 2–41.

Brody, David. *Steelworkers in America.* New York: Harper Torchbooks, 1960.

Buss, Terry F. and C. Richard Hofstetter. Communication, Information and Participation. *Social Science Journal,* 18 (1981), 81–92.

Buss, Terry F. and F. Stevens Redburn. Evaluating Human Service Delivery During a Plant Shutdown: A Decision Seminar Application. *Journal of Health and Human Resources Administration,* 3 (1980), 229–250.

Buss, Terry F. and F. Stevens Redburn. How to Shut Down a Plant. *Industrial Management,* 23 (1981), 4–10.

Buss, Terry F. and Joseph Waldron. *An Early Warning System for Business Retention.* Cleveland: Northeast Ohio Inter-institutional Research Program, 1982.

Buss, Terry F., C. Richard Hofstetter, and F. Stevens Redburn. The Psychology of Mass Unemployment: Some Political and Social Implications. *Political Psychology,* 3 (Fall/Winter 1980), 95–113.

Buss, Terry F., F. Stevens Redburn, and Larry C. Ledebur (eds.). The Economic Revitalization of America. *Policy Studies Review* (1982).

Buss, Terry F., F. Stevens Redburn, and Joseph Waldron. *Mass Unemployment: Plant Closings and Community Mental Health* (forthcoming).

Caplovitz, David. *Making Ends Meet, How Families Cope with Inflation and Recession.* Beverly Hills: Sage, 1979.

Cassimatis, Emanuel. Mental Health Viewed as an Ideal. *Journal of Psychiatry,* 42 (August 1979), 241–254.

Catalano, Ralph and David Dooley. Economic Predictors of Depressed Mood and Stressful Life Events. *Journal of Health and Social Behavior,* 18 (September 1977), 292–307.

Catalano, Ralph and David Dooley. Economic Change in Primary Prevention. In Richard H. Price, et al. (eds.), *Prevention in Mental Health.* Beverly Hills: Sage Annual Review of Community Mental Health, 1980.

Caudill, Harry M. *Night Comes to the Cumberlands, A Biography of a Depressed*

208   Shutdown at Youngstown

Area. Boston: Atlantic–Little, Brown, 1963.

Citibank, N.A. *Monthly Economic News Letter,* 1950-1978.

Clark, Terry N. Community Structure, Decision Making, Budget Expenditures and Urban Renewal in 51 American Communities. *American Sociological Review,* 33 (1968), 576–593.

Cobb, Sidney, et al. The Health of People Changing Jobs: A Description of a Longitudinal Study. *American Journal of Public Health,* 56 (1966), 1476-1481.

Cobb, Sidney and Stanislav V. Kasl. *Termination: The Consequences of Job Loss.* Rockville, Maryland: National Institute for Occupational Safety and Health, 1977.

Cocheo, Steve. Bankruptcy Filings Go through the Roof. *ABA Banking Journal,* August 1980, 48–53.

Coleman, James. *Community Conflict.* New York: Free Press, 1957.

Collins, A.H. and D.L. Pancoast. *Natural Helping Networks.* New York: National Association of Social Workers, 1976.

Collins, John. Save Youngstown: Save America! Joint Strategy and Action Committee. *Grapevine,* 9 (January 1978).

Commerce-Labor Adjustment Action Committee. *Sharpening Government's Response to Plant Closings.* Washington, D.C.: U.S. Departments of Labor and Commerce, November 1979.

Comprehensive Program for the Steel Industry. Washington, D.C.: Steel Task Force, 1977.

Comptroller General of the U.S. *Administration of the Steel Trigger Price Mechanism.* Washington, D.C.: General Accounting Office, July 23, 1980.

Cook, Daniel D. Economic Malnutrition Saps Aging Steel Center. *Industry Week,* April 30, 1979, 42–49.

Council for Economic Development. *Jobs for the Hard-to-Employ.* New York: CED, 1978.

Council for Northeast Economic Action. *Labor and Management: Partners for Progress.* Proceedings of a Conference in Hartford, Connecticut, June 1977, sponsored by the Economic Development Administration. Washington, D.C.: Council for Northeast Economic Action, 1977.

Council on Wage and Price Stability. *Prices and Costs in United States Industry.* Washington, D.C.: Council on Wage and Price Stability, 1977.

Crain, Robert L., Elihu Katz, and Donald B. Rosenthal. *The Politics of Community Conflict.* New York: Bobbs-Merrill, 1969.

Crandall, Robert. *The U.S. Steel Industry in Recurrent Crisis.* Washington, D.C.: Brookings Institution, 1981.

Danielson, Michael N. *The Politics of Exclusion.* New York: Columbia University Press, 1976.

Delbecq, Andre L. and Andrew N. Van de Ven. A Group Process Model for Problem Identification and Program Planning. *The Journal of Applied Behavioral Science,* 7 (Fall 1971), 466–492.

Dooley, David and Ralph Catalano. Economic Change As a Cause of Behavioral Disorder, *Psychological Bulletin,* 87 (May, 1980), 450–468.

Durman, Eugene C. The Role of Self-Help in Service Provision. *Journal of Applied Behavioral Science,* 12 (July–August–September 1976), 433–443.

Employment and Training Administration. *Sharpening Government's Response to Plant Closings.* Washington, D.C.: U.S. Dept. of Labor, 1979.

Ferman, Louis A., et al. *Analysis of the Irregular Economy: Cash Flow in the Informal Sector.* A report by the Institute of Labor and Industrial Relations, University of Michigan, to the Michigan Department of Labor, 1978.

Ferman, Louis A. Regional Unemployment, Poverty, and Relocation: A Social Service View. *Poverty and Human Resources Abstracts,* 6 (1971), 499–517.

Ferman, Louis A. Remarks Delivered before the Committee on Labor and Human Resources on the Role of the Worker in the Evolving Economy of the Eighties, Washington, D.C., September 18, 1980 (photocopy).

Ferman, Louis A. and Jeanne P. Gordus (eds.). *Mental Health and the Economy.* Kalamazoo, Michigan: Upjohn Institute for Employment Research, 1980.

Figueira-McDonough, Josefina. Mental Health Among Unemployed Detroiters. *Social Service Review* (1978), 383–399.

Foltman, Felician M. *White and Blue Collars in a Mill Shutdown.* Ithaca, N.Y.: Cornell University Press, 1968.

Froland, Charles, et al. *Helping Networks and Human Services.* Beverly Hills, California: Sage, 1981.

Galenson, Walter. The Unionization of the American Steel Industry. *International Review of Social History,* 1 (1956), 8–40.

Garland, Greg. Economic Redevelopment after the Collapse. *Warren Tribune,* December 14–20, 1980 (series of articles in seven parts).

Ginzberg, Eli. Manpower Policy: Retrospect and Prospect. In *The Business Cycle and Public Policy, 1929-80.* Washington, D.C.: Joint Economic Committee of Congress, November 1980.

Goodman, Robert. *The Last Entrepreneurs, America's Regional Wars for Jobs and Dollars.* New York: Simon and Schuster, 1979.

Gore, Susan. The Effect of Social Support in Moderating the Health Consequences of Unemployed. *Journal of Health and Social Behavior,* 19 (1978), 157–165.

Greenman, John. Series of award-winning columns, *Warren Tribune,* 1979.

Hallman, Howard W. *Community-based Employment Programs.* Baltimore: John Hopkins University Press, 1980.

Halpern, Howard A. Crisis Theory: A Definitional Study. *Community Mental Health Journal,* 9 (1973), 342–349.

Hansen, Gary B., et al. *Hardrock Miners in a Shutdown: A Case Study of the Post-Layoff Experience of Displaced Lead-Zinc-Silver Miners.* Logan, Utah: Economic Research Center, Utah State University, 1980.

Hargreaves, W.A., C.C. Attkisson, L.M. Siegel, M.H. McIntyre, and J.E. Sorensen (eds.). *Resource Materials for Community Mental Health Program Evaluation: Part IV. Evaluating the Effectiveness of Services.* Washington, D.C.: National Institute for Mental Health, 1975.

Harrison, Bennett and Barry Bluestone. The Incidence and Regulation of Plant Closings. In Redburn and Buss (eds.), *Public Policies for Distressed*

Communities, 1981, pp. 131–169.

Hawkins, Brett W. et al. A Macro-analysis of the Effects of Planning Professionalism on Municipal Planning Outputs. *Journal of the American Institute of Planners,* 41 (1975), 419–424.

Hayes, Linda S. Youngstown Bounces Back. *Fortune,* December 17, 1979.

Hemley, David D. and Lee R. McPheters. Crime as an Externality of Regional Economic Growth. *Review of Regional Studies,* 4 (1974), 73–84.

Holt, Charles C. Unmet Needs for Data on the Demand Side of the Labor Market. *Review of Public Data Use,* 8 (1980), 361–368.

Howard, Robert. Going Bust in Youngstown. *Commonweal,* May 25, 1979, 301–305.

Ignatius, David. Who Killed the Steel Industry? *Washington Monthly,* March 1979.

Industrial Economics Research Institute. *The Feasibility of a Proposed Joint-venture Ironmaking Facility in the Youngstown Area.* New York: Fordham University, June 1978.

Iscoe, I. Community Psychology and the Competent Community. *American Psychologist,* 29 (August 1974), 607–613.

Japan Has Own "Steel Valley." *Youngstown Vindicator,* February 18, 1979.

Jewell, Mike, et al. *Exploratory Evaluation of the Community Mental Health Center Program.* Washington, D.C.: Office of the Assistant Secretary for Planning and Evaluation, U.S. Department of Health, Education and Welfare, March 1980.

Judson, James H. Training Continued through Plant Phase-out. *Training and Development Journal,* 30 (August 1976), 22–23.

Kasarda, John D. The Implications of Contemporary Redistribution Trends for National Urban Policy. *Social Science Quarterly,* 61 (December 1980), 373–400.

Kasl, Stanislav V., et al. Changes in Serum Uric Acid and Colesterol Levels in Men Undergoing Job Loss. *Journal of the American Medical Association,* 206 (1968), 1500–1607.

Kasl, Stanislav V. and Sidney Cobb. Blood Pressure Changes in Men Undergoing Job Loss. *Psychosomatic Medicine,* 32 (January–February 1970), 19–38.

Kelley, Edward. The Merger of Lykes and LTV. Washington, D.C.: Progressive Alliance, 1978.

Kimmel, Wayne A. *Needs Assessment: A Critical Perspective.* Washington, D.C.: Office of the Assistant Secretary for Planning and Education, U.S. Department of Health, Education, and Welfare, 1977.

Kornblum, William. *Blue Collar Community.* Chicago: Chicago University Press, 1974.

Kornhauser, Arthur W. *Mental Health of the Industrial Worker.* New York: Wiley, 1965.

LaRocco, James M. Social Support, Occupational Stress, and Health. *Journal of Health and Social Behavior,* 21 (1980), 202–218.

Liem, G. Ramsay and Joan Huser Liem. Social Support and Stress: Some General Issues and Their Application to the Problem of Unemployment. In Louis A.

Ferman and Jeanne P. Gordus (eds.), *Mental Health and the Economy.* Kalamazoo, Michigan: Upjohn Institute for Employment Research, 1979, 347–378.

Lipsky, Michael. *Street-level Bureaucracy.* New York: Russell Sage Foundation, 1980.

Litvak, Lawrence and Belden Daniels. *Innovations in Development Finance.* Washington, D.C.: The Council of State Planning Agencies, 1979.

Luborsky, Lester, Barton Singer, and Lise Luborsky. Comparative Studies of Psychotherapies. In Robert C. Spitzer and Donald F. Kline (eds.), *Evaluation of Psychological Therapies.* Baltimore: John Hopkins University Press, 1976.

Lucas, William A. and William C. Adams. *An Assessment of Telephone Survey Methods.* Santa Monica, California: Rand, 1977.

Manuso, James S.J. Coping with Job Abolishment. *Journal of Occupational Medicine,* 19 (September 1977).

Marcus, Peter F. and Karlis M. Kirsis. *World Steel Dynamics.* Washington, D.C. American Iron and Steel Institute, 1979.

Marshall, James R. and Donna P. Funch. Mental Illness and Economy: A Critique and Partial Replication. *Journal of Health and Social Behavior,* 20 (September 1979), 282–289.

McCarthy, James E. *Trade Adjustment Assistance: A Case Study of the Shoe Industry in Massachusetts.* Boston: Federal Reserve Bank of Boston, 1975.

McConnell, Grant. *Steel and the Presidency—1962.* New York: Norton, 1963.

Mick, Stephen S. Social and Personal Costs of Plant Shutdowns. *Industrial Relations,* 14 (1975), 203–208.

Nathanson, Josef. *Early Warning Information Systems for Business Retention.* Washington, D.C.: Urban Consortium Information Bulletin, 1980.

National Academy of Science. *Report of the Committee on the Steel Industry.* Washington, D.C.: National Academy of Science, 1978.

National Center for Economic Alternatives. *Youngstown Demonstration Planning Project—Final Report.* Washington, D.C.: National Center for Economic Alternatives, 1978.

Nigg, Joanne and Beverly Cuthbertson. Pesticide Applications near Urban Areas: A "Crisis in Confidence" for Public. *Journal of Health and Human Resources Administration,* 4 (1982), 284–302.

Ohio Legislature. *Proceedings of the Steel Legislature Conference.* Columbus: Ohio Legislature, April 11, 1980.

Parks, Roger B., et al. Citizens Coproduction of Public Services. A paper presented at the American Political Science Association Annual Meeting, August 28-31, 1980, (photocopy).

Pasztor, Andy. U.S. Clears Chrysler Aid. *Wall Street Journal,* June 25, 1980.

Peskin, Dale. After Year, Firm Action is Brewing on Job Picture. *Youngstown Vindicator,* August 24, 1978.

Peskin, Dale. S & T Toughens Policy on News. *Youngstown Vindicator,* May 21, 1978a.

Peskin, Dale. Funding Bids Are Growing. *Youngstown Vindicator,* July 4, 1978b.

Peskin, Dale. Marshall Says Task Force Will Study Valley Appeal. *Youngstown Vindicator,* September 23, 1978c.
Peskin, Dale. Coalition Relights Passion of '60s for Valley's Cause. *Youngstown Vindicator,* September 30, 1978d.
Peskin, Dale. How Carter Signs Memo Is Crucial to Valley Aid. *Youngstown Vindicator,* October 22, 1978e.
Peskin, Dale. Thanks, But No Thanks. *Youngstown Vindicator,* October 29, 1978f.
Peskin, Dale. From the Era of the Trust to the Age of the Conglomerate. *Youngstown Vindicator,* December 10, 1978g.
Peskin, Dale. Dreams and Schemes. *Ohio Magazine,* November 1979.
Peterson, Iver. Public Money and Private Ambition Clash over Future of Steel in Ohio's Mahoning Valley. *New York Times,* December 8, 1978.
Petzinger, T.V. Retrenchment: The Painful Plan to Save Steelmaking. *Youngstown Vindicator,* January 1978a.
Petzinger, T.V. Diversification Is Message of 1977, Strategy for 1978. *Youngstown Vindicator,* January 8, 1978b.
Polivka, Larry, Allen W. Imersheini, John Wesley White, and Lawrence E. Stivers. Human Services Reorganization and Its Efforts: A Preliminary Assessment of Florida's Services Integration "Experiment." *Public Administration Review* (May/June 1981), 359–365.
Pursell, Donald E., et al. *Trade Adjustment Assistance: An Analysis of Impacted Worker Benefits on Displaced Workers in the Electronics Industry.* Memphis: Center for Manpower Studies, Memphis State University, 1975.
Redburn, F. Stevens. On "Human Services Integration." *Public Administration Review,* 37 (May–June 1977), 264–269.
Redburn, F. Stevens and Terry F. Buss (eds.). *Public Policy for Distressed Communities.* Lexington, Massachusetts: D.C. Heath and Company, 1981.
Reindustrialization of America. *Business Week* (special issue), June 30, 1980.
Researcher's Report Hits Campbell Plant Opening. *Youngstown Vindicator,* March 25, 1978.
Rice, A.K. Individual, Group, and Intergroup Processes. *Human Relations,* 22 (June 1970), 565–584.
Rust, Edgar. *No Growth: Impacts on Metropolitan Areas.* Lexington, Massachusetts: D.C. Heath and Company, 1975.
S & T Shutdown Expense Is High. *Youngstown Vindicator,* March 26, 1978.
Samuelson, Robert J. On Mobility. *National Journal,* August 16, 1980.
Samuelson, Robert J. Backwards on Jobs. *National Journal,* February 7, 1981.
Sandburg, Carl. *Smoke and Steel.* New York: Harcourt, Brace and Company, 1920.
Schlozman, Kay L. and Sidney Verba. *Injury to Insult.* Cambridge: Harvard University Press, 1979.
Schmenner, Roger W. *The Location Decisions of Large, Multiplant Companies.* Cambridge, Massachusetts: Joint Center for Urban Studies of MIT and Harvard University, 1980.
Schneider, Mark. The "Quality of Life" and Social Indicator Research. *Public Administration Review,* 36 (May–June 1976), 297–305.

Schultz, George P. and Arnold R. Weber. *Strategies for Displaced Workers.* New York: Harper and Row, 1966.

Sclar, Elliott, D. Social-Cost Minimization: A National Policy Approach to the Problems of Distressed Economic Regions. In Redburn and Buss (eds.), *Public Policies for Distressed Communities,* pp. 15–27.

Sennett, Richard and Jonathan Cobb, *Hidden Injuries of Class.* New York: Vintage, 1972.

Sheppard, L.A., Louis A. Ferman, and S. Faber. *Too Old to Work—Too Young to Retire.* Washington, D.C.: U.S. House of Representatives, Special Committee on Unemployment, 1959.

Silverman, Phyllis R. *Mutual Help Groups.* Beverly Hills, California: Sage, 1980.

Slote, Alfred. *Termination: The Closing at Baker Plant.* Indianapolis: Bobbs-Merrill, 1969.

Smith, Luke M. and Irving A. Fowler. Plant Relocation and Worker Migration. In Arthur B. Shostak and William Gomberg (eds.), *Blue-collar World.* Englewood Cliffs, N.J.: Prentice-Hall, 1964.

Smith, Richard. Decision Making and Non-Decision Making in Cities. *American Sociological Review,* 44 (1979), 147–161.

Sobel, Irvin and Hugh Folk. Labor Market Adjustments by Unemployed Older Workers. In Arthur M. Ross (ed.), *Employment Policy and the Labor Market.* Berkeley: University of California Press, 1967.

Steel's Sea of Troubles. *Business Week,* September 19, 1977, 66–88.

Stern, J. Consequences of Plant Closure. *Journal of Human Resources,* 7 (January 1973), 3–25.

Stone, Judson and Charles Kieffer. Pre-Layoff Intervention: A Response to Unemployment. Detroit: Six Area Coalition, Community Mental Health Center, undated [1981], (photocopy).

Strange, Walter G. *Job Loss: A Psychological Study of Worker Reactions to a Plant Closing in a Company Town in Southern Appalachia.* Unpublished manuscript, October 1978.

Taber, Thomas D., Jeffrey T. Walsh, and Robert A. Cooke. Developing a Community-based Program for Reducing the Social Impact of a Plant Closing. *The Journal of Applied Behavioral Science,* 15 (Spring 1979), 133–155.

Terkel, Studs. *Working.* New York: Random House, 1974.

Thompson, Wilbur R. *A Preface to Urban Economics.* Baltimore: John Hopkins Press, 1965.

Thompson, Wilbur R. Prepared statement, *Hearings on Urban Revitalization and Industrial Policy,* before the Subcommittee on the City, Committee on Banking, Finance, and Urban Affairs, U.S. House of Representatives, (September 16-17, 1980) (photocopy).

Tracy, Eleanor J. There's More Than Ships and Steel in the Lykes Family Vault. *Fortune,* July 17, 1978, 50–56.

U.S. Steel to Trim Fat. *Iron Age,* December 10, 1979, 35–38.

Varenais, Kristina. *Needs Assessment: An Exploratory Critique.* Washington, D.C.: U.S. Department of Health, Education & Welfare, 1977.

Vaughan, Roger J. A Community-based Economic Development Strategy. A paper prepared for the annual meeting of the Council of University Institutes of Urban Affairs, Washington, D.C., March 20, 1980.

Verba, Sidney and Norman H. Nie. *Participation in America: Political Democracy and Social Equality.* New York: Harper and Row, 1972.

Warheit, G.J., R.A. Bell, and J.J. Schwab. *Planning for Change: Needs Assessment Approaches.* Rockville, Maryland: National Institute of Mental Health, 1974.

Warren, Donald I. *Helping Networks.* Notre Dame, Indiana: University of Notre Dame Press, 1981.

Webb, Eugene, et al. *Unobtrusive Measures: Nonreactive Research in the Social Sciences.* Chicago: Rand McNally, 1966.

Wilcock, Richard C. and Walter H. Franke. *Unwanted Workers: Permanent Layoffs and Long-term Unemployment.* New York: Free Press, 1963.

Works Progress Administration. *The Ohio Guide.* New York: Oxford University Press, 1940.

Youngstown Sheet and Tube. *Sheet and Tube's 75th Year.* Youngstown: Youngstown Sheet and Tube, 1975.

Zisk, Betty H. Local Interest Politics and Municipal Outputs. In Harlan Hahn (ed.), *People and Politics in Urban Society.* Beverly Hills, California: Sage, 1972.

Index

economic development, 140, 147, 148, 166-8
Economic Development Administration
(EDA), 24, 27
Ecumenical Coalition, 23-27, 31, 87
Employment and Training Administration,
100
employment policy, priorities, 137
entrepreneurship, 4, 167

Faber, S., 93
"failing company provision," 31
Fatal Accident Reduction Enforcement
(FARE), 73
Federal Community Action, 130
Ferman, Louis A., 93, 99, 102, 113, 115, 143
Figueira-McDonough, Josefina, 54
Folk, Hugh, 91
Foltman, Felician M., 99, 107, 109, 143
Ford, Gerald, R., 18
forecasting, 62
Fowler, Irving A., 107
France, 16
Franke, Walter H., 43, 97, 99, 100, 101, 109,
137, 142
Froland, Charles, 156, 159
Frostbelt, 3
Funch, Donna P., 36

Galenson, Walter, 29
Garland, Greg, 26
General Equivalency Development (GED),
98
General Motors Corporation, 63
Ginzberg, Eli, 147
Goodman, Robert, 3
Gore, Susan, 107
Great Depression, 2
Great Lakes, 3, 138
Greenman, John, 17

Halpern, Howard A., 37
Hansen, Gary, 102-3
Harrison, Bennett, 3, 5, 17, 157
Hayes, Linda, 16, 94
health insurance, 158
Hemley, David D., 73
hidden economy, 115
high technology, 146, 162
Houston, Texas, 106
"human resources investments," 133, 140

ideology, 26
Ignatius, David, 16, 18
"illegal jobs," 115
income maintenance, 158
Indiana Harbor Works, 106
"industrial hostage laws"
"informed consent," 157
innovation, 4
Institute for Policy Studies, 23
"institutional isolation," 161
interorganizational systems theory, 122
intervention, 133, 136, 139, 150, 151, 155,
157, 161

Jamestown, New York, 145
Japan, 16
job discrimination, 114-5
job loss
age, education, race, 52;
alcohol abuse, 76;
bankruptcies, 82;
behavioral disorder, 36, 37;
bureaucratic competency, 114;
charitable contributions, 77;
crime, 73-5;
financial, 56-7;
general model for, 36-7;
general public, 86-88;
interplant transfers, 106;
job safety, 54-6;
marital status, 53-7;
mediating factors, 40-1, 43;
mill closings, 45-57;
mortality, 44, 75-6;
physiological, 44;
research designs, 36-7;
self-esteem, 35-6;
shame of, 40;
"share-of-state analysis," 63;
social class, 38;
social/community, 60-88;
social indicators, 61;
stress, 43-5, 47, 52-3;
suicide, 44;
Supplemental Unemployment Benefits,
57;
temporary employment, 106;
timing, 47-9;
Trade Readjustment Assistance, 57;
unemployment rates, 61-73;

P